MW00583643

The Structure of Theological Revolutions

The Structure
of Theological
Revolutions

*How the Fight Over Birth Control
Transformed American Catholicism*

MARK S. MASSA, SJ

OXFORD
UNIVERSITY PRESS

OXFORD
UNIVERSITY PRESS

Oxford University Press is a department of the University of Oxford. It furthers the University's objective of excellence in research, scholarship, and education by publishing worldwide. Oxford is a registered trade mark of Oxford University Press in the UK and certain other countries.

Published in the United States of America by Oxford University Press
198 Madison Avenue, New York, NY 10016, United States of America.

© Oxford University Press 2018

All rights reserved. No part of this publication may be reproduced, stored in a retrieval system, or transmitted, in any form or by any means, without the prior permission in writing of Oxford University Press, or as expressly permitted by law, by license, or under terms agreed with the appropriate reproduction rights organization. Inquiries concerning reproduction outside the scope of the above should be sent to the Rights Department, Oxford University Press, at the address above.

You must not circulate this work in any other form
and you must impose this same condition on any acquirer.

CIP data is on file at the Library of Congress
ISBN 978–0–19–085140–8

1 3 5 7 9 8 6 4 2

Printed by Sheridan Books, Inc., United States of America

To C. Conrad Wright, optime magister
and
Ruby Hugh and Jim Bretzke, optime amicae

If we want everything to stay the same, everything has to change.
—Giuseppe Tomasi de Lampedusa, *The Leopard* [1]

Contents

Contents

PART IV: *So Now What?*

Introduction

On How and Why Theology Changes

*The development of Christian doctrine does not progress
in a linear fashion.*

—PETER TOON[1]

A. Paradigms and Their Revolutions:
The Micro-Tradition of Natural Law

How does theology—the study of God, whose nature is imagined to be
eternal and unchanging—change over time? And why? These are the essential
questions this book seeks to answer. To do so, I draw on a concept from the
history and philosophy of science: the paradigm shift, a term coined by the
scientist and philosopher Thomas Kuhn, but a term that has now entered the
popular lexicon. This is a book, then, about paradigm change, and even more
specifically about theological paradigm change. And to be even *more* specific
than that, it is an examination of how micro-traditions in theology (in this
case, the tradition of natural law discourse) operate within the macro-tradition of Catholic theology. If we take the vast category of Catholic theology to
be a "macro-tradition" within the even larger category of Christian theology
(made up of many macro-traditions), then the ancient tradition of natural law
represents an important subcategory (what this book will call a "micro-tradition") within it.[2]

The word "paradigm" is actually a fairly old, Greek-derived word that
today is often used interchangeably with the word "model" to describe a fairly
broad range of things—paradigms of historical change, paradigms of democracy, and so forth. As it was utilized by Kuhn, however, "paradigm" had a very
specific meaning—a meaning at once more specific and more complex than
simply another word for "model." Indeed, Kuhn became progressively more
upset when people increasingly (if mistakenly) used paradigm as simply another way of talking about models. We will dig into this detail later on. But for

now suffice it to say that this book will look at changes in Catholic theology through the lens of Kuhn's work.

The title of this book quite consciously riffs the title of Kuhn's *The Structure of Scientific Revolutions.* That book is now considered a landmark in the history of science because it challenged older understandings of how and why the disciplines of physical science "progressed." That word has been framed by quotes because an important part of Kuhn's theory rejected the idea that science progressed in a linear and serene developmental fashion.

Kuhn argued that science *doesn't* evolve in anything like a continuous manner, in which each development builds neatly on what has come before—a presupposition that most people hold when they use the word progress. This book is written in the belief that Kuhn's insights into the history of science offer an important analogy for understanding Catholic debates about natural law in the United States since Vatican II.

The argument in the following pages rests on the conviction that what Kuhn was arguing about with regard to the macro-traditions of physical science are replicated in both macro- and micro-traditions outside of science as well, in this case the micro-tradition of natural law.

Natural law was a philosophical concept long before it became an important theological term. It originated with Aristotle centuries before the birth of Christ. But thanks to the epochal intellectual project undertaken by St. Thomas Aquinas in the thirteenth century, natural law became central to the Christian theological undertaking. Indeed, since the Reformations of the sixteenth century, natural law has become *the* privileged Catholic way of talking about moral theology, particularly Catholic ways of talking about sexual morality. For a number of centuries, then, natural law was (more or less) the only way in which Catholic theologians discussed some of the most important issues of Christian morality.

Chapter 1 will examine how Aristotle's theory of natural law came to be baptized by Aquinas sixteen centuries later. But this book is *not* a history of Catholic moral theology any more than it is a history of Catholic understandings of natural law. There are a number of very fine studies of the history of Catholic moral theology. But in this study both moral theology and natural law will be examined as something like theological guinea pigs (if that's not too undignified a metaphor for so ancient and revered an intellectual enterprise as moral theology) to explore the applicability of Kuhn's theory well outside the physical sciences. The development of natural law discourse is often seen as a steady progression. Drawing on Kuhn helps us see it in a new light.

One of the goals of this book, then, is to explore exactly how much rupture and *discontinuity* can be fitted into an even capacious understanding of a discipline before it becomes impossible to talk about a "natural law *tradition*" (in the singular). My own sense is that there is indeed an ancient and revered tradition (in the singular) of exploring how ethical questions rest on more basic patterns of meaning in the real world (often, but not always, termed "nature"); but to label that ancient and broad enterprise by the singular form of "natural law *tradition*," is problematic. More, too, on this to come.[3]

Just as Kuhn's work utilized the history of science as the narrative clothesline for laying out his argument regarding paradigm revolutions, so this work proceeds in an analogously historical fashion, moving from earlier paradigms of natural law to later ones. As Kuhn argued, history provides an easy-to-understand way of organizing the complex welter of ideas and evidence that is the real world. But the study that follows is organized historically also because its author is a church historian (actually, a historian of religious ideas, to be quite specific), and thus history is the default mode of organization when I am faced with a wide variety of ideas and models. Therefore this book proceeds in a roughly historical fashion from 1968 to the present, although how "rough" that order is will be up to individual readers to decide.

The year 1968 is offered as the starting point for the narrative that follows because that was when, in the United States, the unquestioned dominance of the specific type of natural law discourse (neo-scholasticism) that had defined Catholic moral theology for generations came to a dramatic end with unnerving specificity. And by "unnerving specificity" I simply mean that we can date the dramatic demise of that dominant form of natural law discourse to a very specific date in Catholic history: July 25, 1968. The study that follows therefore begins on that famous July afternoon, when Pope Paul VI's letter about contraception was published in the United States; this book explores some of the most important aftershocks in the field of moral theology that followed.

The reactions to Paul VI's famous encyclical resounded throughout the Catholic world, and one can easily make a compelling case that the most important responses to Paul VI's encyclical were produced *outside* the United States by Catholic theologians in Italy and Germany. Magisterial figures like Bernard Haring, Josef Fuchs, and Klaus Demmer—Europeans all—crafted an early response to neo-scholasticism well before any of the American theologians considered here even began their careers. Indeed, figures like Haring and Fuchs served as the mentors to important North American voices like Fr. Charles Curran. But this book focuses on the distinctly American responses to Paul VI's letter after 1968. This comparatively narrow focus does not imply that other, non-American, responses were either unimportant or of less intellectual cogency than the North American ones, or had less influence on the theology of the universal church. It is simply a reflection of the interests (and competence) of the author, a historian of US Catholic thought and practice in the twentieth century, and of the fact that the response within the American Church is interesting and instructive in its own right.

Why, then, write about how and why theology changes (a very broad topic) focused just on American Catholic models of natural law (a fairly circumscribed topic)? There is a fairly simple answer: I wanted to see whether the application of Kuhn's ideas to the heated Catholic debates over natural law—debates that stand comparison with any other religious tradition with regard to passion, acrimony, and misunderstanding—might offer a more dispassionate, and less heated, way of understanding the development of a "micro" theological tradition. The focus just on the United States, then, was undertaken as something like a "control" sampling of representative Catholic scholars. My own sense is that the results of this experiment warranted the fairly narrow focus. But—yet again—readers will have to decide for themselves whether that's correct.

I believe that Kuhn's now-famous understanding of how physical science develops contains important resources for understanding the history of theology. In the pages that follow I will attempt to show that theology does not progress in anything like a linear fashion from generation to generation, any more than Kuhn believed that about the physical sciences. Rupture and discontinuity are *at least* as important as continuity and linear development in narrating the history of Catholic natural law discourse in the United States during the past half century.

This book argues that the micro-traditions of theology (most specifically the micro-tradition of natural law) do *not* build seamlessly on each other. There is no clear line tracing natural law discourse from Paul VI in 1968 to graduate students writing their dissertations today. The past fifty years have seen serious rupture and reformulations—ruptures and reformulations that warrant a second look understanding theological "progress." That is, this study rejects an understanding of theology as an unbroken and ongoing conversation in which one single model provided the base on which succeeding generations of theologians built their "additions." Indeed, this study proceeds on the belief that *that* very model of the evolution of theology is not only naïve but also—on some basic level—untrue, and unhelpful in understanding the theological task.

Yes, of course there *is progress* in a very specific and circumscribed sense in the discreet subfields of theological research over time: biblical scholars find new archeological evidence—as at Qumran—on which to develop their theories about the "tradition history" of early Christianity and specific themes in the New Testament; scholars engaged in the project of discovering the "Historical Jesus" develop more sophisticated criteria that complicate the earlier, simplistic "Liberal Quest" undertaken in the nineteenth century; liturgical scholars discover lost or forgotten documents that shed new light of how earlier Christians understood "real presence" or the presence of the Holy Spirit in the Eucharist; church historians unearth documents lost or hidden about the role of Pius XII during World War II, or the role of the pope in calling the First Crusade. Progress in the specific fields of theological inquiry *is* made in a clearly circumscribed, narrowly defined, and technical sense. But as Kuhn argued in laying out his own theory of paradigm change, the "progress" made in these discreet areas contributes not only to greater knowledge about specific issues but also, simultaneously, to a growing awareness that the reigning paradigm holding all that knowledge together becomes increasingly untenable in light of new data and new discoveries. The overarching narrative holding all those facts together increasingly comes to be seen as problematic, or limited, or unable to explain a spectrum of new data; indeed, the reigning paradigm eventually comes to be seen as unbelievable and no longer useful for explaining the tradition. It is precisely when scholars come to realize that the "center will not hold" because of the sheer weight of the anomalies encountered by utilizing the older grid that a new paradigm becomes necessary to explain the data and experience at hand.

It is in this sense that this study argues that the micro-traditions of theology (and even the larger tradition of Catholic theology) *don't* "progress" or develop in an orderly, linear way over time. Rather, it argues that the history of theology has been marked by a regular series of ruptures, rejections, and reinventions, in which newer models are offered to replace the older ones, the latter no longer understandable in light of the new insights and data. This is, then, a book about how theological *revolutions* are structured, and why such an understanding might be helpful in understanding the theological task. And as Kuhn observed in making his own case, such a theory can only be proved *in practice*—that is, by how well (or badly) that theory explains the data and experience at hand.

It seems to me that four objections might be made at the outset to the experiment proposed here. *First:* some might object that a better way of talking about all of this should be termed an *evolution* rather than a revolution. After all, the word "revolution" is usually invoked to describe dramatically discontinuous events—as in the American or French Revolution. These skeptics might argue that even given the dramatically different shapes that natural law discourse has taken over the past fifty years, all the theologians engaged in that task were working toward a common end: the furthering of individual flourishing in community. Given that same end or object, is "revolution" actually the best way of talking about their respective projects? After all, all of them took as axiomatic the centrality of the Lordship of Jesus, the goodness of creation, human beings as created in the image of God (*Imago Dei*), and so forth. Wouldn't "evolution" work better here: one model evolving from the previous one?

This is a very good argument that should be taken seriously. My answer is that it's a question of calibration: how important are the respective categories of continuity and change when measuring a tradition? As the last two generations of American historians have labored to document, the American "Revolution" left the thirteen former colonies more similar than different from their identity in 1775. Many have argued that it was a "conservative revolution," which left British Whig political ideas in place for another half century after the colonies separated from Great Britain. Some have gone as far as to argue that perhaps a better term might be the "American Evolution." But historians of the French "Revolution" narrate a very different tale, one in which the discontinuities between "before" and "after" are far more dramatic: France under Robespierre and even the Bourbon kings who followed Napoleon was a very different place than France under Louis XVI—so different that historians mark 1789 as the dividing line between two different eras of Western history. For many, "modern history" begins in 1789, leaving behind the essentially medieval world of the divine right of kings in the eighteenth century. When is the application of "revolution" appropriate—the American or the French? Or both? Was the American event more an "evolution" than a revolution? How radical does a newer form have to be before it is termed a revolution? As in most things, revolution is in the eye of the beholder. Readers will similarly have to decide for themselves whether the application of that term "revolution" to the micro-tradition of Catholic natural law fits or not, but I make the case for it throughout this book.

Second: some may argue that debates about continuity and discontinuity within the Christian and Catholic traditions have a long and distinguished pedigree, so that this is hardly a new question: Newman's *Essay on the Development of Christian Doctrine* and John Noonan's own magisterial *Church That Can and Cannot Change* have already weighed in brilliantly on the question of the continuity (and the ruptures) of the Christian tradition. And both took as axiomatic that there was room for rupture—even dramatic rupture—within a capacious understanding of development and (dare I say) "progress." Does rupture *necessarily* imply complete discontinuity? And is the concept of paradigm revolution therefore the best way of describing the process of Catholic theology?

I think Kuhn's idea offers a helpful amendment to the insights of both Newman and Noonan: both were right (in part, anyway); but both were too sanguine (in my view) in their overly serene understanding of the development of the tradition and its micro-categories. Both were too quick to understand "development" in the way that many nonscientists understand "evolution": as a linear development in which "things are getting clearer and more defined." But no physical scientist would define the word in that way: reality is far more random and dangerous than would warrant a safely optimistic description of its "development." And they would further argue that the "end" of evolution is far more plastic and open than a serenely confident trust in the processes of evolution would allow. Kuhn's theory of paradigm revolutions, then, can serve to nuance—not to necessarily displace—Newman and Noonan's understandings of the "development of doctrine." At the end of this book readers may very well decide that "revolution" has its own problems when applied to the micro-tradition of Catholic natural law, but they will hopefully *also* appreciate the deep problems inherent in any model of the "linear development" of Catholic theology and doctrine. My position, then, is that Newman and Noonan were right—but only in part, and with lots of caveats. This book will, I hope, help to spell out those (sometimes large) caveats.

Third: one of Kuhn's favorite mantras, scattered throughout his book, is "reality is more complex than any model we can construct to explain it." That mantra would seem to imply that the human models constructed to explain the physical universe are not really rooted in any meaningful way in the reality "out there": they're just human language games unanchored to the hard-and-fast reality of the stars in their courses. Kuhn's mantra would seem to imply something like, "we'll construct a model to explain gravity as best we can, but we know it bears no relationship to how gravity *actually* works. Indeed, the word gravity itself is just a human construct to explain patterns we don't really understand in the physical universe." Catholic Christians might object to using Kuhn to analyze their tradition because it has always been rooted in a "theological realism"—the idea that ethical statements about right and wrong, and creedal formulas affirming the identity of Jesus as "true and true man," are more than just human affirmations: they refer in some *real* way to how things actually are, and how the universe is *really* patterned.

I would answer this objection in two parts. First, I think that Catholic theology is far too confident regarding the univocal truth of its creedal arguments, and a tad more modesty might be in order—what Margaret Farley so memorably termed the "grace of self-doubt." Aquinas was at pains to remind his students that his theology was "analogously true." That is, Aquinas consistently argued that his theological constructs had the same strengths and weaknesses as every kind of analogy: they were true insofar as they shed light on a subject that was ultimately mysterious, and the light they shed offered *real*—if partial—knowledge. But Aquinas was also at pains to remind his students that—precisely because his arguments were *analogical*—important parts of the reality illumined remained hidden, and unknown. My sense is that Kuhn's approach to paradigm construction offers us a salutary reminder of the need for theologians to pray for the grace of self-doubt, a grace that Aquinas had in abundance.[4]

But secondarily, even if Kuhn was a thoroughgoing relativist (and I don't believe he was), I remain fairly confident that applying his method to Catholic natural law nonetheless offers important insights into the realist tradition of Catholicism, (add "a" here) tradition that tends to be too quick by half to flout its realist credentials. A tad more mystery might be salutary, after all. And besides, analogy, too, resides in the eye of the beholder.

Finally, a skeptic might observe that natural law debate (like the larger Catholic theological tradition of which it is a part) never takes place in isolation. Catholic theologians, after all, learn their trade in graduate schools, where they are taught by senior scholars both the language and the arguments in which they will pursue their scholarly careers. Further, when minted with their doctorates and placed in tenure-stream positions, they develop their distinctive scholarly voice in a densely textured network of other scholars, some of whom are long-since deceased (like Aquinas) and some of whom work in offices next door to them. To focus on a group of *individuals* and their individually crafted scholarly work (as this study does) might imply that one's work is done without the conversation of provocateurs and partners. As my own dissertation director always reminded me, no one's scholarly work is ever entirely one's own.

My answer is simply that such an observation is obviously true—too obviously true to even question. Of course the individual theologians considered in the pages that follow—John Ford, Charles Curran, Germain Grisez, Jean Porter, Lisa Sowle Cahill—were integrated into their field by both deep reading and brilliant mentors (oftentimes at "secular" schools like Yale and the University of Chicago), and were initiated into their discipline by debate with a broad range of thinkers. But my focus on the following *individuals* to trace paradigm production in no way questions the obvious truth of the communal production of knowledge; what it does allow for is opportunity for the dramatic differences in their respective paradigms to stand in stark relief to each other. My end in proceeding in this way is not to imply that the paradigms considered were created in isolation, or written outside of dense networks of conversation and debate; it is rather to show why (and perhaps even how) rupture and disjunction play at least as important a role in the micro-traditions of theology as continuity, so that "revolution" might not be an altogether inappropriate way of talking about natural law debates in the Catholic community.

I further want to open a conversation about the degree to which natural law discourse was (or wasn't) a linear tradition in Catholic theology. All of the models considered here are labeled as being "in the natural law tradition" by their creators—a unified label that hides dramatically different understandings of what it means to be part of that tradition. Indeed, my suspicion is that the label partakes of false advertising if the tradition it points to is thought of as a single, unified stream. After all, Thomas Jefferson, Frederick Douglas, and Walter Rauschenbusch all fervently believed that there was a pattern or "grid" in the real world to which human beings were required to conform their actions for right living, the end of which was usually voiced as some variation of "flourishing" (e.g., "achieving full personhood," "reaching full stature as disciples"). Neither Douglas nor Rauschenbusch ever thought of themselves as participants in any kind of natural law "tradition," and neither (both voluminous writers) ever used the phrase "natural law." Jefferson famously referred to "nature and nature's God" in his work, but what he meant by that was worlds removed from what Aquinas and any of the authors considered here meant in referring to nature. He is often labeled as a "natural law deist," but such an identity, if related at all, was a distant third cousin to the Thomistic brand, so that to refer to both Aquinas and Jefferson as "natural law theorists" (precisely the claim voiced by John Courtney Murray in *We Hold These Truths*) actually raises more problems than it solves. Whatever is gained by such a common identification also contributes to confusion if the common label is understood to underscore linear progress, or organic development in which disjunction and discontinuity do not take primary roles.

Perhaps the fact that Catholic thinkers tend to be the last group to utilize such language lends a comforting coherence to thus labeling themselves as belonging to the same family—but I nonetheless have my doubts about how close the members of that family really are—maybe third cousins once removed? Readers will have to decide for themselves whether my doubts are warranted.

So now let's turn to some experiments.

PART I

1968

The End of the Catholic Nineteenth Century in 1968

In a higher world it is otherwise, but here below to live is to change, and to be perfect is to have changed often.

—CARDINAL NEWMAN[1]

A. The One-Hoss Shay

Students studying the ups and downs of natural law discourse in American Catholicism during the twentieth century might do well to begin their study with a reading of Oliver Wendell Holmes' picturesque poem entitled, "The Deacon's Masterpiece, or The Wonderful 'One-Hoss Shay.'" On one level the poem offers an arch and amusing recounting of a New England preacher's wonderfully constructed one-horse carriage "that was built in such a logical way/It ran a hundred years to the day." As fans of the poem (like myself) know, the seemingly indestructible chaise "went to pieces all at once/All at once, and nothing first/Just as bubbles do when they burst." Thus occurred the end of the wonderful one-hoss shay, but not without "scaring the parson into fits/Frightening people out of their wits."[2]

Scholars of American literature have reminded us that Holmes' famous poem actually had nothing to do with modes of transportation, one-horse or otherwise. What the poem does offer—quite effectively in fact, given its vivid Yankee speech patterns and colorful images—is a lively commentary on the disappearance of Calvinism in a culture founded and nourished by John Calvin's English "stepchildren." New England had been settled by fervent British Congregationalists in the seventeenth century, precisely as a haven for those who took their religion like they took their liquor: neat, without anything to water it down. The great-great-grandchildren of those very same Reformed Protestants, however, suddenly discovered, in the mid-nineteenth century, when Oliver Wendell Holmes was penning his witty verse, that they were Yankees, and no longer Puritans, Calvinist, or otherwise.

The vast Puritan theological edifice embodied in creeds like the *Westminster Confession of Faith* (1646)—which had been painstakingly carried over the Atlantic in the seventeenth century by the zealous founders of Plymouth and Boston, and carefully nourished by intellectual giants like Jonathan Edwards in the eighteenth century—"went to pieces all at once" two centuries later, seemingly overnight. What had been considered in its day one of the most brilliant Christian theological systems ever conceived— a system regarded by both its adherents and its detractors as marked pre-eminently by its rigorously exact and detailed presentation of Christian belief—suddenly appeared ridiculous and (more to the point) irrelevant, after centuries of unquestioning adherence. And for a system of Christian belief that was considered so perfect that its adherents believed it would stand for a thousand years (or until Jesus returned), its demise—shockingly—was not marked by a long illness. In less than a generation, many of the oldest Protestant churches in Massachusetts (those white-steepled "first parishes" that grace village greens all over the Bay State) suddenly slipped away from their moorings and became Unitarian. As Oliver Wendell Holmes ironically observed at the end of his poem (riffing on Calvinism's purported strength as a rational system of belief that would never be supplanted): "Logic is logic. That's all I say."[3]

The American Catholic community experienced a very similar, and seemingly equally quick, disappearance of a revered theological system after 1968. What passed from the scene was, as in the earlier case, a rigorously systematic, even logical, theological system, which has traditionally been labeled "neo-scholastic natural law."

As a distinctive intellectual system, natural law can be dated to the emergence of Western philosophy in ancient Greece—most notably to Aristotle in the fourth century B.C. In his great work entitled *Rhetoric*, Aristotle asserted that human beings possess certain rights apart from, and antecedent to, the rights and protections granted by rulers or governments ("positive law"). These universal natural rights are inherent in the nature of being human and could be discovered through the exercise of reason. Basing his assertion on the insights expounded by other Greek philosophers (and on the great truths to be found in the dramas produced by Greek playwrights like Sophocles), Aristotle thus argued that—quite aside from the particular rights and protections that each human society sets up—there is something like a "common" law applicable to all people, embedded in their very nature:

> Universal law is the law of Nature. For there really is, as everyone to some extent understands, a natural justice and injustice that is binding on all men, even on those who have no association or covenant with each other. It is this that Sophocles' [character] Antigone clearly means when she says that the burial of Polyneices was a just act in spite of the prohibition [against it]; she means that it is just by nature.[4]

Among the many reasons that Aristotle's idea of a natural law became normative in subsequent philosophical speculation about human nature and human rights for millennia was that such a concept provided a ready means for rising above the multifarious (and often-contradictory) sets of humanly constructed legal systems to talk about certain moral obligations to which every human person, regardless of culture or religion, could be held. What human laws (in the plural) commanded might vary from place to place; but a Universal Law (in the singular) that existed *by nature* (in the sense of *human* nature) was the same everywhere, all the time. Centuries before the rise of global consciousness or multiculturalism, philosophers recognized the utility of a measurement of human goodness that transcended specific cultures: harming the innocent was always wrong, and paying people what they honestly earned was always good, regardless of geography or time frame.[5]

But although built on firm Aristotelean foundations, the recognizably Catholic form of this intellectual tradition took shape in the centuries after St. Thomas Aquinas wrote his magisterial work, the *Summa Theologica,* between 1265 and 1274. The "*Summa*"—the shorthand term that Catholic theologians and philosophers familiarly use to refer to Aquinas' great work— can serve as a convenient placeholder for the emergence of what became a distinct—and distinctively—Catholic "take" on the older Aristotelean tradition. In Aquinas' brilliant hands, Aristotle's idea of natural law became the rock on which much of Catholic moral thought would develop for centuries.[6]

As Fr. Charles Curran so lucidly observed, Aquinas was an "intrinsic teleologist." By that, Curran meant that Aquinas based his ethical system on understanding the proper "end" (*telos* in Greek) of the human project. For Aquinas, that end was human flourishing, wholeness, and completion (*eudaimonia*). Utilizing Aristotle's insights, Aquinas thus elucidated a quite sophisticated and distinctively Catholic version of natural law: for Aquinas, the law component in natural law was not an extrinsic set of commands imposed from the outside by an autocratic God. Rather, Aquinas believed that law was something human beings should observe "because it is good for the individual, and leads to the ultimate fulfillment and happiness of the individual."[7]

Like Aristotle, Aquinas argued that human beings could use their reason to arrive at a proper understanding of both the importance of flourishing and the actions necessary to achieve it. And central to achieving that wholeness and flourishing was living a life of prudence, virtue, and integrity. Arriving at that insight did not require faith in the gods or God at all; but it could be accessed through human reason. It was therefore available to everyone, of any—or no—faith. It is in *this* very specific sense that Aquinas could offer his now-famous formula for ethical living: "the end (telos) of the act determines its goodness or badness." That end was not imposed externally; it could rather be discerned—using human reason—in the structure of human nature itself. Thus both "law" and "nature" had quite distinctive meanings that would (unfortunately) change in the hands of Aquinas' disciples. But Aquinas' legacy to the Catholic tradition was a quite distinctive natural law approach to ethics. To the perennial human question that arises in every culture: "what is it to live a good life?" the Angelic Doctor answered, "it is to achieve fully human flourishing through living a life of virtue."[8]

But Aquinas offered a further, distinctively Christian, "spin" on Aristotle's notion of natural law. Living a virtuous life in accord with the end or purpose of human living, he argued, would never be totally accomplished in this life: achieving such completion would only be accomplished after death, in the beatific vision of God, in God's kingdom. And to achieve such flourishing in the next life, human beings had to develop a range of intellectual and moral virtues that could guide them amid the messiness of history, and its equally messy moral choices. Therefore the Christian life was about developing habits of virtue, focused on a clear understanding of the end of human living. And while natural law was eternal and unchanging, developing the habits necessary to live in accord with it was a fluid and dynamic business, very much inflected by historical circumstances: the natural law that required one to "always tell the truth" didn't change; what "telling the truth" meant in specific historical circumstances, however, was considerably more complex and historically determined.[9]

But in terms of understanding the collapse within the American Catholic community in the decades after the 1960s, there is one further historical wrinkle that needs to be understood. In understanding the events of the

"Catholic 1968," it is important to note that it was not Aquinas himself, nor his famous *Summa*, that shaped the way that Catholic theology and doctrine had been presented in the centuries after his death.

What *did* shape the way that Catholic ethics was presented was a more "positivist" approach to theological discussion popularized by teachers in the medieval universities after Aquinas, teachers who came to be known as "scholastics" (i.e., scholars). In place of Aquinas' quite sophisticated understanding of natural law as an ethical system focused on the goal of human flourishing through habits that evolved and deepened during the life of discipleship, the scholastics increasingly came to present natural law as something given, set, and external to human nature itself: a law *delivered* to humanity from a God outside of history, rather than discerned in human nature. It was a model of law much closer to how lawyers understand "positive law"—that is, human-made law—which was imposed on individuals from above by those who had the authority to do so. These scholastics continued to define themselves as "Thomists"—at least in the sense of claiming Aquinas and his *Summa* as their model and guide. But as a number of historians have noted, Aquinas would have had a difficult time recognizing his own approach to Christian ethics in the works of these scholastics who claimed him as their patron saint.[10]

By the nineteenth century, these scholastic disciples of Aquinas had evolved into something even further removed from Aquinas' approach to natural law. These "neo-scholastics" increasingly came to utilize syllogisms and "proofs" in offering moral teaching, so that Christian ethics was reduced to following formal propositions that applied to everyone, regardless of their place on the Christian journey of discipleship. These neo-scholastics took great pride in the logical nature of applying principles to the Christian life—principles anyone might discover through a syllogistic exercise. Once one had reached the end of the syllogism, the ethical teaching was "proven," and could be assumed to apply to the same situation for everyone, regardless of time or place.[11]

The theology of these new ("neo") scholastics prided itself on its systematic interpretation of Catholic doctrine in light of an unchanging law embedded in an almost objectivist understanding of "nature" by God, discoverable by human reason, the moral implications of which were equally unchanging. But the great twentieth-century moral theologian Josef Fuchs argued that to call the arguments offered by these thinkers "Thomistic" was something of an intellectual stretch; it was, rather, really a form of moral positivism, positing a "static law 'written in nature'" that missed Aquinas' emphasis on natural law as the "living and *active creaturely participation* in God's eternal wisdom." It was this rigid nineteenth-century neo-scholastic natural law tradition that helped to set up the Catholic version of the collapse of the "One-Hoss Shay."[12]

The trauma experienced within the Catholic community by the seemingly swift and unforeseen collapse of neo-scholastic natural law had actually been preceded by a gradual and quiet fraying of neo-scholastic discourse for decades among moral theologians. Thus, while the collapse of this neo-scholastic tradition as the privileged form of Catholic moral teaching appeared to both lay Catholics and to most parish priests to be sudden and without warning, cracks had begun appearing considerably before its fate became publically acknowledged. But even with these historical caveats, the public collapse of neo-scholasticism as the privileged form of Catholic moral discourse can be dated to the afternoon of July 25, 1968 (Rome time). On that seemingly unremarkable afternoon during a typically humid Roman summer, Pope Paul VI ended years of discussion and study by Catholic theologians and bishops by issuing a letter on human sexuality and birth control entitled—innocuously enough—"On Human Life."[13]

B. *"Intrinsically Disordered Acts"*

The 1968 encyclical ("Catholic-speak" for an official letter published by the pope on an important issue) opened with the unremarkable observation that modern science—most especially those branches of the scientific enterprise studying human fertility—had given rise to new questions that demanded Catholic attention. Indeed, it observed that, given the extraordinary progress that modern science had made in addressing issues surrounding pregnancy and fertility, believers must now enter into a new and deeper reflection upon the principles of the "moral meaning of marriage." And it further reminded Catholic readers that it was both the duty and the right of Church leaders—most especially the duty and the right of the "Chief Pastor" of the Church, the pope himself—to lead the conversation about such important issues. And this was so (the encyclical carefully noted) because the Church had received from Christ himself the responsibility of interpreting "the entire moral law—not only the law of the Gospel, *but also the natural law, which are both the expression of God's will for man's [sic] moral life.*"[14]

Given the understanding of neo-scholastic natural law that shaped the understanding of most Catholic bishops and some theologians at the time, nothing stated in the Introduction to that point would have raised many eyebrows. Further, the encyclical's lush and elegant second section—exploring the question of how church teaching needed to underlie and inform moral decisions in light of these scientific advances—began with the unexceptional observation that this very important conversation about the moral meaning of marriage had to balance biological, demographic, psychological, and even sociological perspectives within the broader context of religious faith. That is, the physical and social scientific approaches to marriage and family questions (good in themselves) had to engage in ongoing conversation with what the Church taught about the "ends" and purposes of married love. At this point, the encyclical offered a moving and extended reflection on the love of husband and wife, drawing deeply on the beautiful reflection on such love that had been offered in the Second Vatican Council's "Constitution of the Church in the Modern World," *Gaudium et Spes*.[15]

But by the time readers of the encyclical reached paragraph 10, things became both considerably more interesting and (as it would turn out) more contentious. For in that paragraph the pope observed that genuine love and respect between married partners naturally flowed into "responsible" parenthood. That phrase—responsible parenthood—seemed to open up several possible options as to the encyclical's purpose. For paragraph 10 observed that responsible parenthood required that husband and wife "recognize their duties to God, toward themselves, toward the family, and toward society, in a correct hierarchy of values."[16]

At that point, the pope's argument could have gone in a number of conceivable directions. The encyclical could have argued for a change in the Church's teaching regarding contraception. Might not the decision to limit the number of children in a marriage in order to better care for other children, or to let one spouse care for a sick or hospitalized spouse, evince a "correct hierarchy of values"? Might this not be an instance of recognizing their spousal duties "toward themselves, toward the family, and toward society"? Or, the encyclical could have proceeded toward a reaffirmation of the norms of the past, especially given the serious conjugal responsibility to recognize their "duties to God." Or, the Pope's argument could have outlined some new position on a spectrum somewhere between the first two positions. For example, the Church's prohibition of contraception might remain the norm, but perhaps exceptions could be made for crisis situations like food shortages or epidemics in developing nations, or the development of serious health challenges by either parent.

But in fact the sentence that began widespread Catholic dissent from, and objection to, neo-scholastic natural law as the preferred language for Catholic theology occurred at the end of that same paragraph. For after its

extended reflection on "responsible parenthood," article 10 announced that
married couples were not, in fact, free to proceed completely at will, "as if they
could determine in a wholly autonomous fashion the honest path to follow."
Rather, all Christian couples were expected to *conform their activity to the
creative intention of God expressed in the very nature of marriage and its acts.*"[17]

While the debates generated almost immediately after the publication of
Humanae Vitae focused on a number of statements made throughout the encyclical, most of the "pushback" offered by Catholic theologians in the United
States coalesced around paragraph 10 and the four paragraphs that followed
it. Paragraph 11 announced that Paul VI would stand by previous teaching on
this issue: the Church, "calling men [*sic*] back to norms of the natural law, as
interpreted by her constant doctrine, teaches that *each and every marriage act
must remain open to the transmission of life.*" And paragraph 14 elucidated that
teaching with a quite specific discussion of the kinds of conjugal acts that it
described as intrinsically disordered:

> It is not licit, *even for the gravest reasons*, to do evil that good may follow
> therefrom; that is, to make into the object of a positive act of the will
> something which is intrinsically disordered, and hence unworthy of
> the human person, *even when the intention is to safeguard or promote
> individual, family, or social well- being.*[18]

At various points, the pope's missive had consciously allowed that sexual relations between spouses embodied a range of important values and goods,
goods that included the expression of mutual affection and the physical expression of fidelity and respect. But articles 11 and 14 formed the bookends
of an argument which insisted that, even allowing for these interpersonal
goods that coitus expressed, sexual relations between spouses could never be
judged from the standpoint of affection and respect to the exclusion of an
openness to the possibility of transmission of new life. And it was article 12
that offered the "glue" (as it were) that held together these two bookends in
a coherent way. For article 12 announced (in two of most quoted sentences
in the critical responses which immediately followed the publication of the
encyclical) that

> this teaching is founded on the *inseparable connection*, willed by
> God and unable to be broken by man [*sic*] on his own initiative, *be-
> tween the two meanings of the act: the unitive meaning and the procre-
> ative meaning.* . . . We believe that the men of our day are particularly

capable of seizing the *deeply reasonable and human character* of this
fundamental principle.[19]

Viewed with twenty-twenty hindsight, it is now clear that there were two
phrases in article 12 that unleashed the perfect storm of the reception (or,
perhaps closer to the truth, nonreception) of Paul VI's encyclical in the days
and months that followed. The first was this description of an *inseparable*
connection between the two meanings of sexual relations between spouses
that had to be held together in each and every act of sexual relations between
husband and wife. But it was the second phrase, the one about the *"deeply
reasonable and human character"* of this principle that—unsurprisingly, given
neo-scholasticism's strong emphasis on the profoundly reasonable, and even
logical, nature of its arguments—would cause so much confusion (and, soon,
even anger) among the Catholic faithful.[20]

No Catholic moral theologian in 1968 would have questioned the fact
that there was an important connection between conjugal love and procreation. At least since St. Augustine penned his essays on the duties and
ends of sexual relations in marriage in the fourth century, Catholic theology took such an intrinsic connection pretty much for granted. What
many (and, as it would turn out, the majority) of moral theologians in the
American Catholic community *did* question was the inseparable nature of
that connection in *each and every* act of spousal coitus. More specifically,
they found the natural law "proof" for such a teaching thin—at best. Indeed,
far from assenting to the "deeply reasonable and human character" of such
teaching, an exceedingly large segment of Catholic moral theologians in the
United States (almost all of them priests) found such an argument implausible (or even illogical), and easy to refute. Dubious voices in the theological
guild immediately started asking if these were the best arguments available
to justify what many Catholic couples had already come to view as outdated
church teaching.

But there were other—historical and political—questions that dogged the
reception of *Humanae Vitae* from the moment it was promulgated. Precisely
because it was issued just three years after the conclusion of the Second
Vatican Council, which had privileged a more biblical and less hierarchical
understanding of the Church as the "people of God," the way in which the
encyclical had been promulgated seemed, at best, problematic. In issuing the
encyclical, Paul VI had overridden the majority opinion of a hand-selected
committee that his much-loved predecessor, John XXIII, had appointed. The
majority report of that committee had strongly urged a change in Church

teaching that would allow some forms of contraception. Further, the precise nature of the encyclical's juridical authority as "definitive" church teaching had been muddied at its first public appearance: Monsignor Ferdinando Lambruschini, in presenting the encyclical at a Vatican press conference on July 29, 1968, had declared that, while the encyclical was obviously an important document issued by the man whom Catholics considered the Vicar of Christ on Earth, "an attentive reading of the encyclical does not suggest the theological note of infallibility." If that was so, then what—exactly—*was* its authority?[21]

This last question—of the authority of the encyclical—was the core issue in understanding what followed. For although the collapse of scholastic natural law theory as the premier (and privileged) Catholic approach to moral theory seemed sudden and unaccountably swift in the wake of *Humanae Vitae,* warning signs—quiet, undramatic, and largely limited to Catholic moral theologians—had been gathering for a while. John Lynch, SJ—himself a moral theologian of some note—had voiced concerns in the pages of *Theological Studies'* famed "Notes on Moral Theology" (something like the top-of-the-line trade journal for priests in the theological ethics guild) in 1964 that storm clouds seemed to be gathering over the unquestioned reception of neo- scholastic theological arguments. Lynch—four years before the publication of Paul VI's encyclical—had noted that the Church's prohibition was "based on a single principle: the fact of an established design which God Himself had written unchangeably into the natural structure of the marriage act."[22]

This central principle of an "established design—implanted in nature itself by God, and ostensibly discernable to anyone utilizing human reason, quite independently of religious faith—represented the keystone of the entire neo-scholastic argument about contraception. Further, this principle of an established design had offered a purportedly *reasonable* basis for Catholic teaching, utilized most recently by Pope Pius XII in his 1953 address to Italian midwives. But despite the consistent use of this argument by Catholic authorities (including a number of Paul VI's predecessors) throughout the 19th and 20th centuries, Lynch observed in his "Notes" in 1964 that it was becoming quite common to hear fellow Catholic theologians ask hard questions about the intellectual weight of such an argument. He confessed that it was unsettling to hear the confident prophecy that the Church would have to change its official teaching, "voiced intramurally." Indeed, most unsettling for Lynch was the fact that a number of fellow Jesuit seminary professors had freely confessed to him "that none of the rational arguments advanced in proof of the intrinsic evil of the practice is totally convincing." In the event, Lynch's professed worries about the intellectual thinness of the proofs offered by neo-scholastic theology for the condemnation of contraception proved to be something of an understatement four years later, when *Humanae Vitae* set off a firestorm among Catholic moral theologians.[23]

C. *The Attack on the House of Arrested Clocks*

Even allowing for the fact that the swift and almost universal critique of *Humanae Vitae* in the days following its release was not exactly as surprising as the secular and Catholic press portrayed it, the collapse of the Catholic version of the one-hoss shay *did* unnerve many clergy and lay people, creating a traumatic series of aftershocks much like those described by Oliver Wendell Holmes ("Scaring the parson into fits/Frightening people out of their wits").[24]

According to demographic data, we now know that a quite significant percentage of the Catholic faithful had long been utilizing precisely the kinds of artificial contraception condemned by the 1968 encyclical. But many (probably most) of the faithful utilizing contraceptive devices undoubtedly presumed that this was "sinful practice" in their marriage—at least in the eyes of the Church. Most of them were not aware of the murmuring among Catholic moral theologians that the neo-scholastic arguments used to condemn such practice lacked cogency (or even basic coherence), and could easily be refuted by those in the theological guild. Even granted, then, lay ignorance about the gradual fraying of the neo-scholastic theological edifice, what had happened among Catholic theologians in the years before Paul VI's much-maligned encyclical that could trigger such an immediate and well-thought-out critique of what Catholics considered magisterial teaching—perhaps not infallible, but magisterial (i.e., authoritative) nonetheless?[25]

The short answer to that question is that a very broad intellectual movement had breached the closely guarded battlements of the Catholic fortress, and could not be rebuffed, even by the considerable forces of the papacy. This movement was the dawning of historical consciousness within the Church itself. Historical consciousness, at its most basic level, is the simple awareness that everything in history changes. This may sound obvious, but it was actually anything but. In 1960 it would have been a very safe bet that most US Catholics believed that what they did at mass on Sunday mornings was pretty much like the worship led by Jesus' disciples in the first century. Many (arguably most) also believed that Catholic teaching was unchanging simply because it was unchangeable. Just like the Latin formula that ended most Catholic prayers—*erat in principio, et nunc, et in saecula saeculorum* ("as it was in the beginning, is now, and will be forever")—most Catholics took for granted the timelessness of both their theology and their worship. It was precisely because of this sense of timelessness that so much of Catholic life came under attack by historical consciousness.[26]

Perhaps the person who understood and described that older Catholic worldview, the newer worldview that attacked it, and the stakes involved in the displacement of the first by the second was Canadian Jesuit theologian, Bernard Lonergan. In a brief but extremely important paper delivered at the Canon Law Society of America in 1967, Lonergan outlined that intellectual displacement with breathtaking brevity and elegance. The title of Lonergan's famous address—"The Transition from a Classicist World View to Historical Mindedness"—offers an easy-to-grasp guide for understanding the sometimes-complex debates that followed the publication of *Humanae Vitae*. In his address, Lonergan argued that the battles about authority then roiling the North American Catholic Church over its reception of the documents of the Second Vatican Council really had less to do with worship or church authority than with two worldviews that now battled in what many in the Catholic community considered a life-or-death combat:

> One may be named classicist, conservative, traditional; the other may be named modern, perhaps historicist (though that word unfortunately is ambiguous). The differences between the two are enormous . . . [for] they are differences in horizon, in total mentality.[27]

For Lonergan, then, the real battle underlying all of the discreet skirmishes between what both the secular and Catholic press would come to term "liberals" and "conservatives" in the Church was between two worldviews that found public voice in the Catholic community in the course of the 1960s. For the "classicists" (and here we can substitute the phrase "the writers of the 1968 encyclical") the real world rested on unchanging laws. The Truth (always in caps for such believers) remained substantially the same throughout history. For classicist believers, then, human nature and right action were necessarily static realities because they rested on immutable laws found in nature, whose author was God. And because God had created human reason as well, the *ends* of "human nature" and "right action" (Catholic-speak for the meaning and purpose of human life and behavior) could be appropriated through the rational study of an unchanging natural law that (quite literally) undergirded the real world. Natural law, then, was "out there" in an objective, third-person kind of way, and its very objectivity made it a powerful symbol of God's ordering of the universe. That natural law was both objective (like gravity) and discoverable by human reason.[28]

Toward this static worldview Lonergan sketched out what many called the historicist understanding of reality, perhaps more felicitously termed "historical mindedness." Adherents of this approach saw no changeless realm of static truth undergirding either nature or human evolution. Rather, everything— human persons and institutions, no less than the physical universe itself—was shaped by processes in history. This second approach to understanding reality had, in Lonergan's estimation, largely won the day in Western culture since the eighteenth century—so much so that to be "modern" in popular usage was to understand the human project as developing over, and in, time. The idea that there existed, somewhere either in history or above it, a perfect and timeless model of perfection that could serve as a yardstick for measuring human goodness or rightness now appeared not only naïve but also nonsensical.[29]

In this second (modern) worldview, then, human nature and human values were *not* "fixed, static, and immutable, but shifting, developing, going astray, and capable of redemption." And this was obviously the case (obvious, at least, to those who ascribed to historical consciousness) because *everything* was immersed in the stream of history—even the Gospel message itself. Thus, Lonergan argued, for those with historical consciousness, Jesus' message of redemption had to be framed within the context of "historicity . . . for it is on this level and through this medium . . . that divine revelation has entered the world, and that the Church's witness is given to it." And then Lonergan enunciated an insight that might be taken as the death knell for the uncontested dominance of the centuries-old classicist approach to Catholic thought and practice: that older static conception of reality, he announced, "is no longer the only conception, or [even] the commonly received conception; and I think our Scripture scholars would agree that its abstractness, and the omissions due to abstraction, have no foundation in the revealed word of God."[30]

And as if that were not enough to unsettle the waters of centuries of Catholic teaching, Lonergan observed that Catholic theology was placed in an impossible situation if the foundational insights of modern thought were perceived as impossible challenges to belief: Christian believers could no longer ignore the implications of historical consciousness. Nor could the Church itself in its role as teacher of the faithful.[31]

Long before Lonergan delivered this now-famous address, Catholic moral theologians had recognized the challenges posed by historical consciousness to their craft, and had begun to reshape the Catholic tradition accordingly. Their explorations as to how that consciousness might change the trade of Catholic moral theology were quiet and specialized, and largely outside the purview of the vast majority of both the Catholic faithful and Catholic bishops.

Usually labeled "revisionists" by their colleagues, these scholars recognized that the older, static ("objective") model of natural law now posed insuperable problems to the utility—and even the coherence—of Catholic teaching, and had to be revised along more modern lines. Human history and human experience must now be introduced, they argued, in the presentation of moral arguments, if for no other reason than to make it believable to modern Catholics.[32]

By the 1950s, Catholic moral theologians experienced something like a split within their ranks: a number continued to practice the older "manualist" tradition, centered on the classicist model of natural law, whose aim was to provide manuals for confessors hearing confession. Richard McCormick would later characterize this tradition as "all too one-sidedly confession-oriented, canon law-related, sin-centered, and seminary-controlled." But, increasingly, theologians joined the ranks of the revisionists, who understood that the moral life had to take into account historical developments in the life of the Church, as well as the often-messy historical lives of individual Christians.[33]

Arguably the first major revisionist to achieve widespread attention by moral theologians was Bernhard Haring, whose 1600-page book, *The Law of Christ*, was published in 1954. One of Haring's canniest decisions was to begin his massive, two-volume study of Catholic moral theology with a historical survey of moral theology. While the ostensible purpose of that survey was to show how Haring himself stood under the broad umbrella of the Catholic moral tradition, it implied genuine problems for conceiving of the tradition as a linear one, and this was so because Catholic moral theology *itself had a history,* and that history didn't appear to flow in a single stream. Far from being static, timeless, and linear in development, Haring showed how the various schools of moral theology had developed over the course of history, and how they had often disagreed with each other. As Garry Wills would later observe, the most dramatic insight offered by this kind of historical survey was that it let the cat out of the bag that the "*church changes.*"[34]

Haring's break with the neo-scholastics who preceded him, then, not only involved his rejection of their approach to moral theology as a background for hearing confessions but also, more importantly, took as axiomatically true that moral theology itself had evolved over time, and had dramatically changed its position on certain acts that it had once considered "intrinsically evil" (like charging interest on loans ["usury"]) or, conversely, condemning activities it had once considered morally permissible (e.g., Christians engaging in chattel slavery and the slave trade). Even the categories of "goodness" and "badness," it would seem, had had a history. And with that realization came another—potentially far more unsettling—one: that the classicist appeal to the unchanging nature of church teaching ("as we have always taught") often had a problematic basis in history.[35]

And it was *precisely* that problematic historical appeal to "as we have always taught" that marshalled the revisionist critics of *Humanae Vitae* from the moment of its appearance. Quite contrary to Paul VI's intention and expectations, the encyclical's very appeal in article 11 to the "constant teaching of the Church" in arguing for its position now seemed both unconvincing and even historically naive to revisionist moral theologians, which made their criticism of the encyclical all but certain.[36]

D. *"None of the Rational Arguments Is Totally Convincing"*

Richard McCormick, a much-respected revisionist theologian, immediately recognized the deeply problematic nature of the classicist arguments offered in *Humanae Vitae*, and offered a thoughtful and (in the minds of some, devastating) critique of its teaching in *Theological Studies*.

McCormick began by noting that many of the arguments offered in *Humanae Vitae* rested on an embarrassingly dated and static understanding of biology: the encyclical seemed to "attribute a [moral] meaning to all coitus on the basis of what happens with relative rarity." How could the moral meaning of a physical act be derived from a purportedly fixed and unmovable end—conception—that it actually achieved only rarely, while ignoring the importance of other ends that were arguably achieved with more regularity? This, McCormick averred, made no sense.[37]

But McCormick went even further in assaulting the intellectual incoherence of the encyclical's model of morality: he observed that there was something like a logical contradiction at the heart of the encyclical's argument. The encyclical had strongly condemned all artificial methods of contraception as "intrinsically disordered" (the latter phrase representing a condemnation about as condemnatory as Catholic theology gets). But while so arguing, it also allowed for the moral permissibility of what Catholics had come to call the "rhythm method" (i.e., intentionally plotting cycles of female menstruation to determine "safe" periods during which coitus was less likely to lead to pregnancy). This, it seemed to McCormick, opened up a large realm of logical inconsistencies—an especially damaging observation, given neo-scholasticism's proud claims to be reasonable and even logical, and the pope's own confidence (explicitly voiced in the encyclical) that the "men of our day are particularly capable of seizing the deeply reasonable character of this fundamental principle."[38]

With this very allowance of the rhythm method, McCormick observed, the encyclical seemed "unwittingly to imply a factual separation of the unitive and procreative aspects of human aspects of human coitus during the infertile period." But such a double standard flew in the face of human reason: wasn't *any* separation of the unitive and procreative aspects of sexual relations precisely the thing that the encyclical condemned as intrinsically disordered? And if it allowed for such a separation to utilize the rhythm method, why not for other (equally intentional) methods of controlling contraception? Why was the use of a thermometer and calendar (for charting the infertile periods of a woman's ovulation cycle) somehow *not* a violation of the prohibitions enjoined on Christians ("never frustrate the natural course of sexuality") while the use of a pill consumed orally somehow *was*? This too, he averred, made no sense.[39]

But arguably the most thorough-going of McCormick's criticisms was his questioning of the basic model of neo-scholastic natural law underlying the entire document: natural law arguments, he argued—if nothing else—had to be *plausible*, as they claimed to rest on the reasonable nature of a physical universe created by God. If the analysis and argument offered in authoritative moral teaching using natural law do not support the conclusions of such teaching, what was one to make of those conclusions? *That* was the question posed by moral theologians like McCormick who had come to doubt the intellectual coherence of the older classicist model of natural law. Precisely because the Catholic tradition of natural law since Aquinas had emphasized the essential *reasonableness* of morality, in the process foregrounding the ability of the human intellect to grasp the essential coherence and plausibility of the Church's stance on moral issues like contraception, what were they to make of such teaching when it appeared to rest on illogical and even implausible arguments? And how could Catholic moral theologians defend such teaching when they (as well as the Catholic faithful to whom such teaching was addressed) clearly recognized the intellectual incoherence and existential irrelevance of such a dated, static, and juridical approach to living the Christian life?

> At the very least, very many moral theologians will agree that there are serious methodological problems, even deficiencies, in the analysis used to support the conclusion [of the encyclical]. . . . It says in effect that the authoritative character of the teaching is not identified with the reasons adduced for it. On the other hand, it clearly implies that the certainty of the teaching cannot prescind from the adequacy of the analyses given.[40]

Being something of a star within the guild of Catholic moral theology at the time, McCormick articulated with nuanced precision the confusion of many others in his discipline: if (as Monsignor Lambruschini had stated at the press conference announcing the encyclical) *Humanae Vitae* did not purport to be infallible teaching, how could its teaching be accepted as valid completely independently of the arguments presented to explain it? The model of natural law advanced in it was not only doubtful but also almost risible in its simplistic identification of natural law with "natural processes" in the physical universe. As McCormick and many others would later note, such a moral argument risked being labeled "physicalist"—a largely discredited approach that argued that one could reach an understanding of the moral meaning of human acts by studying their physical embodiment: was *this* really the best the Church could offer on such an important question? Such a simplistic argument was— as Garry Wills would later observe—so intellectually thin as to "make a high school sophomore blush." Being himself an accomplished student of the history of moral theology, McCormick knew that, while the Church's teaching did not claim to be *rational* (i.e., reducible to human reason), Catholic theology had asserted for centuries that its teaching was at least *reasonable* (i.e., understandable to human reason). No Catholic theologian would claim that the authority of Church teaching was *totally* independent of the arguments advanced to explain it. Indeed, the Church (after a fair amount of internal debate) had embraced natural law in the thirteenth century precisely *because* that tradition promised the possibility of explaining (or even justifying) its moral teaching by an appeal to its essential "reasonableness." Given that long and distinguished history of moral teaching, what was one to make of the authority of an encyclical like *Humanae Vitae*? What authority, indeed.

PART II

Paradigm Revolutions, 1960 to 1966

2

The Structure of Scientific Revolutions

A. "Forcing Nature into Conceptual Boxes"

Richard McCormick's powerful critique of the "authoritative teaching" about human reproduction offered in *Humanae Vitae* unites the two movements around which this book is structured. While most Catholics experienced the widespread critique of the 1968 encyclical as a sudden (if welcome) rejection of the kind of theological argument that the Church had utilized in its moral teaching for several centuries, the cracks in the foundations of that older approach to natural law had appeared considerably before 1968. The emergence of a *historicist* approach to moral theology in the decades before the promulgation of the encyclical thus contextualizes the rocky reception accorded it, allowing us to see that rocky reception within a much larger historical framework. The arguments offered as "proof" that the practice of contraception was "intrinsically disordered" rang false for most of the encyclical's readers, including among the most respected moral theologians in the American church. Its static and ahistorical teaching regarding the unchangeable "design" implanted in "nature" by God's own self seemed unsupported by the actual experience of married couples, who experienced their history of sexual relations as bearing *many* meanings. Further, even the guild of moral theologians had come to a much more nuanced understanding of what could be (and what could not be) "unchangeable" in Christian ethics. As the great scholar Bernard Haring illustrated so well in a book published more than a decade before *Humanae Vitae*, both moral theology and the Church's teaching on a number of important moral issues had a history, and the word "unchangeable" didn't seem to correctly apply to those teachings. Further (and equally to the point), the meanings or "ends" of those acts seem to have changed, too.

But historical consciousness, in itself, does not serve as well in explaining the debates that fractured the Catholic community in the half century *after* the promulgation of *Humanae Vitae*. To explain those intramural debates after 1968, turning to the insights of a second intellectual movement (whose emergence was contemporaneous with that of historical consciousness among moral theologians) might serve the purposes of this study more effectively. This second intellectual movement had no discernable impact at all on shaping the immediate reactions to Paul VI's encyclical; but it nonetheless offers important resources for explaining the scramble undertaken by Catholic theologians to *both* critique *and* buttress *Humanae Vitae* in the decades after its promulgation. And it is this second intellectual movement that will significantly shape the narrative in the pages that follow.

In one sense, this second (science-based) movement represented a very similar emergence of historical consciousness among scientific researchers in ways that paralleled the rise of historical mindedness among Catholic theologians like Bernard Lonergan and Bernard Haring. But in another sense, the implications of this second intellectual strain of thought are arguably even more far-reaching and revolutionary in the realm of epistemology—that is, in explaining how human beings come to know the world around them. For this second intellectual impulse, sponsored by historians and philosophers of science, raised profoundly disturbing questions about how human knowledge could be conceived of as linear and accumulative. And to that extent, it seemed to raise equally vexing questions about utilizing the word "progress" in understanding the world around us.

Thomas Kuhn (himself a historian of science at the University of California in Berkeley) produced what many consider the most lucid announcement of the arrival of this second intellectual movement in his 1962 bestseller, *The Structure of Scientific Revolutions*. In the Introduction to that work (entitled, "A Role for History"), Kuhn noted that there had been a "decisive transformation in the image of science by which we are now possessed." This transformation had led Kuhn—and seemingly many other physical scientists as well—to believe that scientists had been "misled in fundamental ways" about how science explained the laws of the physical universe. And he therefore announced that he was proposing a "quite different concept of science that can emerge from the historical record of research activity itself."[1]

Basic to Kuhn's argument in the book was that an older model of science had posited a cumulative process in understanding how scientists came to understand how the physical world worked. That older model understood the "great discoverers" in science as standing on the shoulders of their scientific predecessors in advancing knowledge: according to this older model of how science had progressed, Galileo had built on and extended the insights of the ancients like Aristotle in exploring what made falling bodies fall, while Isaac Newton in turn had built on Galileo's insights in explaining gravitational forces. Thus the progress of science (at least according to the older linear, cumulative narrative) extended backward to the very beginnings of Western speculation about the physical universe in ancient Greece, and forward to very contemporary explorations into the gravitational forces affecting superconductors. This "grand march of science" approach to understanding how humans had gathered reliable information about the physical universe around them thus posited an unbroken narrative that stretched over centuries and a wide variety of cultures. And it took as axiomatic the belief that Aristotle, Galileo, Newton, and the post-Newtonians working in laboratories adjacent to Kuhn's office were *all* engaged in the same scientific pursuit, seeking answers to same kinds of questions about the physical universe (albeit with very different kinds of scientific instruments), and all contributing to the same scientific project. Indeed, Kuhn argued that a central component of the older model's understanding of science was that the most basic *questions* that governed scientific research and experiment never changed; rather, the *answers* to those questions progressed in clarity, reliability, and intellectual elegance.[2]

But Kuhn argued that historians and philosophers of science in the decades before the appearance of his book had come to have significant doubts about the validity of that model. These scholars had now begun to trace "different, and often less than cumulative, developmental lines for the sciences." Kuhn's description of how science *actually* worked was far more historically disjunctive, and far less cumulative, than the model of the grand march of science approach had led scholars to believe: yes, he allowed, Aristotle, Galileo, and Newton had all studied falling bodies. And all three had sought to arrive at a theorem (or at least a theory) to explain why such bodies did fall. But Kuhn argued that they were *not* engaged in the same scientific pursuit; nor was their understanding of the laws governing such bodies in any way cumulative, or even analogous to each other's speculations.[3]

Kuhn's example of Galileo and Isaac Newton might serve as a decisive instance of this point regarding the noncumulative nature of science. Newton (usually presented in high school science texts as the hero of modern mathematics) had asserted that it was Galileo who had actually discovered the relation of gravity to the speed of falling objects ("the constant force of gravity produces a motion proportional to the square of the time"). And Kuhn points out that Galileo's discoveries in the seventeenth century *did* agree with that kinematic theorem ("the constant force of gravity . . .") when they were embedded within Newton's mathematical equations a century later. But Galileo had said nothing explicitly about how the constant force of gravity affected falling bodies for the simple reason that the very concept of a "uniform gravitational force" was not proposed until a century after Galileo—by Newton himself. Galileo had sought an explanation to the puzzle of falling bodies that lacked the reliable mathematical information about gravitational force that Newton would provide later, and thus had constructed an answer to that puzzle by constructing a very different model of the physical universe from Newton's—a model that proposed no role at all for the crucial factor of a constant gravitational force. Thus from Kuhn's point of view, Galileo had (almost literally) lived in a different universe than Newton. Newton's brilliant formulations, then, didn't contribute to a cumulative line of research about falling bodies that included Galileo and even earlier scientific experimenters. The paradigm that Newton constructed to explain why falling bodies fall didn't build on Galileo: it replaced Galileo's paradigm with a completely different one. Kuhn observed that by crediting Galileo with the answer to a question that Galileo's own scientific paradigm would not have been able to formulate, Newton had unintentionally hidden

> the effect of a small but revolutionary reformulation in the questions that scientists asked about motion as well as the answers they felt able to accept. But it is just this sort of [revolutionary] change in the formulation of questions and answers that accounts, far more than novel empirical discoveries, for the transition from Aristotelian to Galilean and from Galilean to Newtonian dynamics. By disguising such changes, the textbook tendency to make the development of science linear *hides* a process that lies at the heart of the most significant episodes of scientific development.[4]

Kuhn, like most of his colleagues engaged in scientific research, understood the day-to-day working of laboratories to rest on a shared understanding of the basic rules of the physical universe, an understanding that Kuhn labeled "normal science." Normal science rested on an agreement reached among a majority of scientists in any given discipline (e.g., biology, physics, chemistry) that they could articulate an overarching model of how the universe actually operated, and could utilize such a model in constructing their own discreet research projects. Kuhn labeled that overarching model the "paradigm" of scientific research, utilizing an ancient Greek-derived word to do so. But in using that term Kuhn also (unintentionally) opened the floodgates for the popular—and usually incorrect—usage of paradigm that Kuhn found annoying. Basic to Kuhn's argument about the paradigms that governed scientific research was his belief (supported by numerous examples in his book) that this basic model *never* claimed the loyalty of all scientists at any given moment, even in the same discipline. Such paradigms rather claimed the loyalty of a majority of scientific practitioners in their trade. That meant that there were always outliers in any scientific discipline who rejected the normativity (or even the coherence) of the reigning paradigm in explaining how the physical universe operated. This point seems minor but is, in fact, key to Kuhn's later argument.[5]

And the reason this point was anything *but* minor—just like the reason there were always outliers who rejected the reigning paradigm that governed normal science—is that, as Kuhn understood it, science could never legitimately claim to offer a definitive and final model of the real world. Indeed, it was conceptually impossible to offer such a model; and this was because, as Kuhn repeatedly reminded his readers, "reality" (a word always used in "scare" quotation marks) was always more complex than any model that could be offered to explain it. Rather than offering a blueprint for the physical universe (like a carpenter's blueprint for building a house), Kuhn argued that science proceeded on the basis of a humanly constructed, provisional model for predicting the likely outcomes of experiments. And this basic model—the reigning paradigm of scientific research—was never totalistic: there were always parts of the physical universe that eluded its explanatory powers. Indeed, there were often results in normal scientific research that seemed to imply not only that the paradigm was incomplete but also that it might be wrong. And for that reason, there were always practitioners—outliers—who nursed profound doubts as to the paradigm's worth and veracity, who in fact offered contrary models for explaining the process of evolution or the behavior of neutrons. It was in that sense that the paradigm informing normal science was confessedly arbitrary, provisional, and humanly constructed.[6]

But even granted the provisional and arbitrary character of any scientific paradigm, Kuhn argued that there were considerable benefits to scientists buying into it. Such an acceptance of a common overarching model of the physical universe (however provisional) freed scientists to engage in the "strenuous and devoted attempt to force nature into the conceptual boxes supplied" by the reigning paradigm. That strenuous and devoted undertaking is how Kuhn defined the vast majority of scientific experiments—the day-to-day activities of laboratories across the globe attempting to reach a clearer under-standing of the forces that governed the behavior of subatomic particles no less than the stars in their courses. *This,* he averred, was what normal science was all about. And it was this model of experiment that exhausted the word "science" for nonscientists (and even for many scientists themselves).[7]

B. *Paradigm Revolutions*

But with that observation, Kuhn undertook the delivery of what many thought of as a series of radical propositions that punctuated his book, bringing it al-most instantly to the attention of scientists and nonscientists (the latter not in the habit of reading about physics or chemistry experiments). The first of these was his critique of the purported "objectivity" of the model offered by normal science: the reigning paradigm governing and underlying the kind of day-to-day scientific research undertaken by normal science did not (because it could not) offer any kind of one-to-one description of some real world "out there" in any simplistic sense. The laws formulated as a result of scientific research, then, were misunderstood if conceived as being somehow discov-ered in nature—as an apprentice might take apart a clock and discover what made it work. There were no such objective laws waiting to be discovered in nature (which was precisely why science was not about discovering them). The theories and formulas that resulted from regular scientific experiment, then, were misunderstood if conceived to be embedded in some objective order independent of human reason. Rather, those theories and formulas might be better understood as predictive strategies for exploring how phys-ical phenomena operated under certain, specified, conditions. They were not laws embedded in the physical universe, but rather human strategies for predicting the likelihood of the outcomes of experiments, based on previous experiments.[8]

But Kuhn then proceeded to immediately offer yet another radical prop-osition, this one about the "cumulative" nature of the scientific enterprise. Yes, he said, the ongoing scientific effort of "strenuously forcing nature into the conceptual boxes" offered by the reigning paradigm did foster a kind of progress in specific scientific areas. Advances were made in a variety of areas studied, and more sophisticated tools—crafted to discover even more in-formation about the universe—became more successful in forcing an even broader array of data into the boxes supplied. In *this* quite specific if narrow sense, normal science *had* extended the frontiers of human knowledge in a variety of areas. And in that quite specific sense, at least, normal science *was* cumulative and progressive: one scientist might build on and extend the insights of predecessors' experiments, in the process widening the human understanding of how (and in more rare cases, even why) physical phenomena operated within a quite structured set of circumstances. But such accumulation of scientific knowledge was always bounded by the inevitable appearance of experimental results that failed to behave in a manner which the reigning paradigm predicted they would. Thus the results of scientific research might be considered "progressive" (a word that physical scientists tended to avoid) because those results proved the hunches of the scientists undertaking the experiments to be true in a significant number of experiments. But, Kuhn noted, exceptions inevitably appeared in research, and these exceptions to the expected outcomes always posed (at least in theory) a challenge to the ability of the overarching paradigm to explain the real world.[9]

Kuhn called these exceptions to the expected and predicted outcomes of experiments *anomalies*—that is, challenges to the expected (and predicted) order of things as defined by the paradigm. And this understanding of scientific anomaly constituted Kuhn's third dramatic proposition. Normal science therefore did not aim at novelty—on discovering "new things in nature" (which was, of course, precisely how most nonscientists would describe the enterprise of science). Rather, according to Kuhn, scientific research was inherently conservative: it was dedicated to buttressing the status quo by supporting with yet more data the model of the universe laid out in the paradigm. For Kuhn, then, science was dedicated to more or less discovering what it expected to discover. Kuhn therefore observed that genuine novelty (unexpected discoveries) in science emerged only with difficulty, when data *resisted* explanation by the reigning models of how things should behave. These anomalies therefore emerged not when things went right (i.e., when things behaved according to how the paradigm predicted they would behave), but rather when things went awry. "Novelty" or anomaly was what happened when the phenomena being studied did not behave as the paradigm predicted they would. And far from being welcomed by experimenters, these exceptions raised the unsettling possibility that the experiments that produced such new information were misguided or perhaps even counterproductive in generating useful and reliable data about the physical universe.[10]

And anomalies in science, Kuhn noted, take some time to be recognized as such. Initially, exceptions to the expected outcomes of scientific experiment were either explained away as being due to faulty equipment, or to mistaken measurements, or to the broad array of errors that all human beings (even scientists) are heir to. Equally often, anomalies were initially missed or

overlooked entirely because "only the anticipated and usual are experienced—
even under circumstances where anomaly is later to be observed." It was
only later, when a pattern of unexpected outcomes emerged from repeated
experiments, that an awareness develops in the experimenters that something
has gone wrong, or at least that the outcome of the experiment seems to defy
what the paradigm said *would* happen. And in the early stages of recognized
anomalies, the unexpected results of certain experiments are often built
into a slightly expanded (or "corrected") version of the reigning paradigm,
at least for a while: "normally, x and y result from the experiment" scientific
experimenters would say, "except under these conditions, when z happens,
although we don't yet know why."[11]

Thus the original model is stretched or expanded to include the anomalies,
usually with the tacit understanding among scientific researchers that the basic
model was still fine; "yes, there are these exceptions, but when our knowledge
has advanced somewhat, we'll be able to explain why these exceptions occur."
And this resistance to rethinking the overarching paradigm too quickly, Kuhn
observed, had its own salutary benefits: "by ensuring that the paradigm will
not be too easily surrendered, resistance guarantees that scientists will not be
lightly distracted" from the important research of normal science. Further,
Kuhn drily observed, scientists dedicated to defending the reigning paradigm
will, at that point, do what historians, social scientists, and hosts of other
experts do in similar situations: "they will devise numerous articulations
and *ad hoc* modifications of their theory in order to eliminate any 'apparent'
conflict."[12]

But for an anomaly to evoke a genuine crisis of confidence in a paradigm's
utility as the guiding model for scientific research, it must come to be seen as
more than just a single exception. Most scientists understand that there will
always be difficulties in the "paradigm-nature" fit: exceptions or difficulties
in making physical processes fit into the conceptual boxes supplied by the
paradigm are encountered every day in normal science, and often result in
solidifying the dominance of the reigning paradigm by forcing researchers
to try new experiments, or to develop new equipment, ultimately providing confirmation for the veracity of the reigning model by expanding the
community's understanding of the paradigm's complexity or the subtlety of
its conceptual reach.[13]

But at the point at which the number of anomalies grows widespread, and
when the exceptions come to be seen as touching on fundamental assumptions
on which the paradigm rests, questions begin to be raised within the scientific community as to the reliability (and thus the utility) of the overarching

paradigm. At that point, scientists begin to consider: "perhaps our paradigm of how the universe functions doesn't actually provide the kind of verifiable predictive map we had thought." Perhaps the paradigm itself—and not just the discreet experiments based on it—needs to be rethought. Precisely because questioning the reliability of the paradigm would require a number of major shifts—in the kinds of experiments that scientists undertake, as well as in how scientists would explain what those experiments revealed about the physical universe,

> the emergence of new [paradigms] are generally preceded by a period of pronounced professional insecurity. As one might expect, that insecurity is generated by the persistent failure of the puzzles of normal science to come out as they should. *Failure of existing rules is the prelude to the search for new ones.*[14]

Widespread perceptions of fundamental problems with the *entire* paradigm are rare, Kuhn argued, as such perceptions mark moments in the history of science when the fundamental assumptions about how the physical universe operates are reexamined in a sustained way. Thus, unlike encountering anomalies in research (which are an almost daily occurrence), the emergence of questions about the veracity of the overarching paradigm occur so rarely that they can de dated, and mark what Kuhn calls "turning points" in the history of science. Kuhn labeled this period of intellectual insecurity in the field "the period of crisis," and his delineation of that period constituted Kuhn's fourth radical proposition.[15]

Kuhn described that period in scientific research as involving a period of "extraordinary, rather than normal, research." That period witnesses a "proliferation of competing articulations, and the willingness to try anything." But what really marked that period as one of crisis was the widespread willingness among scientists to turn to *philosophy* and even a willingness "to debate over fundamentals." Thus "scientific revolutions"—turning points in the history of science that the book's title refers to—do occur, but they occur only after a significant number of practitioners are willing to *debate fundamentals*—a debate that may seem to have much more in common with philosophy than with the exigencies of physical science.[16]

When anomalies occur regularly, and repeatedly, and among a wide group of practitioners, and a willingness emerges among the most respected members of the field to "turn to philosophy, and even a willingness to debate fundamentals," the once-unthinkable suddenly becomes thinkable, and even attractive: a significant number of scientists (usually, at least initially, the "stars" in their field, whom other scientists respect) reluctantly agree that the reigning paradigm is now so problematic that its usefulness for explaining the data produced by scientific experiment is at an end, and "a new basis for the practice of science" now becomes necessary. And this fifth dramatic proposition offered by Kuhn (the way in which a new paradigm comes to replace an older one) is critical for understanding his most basic thesis regarding the "structure" of scientific revolutions.[17]

Basic to understanding Kuhn's fifth radical proposition is his repeated assertion that a paradigm "is declared invalid only if an alternate candidate is available to take its place." This assertion appears, on the face of it, to be an easy point to understand, but—like so much else in Kuhn's narrative—this is not the case.[18]

Kuhn goes to considerable lengths to unpack this fifth insight, so it might be worth pausing to explain the implications of his assertion. One of the most radical implications of this fifth assertion regarding the necessity of an "alternate candidate" before an older paradigm can be rejected is Kuhn's belief that the historical study of scientific development offers no evidence of what he terms "falsification by direct comparison with nature." That is, Kuhn is at pains to explain that no specific paradigm—by itself—can be evaluated by comparing it with what a scientist might encounter "directly" in the natural world. In Kuhn's understanding, such a direct comparison would be fruitless because "nature" is a humanly constructed entity in science.

The random sets of data produced by scientific experiments are "ordered" and explained by scientists themselves: there is no order implicit in nature apart from the scientific lenses used to study it. Or, perhaps closer to the truth, if there is such an order in nature, it is inaccessible to human understanding without some grid—some exploratory pattern—constructed to explain what (at least initially) is experienced as random data. Thus the decision to abandon one paradigm for another as the new basis for science is at least as much a comparison between the *two paradigms themselves* as it is a comparison with the "facts of nature." It is therefore inevitable that

the act of judgment that leads scientists to reject a previously accepted theory is always based on more than [just] a comparison of that theory with the world. The decision to reject one paradigm is always simultaneously the decision to accept another [because] the judgment leading to that decision involves the comparison of both paradigms with nature *and* with each other.[19]

And this is so, Kuhn asserted, because most scientists understand that the paradigm that informs and gives intellectual cohesion to their work is provisional and arbitrary: paradigms articulate the smartest and most comprehensive set of explanations for how and why their experiments are related to the experiments of other scientists everywhere, and how and why all of their experiments together help to explain the physical universe.[20]

Thus any simple comparison between a given paradigm and "nature" will reveal what scientists already know: that the paradigm explaining how and why the physical world seems to operate as it does is different from nature itself. The "laws" articulated in paradigms to explain the physical universe, then, are not "nature's laws," but rather science's laws—formulated after many experiments on discreet sets of phenomena to predict and explain what will (most probably) happen under certain sets of circumstances. The decision to abandon one paradigm, then, is always *simultaneously* the decision to accept another because the only way to engage the physical world in any scientific undertaking is through the medium of a humanly constructed model—a paradigmatic lens—that reduces the sheer welter of millions of pieces of data to some kind of order and meaning.[21]

Kuhn therefore contended that any model of science in which practitioners go "directly" (again, always in scare quotes) to nature to find out the properties of the physical universe is both naïve and profoundly unscientific. What one would encounter by undertaking such a direct engagement of the physical world without some agreed-upon model of how things work would be both overwhelming and meaningless because of the sheer amount of observed data. Thus in Kuhn's description of both science and its "revolutions," the very nature of the scientific enterprise requires and presupposes workable paradigms. And when those paradigms no longer function to explain an increasing amount of data generated through scientific experiment (anomalies), another paradigm has to take its place before any kind of normal science can continue. But Kuhn is at pains to emphasize that such paradigm change is not cumulative and gradual; it is, rather, sudden and revolutionary:

A new theory, however special its range of applications, is seldom or never just an increment to what is already known. Its assimilation requires the reconstruction of prior theory and the re-evaluation of prior "fact," an intrinsically revolutionary process that is seldom completed by a single man and never overnight.[22]

But Kuhn also presented a sixth radical proposition directly pertinent to the study of natural law that follows, and this was his idea of "incommensurability." And by that term he simply meant that scientists could not decide which of the paradigms was "truer" by simply comparing them with each other. This counterintuitive insight was important for Kuhn because he was at pains to show that, while new paradigms ordinarily incorporate much of the vocabulary and scientific apparatuses of older scientific paradigms,

> they seldom employ these borrowed elements in quite the traditional way. Within the new paradigm, old terms, concepts and experiments fall *into new relationships one with the other. The inevitable result is what one must call . . . a misunderstanding between the two competing schools.*[23]

And the historical example he offers to prove this point of incommensurability is the dramatic one of Albert Einstein's general theory of relativity. Kuhn observes that the initial scoffing that greeted Einstein's theory—space could not be "curved," his critics argued at the time, as Einstein had proposed—was not wrong or mistaken, at least according to the reigning paradigm of (Newtonian) physics at the time. Mathematicians, physicists, and philosophers who attempted to develop a version of Einstein's theory based on Newton's model of the laws of physics were—of course—doomed to failure:

> What had previously been meant by "space" was necessarily flat, homogenous, and unaffected by the presence of matter. Newtonian physics could not have worked [using such a model]. To make the transition to Einstein's universe, the whole conceptual web whose strands are space, time, matter, force, and so on, had to be *shifted and laid down again on nature. Only men [sic] who had together undergone or failed to undergo that transformation would be able to discover precisely what they agreed or disagreed about.*[24]

As Kuhn argued it, a new paradigm—like the one offered by Einstein to replace the Newtonian one—was an entirely new way of regarding the problems of physics and mathematics, one that necessarily changed the meaning of words like "space," "time," and "matter." Without those changes the very concept of "curved space" was ridiculous. Thus from Kuhn's point of view, the proponents of the two paradigms used almost exactly the same terms and phrases in making their arguments; but they practiced their sciences in two very different—incommensurable—worlds. One was embedded in a flat, the other in a curved, model of space. Thus "practicing in two different worlds, the two groups of scientists *see different things* when they look from the same point in the same direction."[25]

The process Kuhn describes therefore is *not* the structure of scientific progress or advance, but rather the structure of scientific *revolutions*. The widespread acceptance of a new basic model for the scientific enterprise is thus "far from a cumulative process, one achieved by an articulation or extension of the old paradigm." It is, rather, a *reconstruction* of the entire field on a completely new basis, from the ground up. And that reconstruction inevitably changes some of the field's most elementary and fundamental theories no less than it changes the kinds of experiments undertaken. The revolution, then, changes the kinds of arguments offered in "proof" of the success of experiments, no less than the parts of the physical universe studied to arrive at those proofs. The new paradigm, correctly understood, does not build on or *extend* the older arguments of how the physical universe works; it replaces them with entirely new arguments and models.[26]

And during the initial, always-contested, period when a new paradigm has been at least provisionally accepted to replace an older one, adherents of the older model will point out—correctly—a large but never complete overlap between the problems that can be solved by *both* the old and new paradigms. This last attempt on the part of the older paradigm's devotees to call their colleagues back to the older "orthodoxy" informing scientific research is both justified and poignant. It is justified because the small but vocal group of practicing scientists who will never render allegiance to the new model will continue to point out—again correctly—how the older paradigm *did* contribute to significant advances in understanding some workings of nature. But it is also poignant because, while the older model will continue to hold the allegiance of at least some members of the scientific community, the majority of practicing scientists will have already, in a sense, "moved on," and will increasingly come to view the arguments on behalf of the older paradigm as misguided, or even as willfully anachronistic. And that is because the newly adopted paradigm does not build on the honest gains in knowledge garnered by the older model; it rather represents

a reconstruction of the field from new fundamentals, a reconstruction that changes some of the field's most elementary theoretical generalizations as well as many of its paradigm methods and applications. . . . When the transition is complete, the profession will have changed its view of the field, its methods, and its goals.[27]

C. Theology, the Queen of the Sciences

At least since the High Middle Ages, Catholic Christians have labeled theology as the "queen of the sciences." Such a designation—however counterintuitive to contemporary ears—built on firm foundations laid by St. Augustine (arguably the father of Christian theology in the West), who had argued in the fifth century that a "science" was any reasoned study of the real world. Building on those firm Augustinian foundations, medieval schools of higher education like Oxford and the University of Paris had sought to order a reasoned understanding of the real world around two large areas of study: the "Trivium" (the study of grammar, logic, and rhetoric) and the "Quadrivium" (arithmetic, geometry, music, and astronomy). But the intellectual giants of those university foundations—including the Angelic Doctor himself, St. Thomas Aquinas—had argued that these various branches of learning needed an overarching standard—a paradigm, if you will—that could order and provide intellectual cohesion to the welter of information gathered and passed on in the trivium and quadrivium. A succession of thinkers argued that the discipline of theology could provide just such an overarching model for fitting the discreet areas of study of the real world into something like a synthetic whole: of all the sciences studied at the great intellectual centers of Oxford and Paris (logic, arithmetic, geometry), theology seemed to promise the largest and most capacious category for organizing the other (lower) sciences into a coherent and understandable larger pattern of meaning.[28]

Thus it was that Catholic universities everywhere inevitably displayed statues, paintings, or sculptures of a crowned and seated woman with an open book, teaching other figures (invariably male) seated below her. Such artistic creations provided a physical instantiation of what students studying at those institutions already knew: that theology was the discipline around which the curriculum was organized—that theology was literally (at least in those artistic displays) the Queen of the Sciences.

It strains the obvious to observe that theology and—say—physics are both "sciences" in very different ways. While theology purports to construct a reasoned model of the "real world" of ethical obligations and personal duties based on observed, experiential data, it does not do so by utilizing the kinds of quantitative methodologies that inform the disciplines of quantum mechanics and optics. Nonetheless, the methodological foundation of the discipline of theology—"*Lex orandi lex credenda*"—articulates the explicitly experiential basis for the *science* of theology. That methodological formula, proposed by papal secretary Prosper of Aquitaine in the fourth century, is usually translated as "the law of praying grounds the law of believing," and reminds Catholic theologians even today that the formulations and explanations of their discipline are very different from those offered by the discipline of philosophy. While philosophy might offer purely speculative answers to the "big questions" of human existence ("What is the good person?" "What is the best political ordering of human societies?"), theologians were tied to a much more practical and concrete standard. Their task was to offer a *lex credendi*—a reasoned explanation of why Christians believe the doctrines that define their religion—based in a rigorous analysis of the concrete, actual experience of Christian believers. Theology, then, must be rooted and anchored in the lived religion of prayer, worship, and life of actual believers (the *lex orandi*). Theology, then, proceeded on the belief that it could offer explanations for its faith that were *reasonable*, if not technically rational.[29]

Theology therefore, as the effort to offer a reasoned explanation for the "law of believing," had to be rooted in a careful and rigorous examination of experience. And to that extent, at least, theologians claim to be practicing a "science": a reasoned, systematic analysis and explanation of observed human behavior, systematized and ordered into a larger model and pattern—again, something like a paradigm—that orders the various doctrines and practices of religious belief.

And to the extent that theology *is* a science—a reasoned attempt to explain the lived experience of believers—the insights offered by Kuhn regarding paradigms and the revolutions that occur to "fit" them more closely with observed data might be useful in understanding the fractious debates over models that occur in the discipline of theology as well. Indeed, Kuhn's brilliant and ideologically neutral account of how and why an older paradigm is eventually replaced with a newer one might help historians of religious ideas to narrate debates every bit as heated and divisive as those found in the physical science community in a more even-handed way: scholars can avoid the invidious labels of "liberal" and "conservative," "orthodox" and "progressive" in describing the fraught debates that have punctuated the history of theology. More specifically, the promise of Kuhn's approach to describing how models of the real world are worked out would seem to be especially promising in narrating the debates over the micro-tradition of natural law in the Catholic moral theology community.

Perhaps even more important for understanding contemporary Catholic natural law discourse, Kuhn's hermeneutic of "paradigm revolutions" might help to clarify the process and structure of how natural law thinking and argument actually operate within the Catholic academy. One of the many factors leading to the contemporary confusion in natural law debate is the deeply held belief that natural law discussion has progressively evolved, and represents a linear, cumulative process in which the original insights of Aquinas have been clarified and strengthened by successive revisions and insights by scholars in close conversation with each other. Many of the claimants to Aquinas' mantle would fervently maintain that they were all, nonetheless, involved in the very same project, playing by the same rules (more or less), and seeking a common end to a moral theology project. But what immediately strikes the reader of these various (and varied) models of natural law is that many of them are *not* cumulative and progressive, but rather rest on mutually exclusive or (altogether different) presuppositions about where and how one can access Christian experience, and what one can make of it. Likewise, many of the models of natural law that define the micro-tradition seem to imply that the ends or purposes of human flourishing are varied (or, at least, various): they fail, in other words, to present a common understanding of what "human flourishing" is, and how it can be achieved; and in a few cases, the model implies that human flourishing might be too optimistic a goal for undertaking the project. Yes, many of them continue to claim the revered mantle of "Thomist" as their preferred designation. But that designation would seem to be the most significant feature they share with other claimants.

As Kuhn so carefully argued, the "structure" of his argument focused not on scientific progress or revision, but rather on scientific *revolutions*. Older paradigms were not "corrected" or nuanced; they were replaced from the bottom up with an altogether different basic model that largely redefined the field and the "legitimate" experiments one could undertake in it. The ultimate test for the utility of a paradigm, then, was not its claim to a revered designation ("Aristotelean" or "Newtonian"), or its ability to prove its intellectual paternity; the ultimate test was rather its proven ability to make sense of more data in a unified way—its ability to fit even more of experienced reality into conceptual boxes that made sense of experience and observed data.

Viewed through Kuhn's lens of paradigm revolutions, then, the critical review offered by moral theologian Richard McCormick shortly after the appearance of Paul VI's encyclical can be understood as neither rebellious nor unfaithful to Church teaching: he was being neither liberal nor conservative, neither progressive nor orthodox. McCormick's critique of

Humanae Vitae—viewed through the lens of Kuhn's model of how intellectual revolutions take place—might rather be seen as an attempt to address the spectrum of troubling anomalies in the paradigm informing teaching that now appeared jarringly out of sync with how Catholics actually sought to live the life of discipleship. The "exceptions" that immediately became apparent in the encyclical's presentation of the moral life—its "physicalist," outdated model of biology that moral theologians recognized as simplistic and implausible; its problematic cementing of the unitive and procreative aspects of human sexuality that flew in the face of the actual experience of believers eager to follow church teaching; its hapless appeal to human reason to shore up its sanctions; its position that the purpose (the "end" or purpose) of human sexuality was procreation, nothing more and nothing less—led McCormick to argue that the paradigm of natural law informing the encyclical now appeared more problematic than helpful, and that moral teaching in the Church had already entered into what Kuhn would have termed "a period of crisis."

Viewed through the lens of Kuhn's thesis, then, McCormick's revisionist critique of the classicist arguments offered in the encyclical simply solidified and articulated what many Catholic moral theologians had been talking about in seminary rec rooms for a while—doubts "voiced intramurally" about the utility of the older paradigm, as Jesuit moralist John Lynch had observed in 1964. The older, static model of neo-scholastic Thomism that had provided the framework for Catholic ethical teaching—*and* had provided the framework for the condemnation of contraception in Paul VI's encyclical—now appeared simplistic, and (more to the point, at least in the minds of both moral theologians and many of the Catholic faithful) no longer helpful in framing the moral life. The model on offer in the encyclical to order and explain important ethical questions in the Christian life now seemed strained, and even implausible, in navigating the complexities of an ethical life in the world. It failed to account for too many demands and exceptions that Christian couples themselves reported about their "bedroom relationships." The anomalies, in other words, now outweighed the benefits provided by the classicist model of neo-scholastic moral theology.

McCormick's famous article in 1968 did not purport to offer what might be considered a new paradigm to replace the one that had (problematically) ordered the arguments of *Humanae Vitae*; but it represented one of the first warning signs that the public phase of the "period of crisis" that always preceded the articulation of a new paradigm had already arrived. That period of crisis would extend over a number of decades, and forms the subject of the chapters that follow.

"A Period of Crisis"

*It is a perennial mistake to confuse repetition of old formulas
with the living law of the Church.*

—JOHN NOONAN, *Contraception*[1]

A. *"An Inadequate Concept of Natural Law"*

On the very afternoon when *Humanae Vitae* was publically presented to
the press in Rome—July 29, 1968—a rising star in the world of American
moral theology obtained a copy of the entire text. Fr. Charles Curran,
then a junior professor teaching at the American bishops' own academic
institution, the Catholic University of America (CUA), immediately
called a meeting of his colleagues in CUA's faculty residence for priests,
Caldwell Hall. In what now seems like lightning speed in the age before
the Internet and I-Phones, Curran and his colleagues read through the
text of the encyclical and drafted a critical response to it in the course of
just two days.[2]

That the assembled clerics present at that hastily organized Caldwell Hall
meeting could produce a carefully reasoned, technical document between
July 29 and July 30 witnessed to the fact that the internal critique of the
older model of neo-scholastic theology—a critique that had been "voiced
intramurally" for some time—had reached the stage of paradigm criticism
that Thomas Kuhn had labeled a "period of crisis." The anomalies resulting
from the application of that older paradigm to the lived experience of
faithful Catholics, anomalies that revisionist moral theologians had been
commenting on for years, leaped from the pages of an encyclical promulgated
that very day when presented in summary form. What their hastily composed "response document" represented was a public announcement that
the utility of the received neo-scholastic paradigm undergirding the "ordinary magisterium" of the Church was now perceived to be at an end (or at

least perceived to be such by the teachers formally designated to pass on that teaching to seminarians), and a new paradigm was now needed to take its place.[3]

Curran had asked his colleagues at the July 29 meeting in Caldwell Hall to contact fellow moral theologians across the country to gather further input for their document, and indeed by 3:00 A.M. on the morning of July 30, something like the final version of their text had taken form. Curran and his colleagues had managed to garner 87 signatures of Catholic moral theologians supporting their response document as a result of this nationwide consultation, as well as the signatures of 100 clergy who were members of the Washington Association of (Catholic) Priests—all of this in 48 hours. Several hours later, Curran presided at a hastily called press conference at the Mayflower Hotel in Washington, DC. It is safe to say that nothing like this had ever been seen in the 300-year history of the Catholic Church in the United States.[4]

As Kuhn had so saliently observed regarding the frequency of paradigm revolutions, the widespread recognition of the need for a new basic model for any discipline was quite different from the expected day-to-day frustrations of finding data that refused to fit neatly into the accepted pattern—that is, of finding "anomalies"—a truth that defined the world of moral theology no less than that of normal science. Moral theologians, like their colleagues in the physical sciences, were accustomed to encountering such anomalies in working out what they called "cases of conscience"—that is, in applying the standards of Catholic moral theology to specific cases of human behavior that needed a "line call" regarding their goodness or badness. Such anomalies occurred every day, requiring finesse and creativity on the part of theologians: "yes, this case does pose some special problems that the usual moral norms don't seem to cover," they would say, "but that's why we need to study it more carefully." Anomalies were one thing, just as Kuhn had noted. But the widespread sense among experts in the field that the accepted "micro"-paradigm no longer appeared helpful, or even true—that was something else again. And that widespread sense occurred so rarely that Kuhn argued that one could number them: they represented "turning points in science." And Kuhn had offered a fairly short list of those turning points in, say, physics: Aristotle, Galileo, Newton, Einstein, Heisenberg. Those turning points, Kuhn further argued, always generated a "period of crisis" before a new paradigm arose to replace the old one—a new paradigm that could make sense and "order" the spectrum of anomalies that had multiplied under the old paradigm.

Thus, whatever else the Mayflower press conference may have meant within the world of Catholic moral theology, it represented the first public announcement—to be followed several months later by Richard McCormick's article in *Theological Studies*—that the older micro-tradition of neo-scholastic natural law was already acknowledged by the specialists trained to pass it on as no longer useful, and that the period of crisis that always followed such a recognition had arrived. And Curran's structuring of the conference on the morning of July 31 fits perfectly within the schema articulated by Kuhn as marking such periods of crisis: the "response document" crafted by Curran and supported by the signatures of well over 100 Catholic theologians and priests articulated the widespread sense that there had been (in Kuhn's words) a "persistent failure of the reigning paradigm to explain observed phenomena." The encyclical's application of moral principles to the sexual lives of married couples was now seen as so problematic and flawed that Catholic theologians now announced (again in Kuhn's words) their "willingness to debate fundamentals." Indeed, the recognized "experts" within the guild of moral theology now publically announced the need to "reexamine the fundamental assumptions about how the universe operates in a sustained way." What Curran did not state at the press conference—because he could not have foreseen this at the time—was that there would be a "proliferation of competing articulations" of what a new paradigm might look like during the confusing interlude that Kuhn termed "the time of crisis."

Just as Kuhn had noted that the first members of a scientific community to question the utility of an older paradigm would be the field's most respected practitioners, so the "Mayflower document" observed that the "Christian tradition assigns theologians the special responsibility of evaluating and interpreting pronouncements of the magisterium in light of the total theological data operative in each question or statement." And in the opinion of the signatories who represented something of a "who's who" of the moral theology world, significant anomalies resulted from evaluating the encyclical's arguments "in light of the total data." Indeed, the specific applications of Paul VI's teaching in the encyclical were so problematic and counterfactual to the lived experience of actual married couples that it led the signatories to assert that it was based on "an inadequate concept of natural law." Thus, in what was read at the time—by both the press present at the Mayflower Hotel and by millions of others who read about the event in the *New York Times*—as merely prefatory remarks to the main event, in retrospect actually contained the most important announcement of the meeting: the experts in the field of moral theology (many of whom had been at the impromptu meeting in

Caldwell Hall a few days previously) now declared the older micro-paradigm of natural law, utilized in *Humanae Vitae*, as not only inadequate but also perhaps even *wrong*. The most basic model undergirding the arguments of the pope was now rendered obsolete, and a newer paradigm was needed to take its place.[5]

Too much lived experience of the faithful at prayer and in living out the Christian life (the *lex orandi*) been ignored or overlooked in applying the older paradigm to make the *lex credenda* offered in the encyclical believable, or even coherent. The encyclical's condemnation of artificial contraception seemed to be based on a number of problematic assumptions that rendered its most basic model not only inadequate but also even "erroneous": this latter word is important in understanding why the response of the theologians at the Mayflower Hotel was not an "evolution," but rather a represented the opening movement of a revolution in micro-paradigm production. The most basic presuppositions of the older paradigm—that one could identify moral meanings in physical acts; that the Church was obliged to teach authoritatively in light of those physical acts; that the ultimate purpose of human coitus was openness to the propagation of the species—all of these were now determined to be *not* only unnuanced or overargued but also rather "erroneous." Further (and even more to the point), the theologians who had signed the response document announced (in the very act of signing it) that they sensed the need for a completely new understanding of what "human flourishing" might look like in Catholic teaching.

With the benefit of hindsight, we can now recognize in this passing statement something of a tectonic shift beginning within the Catholic theological community. If the signatories had been physical scientists rather than moral theologians, Kuhn would have simply observed that a "turning point in science" was now widely perceived to be necessary. The older paradigm didn't need "tweaking" or refitting: it needed to be replaced.[6]

It was precisely the failure of the underlying model of the encyclical to explain the *data* of the lived experience of married couples—the failure of the paradigm to "explain the results of rigorous observation and experiment," in Kuhn's terms—that led the signatories to voice public doubt as to its utility. The fourth paragraph of the Mayflower Statement homed in on just this issue in a way that Kuhn would have considered supportive of his model of how intellectual revolutions take place: how could Paul VI's encyclical appeal so repeatedly to the "Church's experience" in condemning contraceptive practice when the experience of so many devout married couples had been ignored? *Whose* lived experience, they asked, was being utilized to ground this argument? If the actual experience of married people (including the experience of Pat and Patty Crowley, a married couple on the committee who had voted in favor of the majority report rejected by Paul VI) was overlooked or rejected, what did it mean to say that "the Church," reflecting on its experience, understood its moral tradition to prohibit contraception?[7]

Vatican II's "Dogmatic Constitution on the Church in the Modern World" had defined "the Church" as the "People of God"—everybody: pope, moral theologians like McCormick and Curran, lay couples like Pat and Patty Crowley. What "church" was the encyclical talking about, and just how was the "experience" of that church understood? That very appeal—to the "experience of the Church"—now seemed specious (at best), and perhaps something even more intellectually troubling:

> The encyclical consistently assumes that the church is identical with the hierarchical office. No real importance is afforded . . . *the life of the church in its totality; the special witness of many Christian couples is neglected.* . . . Furthermore, the encyclical betrays a narrow positivistic notion of papal authority, as illustrated by the rejection of the majority view presented by the commission established to consider [just this] question, as well as by the rejection of the conclusions of a large part of the international Catholic theological community.[8]

But the criticism of the encyclical aimed at far more basic issues than simply the process and consultation that shaped its promulgation: the signers of Curran's document argued that the conclusions of *Humanae Vitae* rested on "*an inadequate concept of natural law.*" The fact that there were now other, less static and propositional models of natural law that had been ignored raised troubling questions about the intellectual coherence of the Vatican teaching office. And as the signatories pointed out, those other paradigms of natural law "come to different conclusions on this very question."[9]

The things that had made the neo-scholastic paradigm so attractive to some moral theologians since at least the 18th century—its "classicist" understanding of natural law as static, propositional, and timeless, which offered an ease of utility in laying it out and passing it on; it's ahistorical character, which made it applicable to all cultural situations and moral actors, making it seem universal and above cultural differences; its legalistic understanding of an eternal law as a the source of obligations and restraint, which seemed to offer clear and certain *propositions* to often-difficult and messy ethical situations—were now declared to be fatal flaws that were profoundly inadequate, "or even erroneous." And the Catholic theologians who had signed the text on July 31 pointed out that there were now other, less static and nonpropositional understandings of natural law that "come to different conclusions on this very question [of contraception]."[10]

It is well worth pausing to recognize that this last assertion—pointing out that were already "other" understandings of natural law, that came to very different conclusions regarding the ethical meaning of contraception—represented something of a revolutionary statement. What the signatories of the Mayflower Document announced in that seemingly neutral observation was not only that the "period of crisis" was well under way but also that other paradigms were *already* being "floated" within their professional community—a community dedicated to the task of maintaining what Kuhn would term "normal science" under a new (incommensurable) paradigm. And those "other" paradigms needed to make sense of the anomalies encountered in considering the cases of conscience of actual, living Catholic married couples. Utilizing the lens of Kuhn's narrative, we might now recognize that the practitioners entrusted with the duty of overseeing and guarding the intellectual tradition of moral theology in the Church (almost all of whom were priests) had already decided that "other" paradigms needed to be experimented with for explaining Catholicism's moral tradition.

Almost all of those "other" models of natural law referred to by the Mayflower signatories would, of course, claim St. Thomas Aquinas as their model. This is in no way surprising, given the sacrosanct nature of the designation "Thomist" among Catholic theologians. To claim that mantle was to announce that one stood well within a theological tradition that had been maintained for seven centuries, and few Catholic moral theologians desired to stand outside that circle. But many of the "Thomistic" models they referred to differed in as many points as they shared, stretching the label "Thomistic" almost to the breaking point. This last point is important to bear in mind when reading the "Text of the Theologians" (as the *New York Times* referred to the Mayflower Document). But what the signatories all had in common was the sense that the older paradigm of neo-scholasticism could no longer hold up under the bright light of day. It was for that reason—the failure to pass the "probability" test of paradigm utility—that they declared that the encyclical's "conclusions have been called into question for grave and serious reasons." But in making their dissent known for "grave and serious reasons," they also dryly observed that it was, to say the least, surprising that what was alleged to be the design of God could only be discovered in the utmost secrecy of a military character and without subjecting the statement of the alleged design of God to the scrutiny of moral theologians who are experts in the matter, or the comment of the faithful; who would be expected to carry out the orders given.[11]

As Kuhn noted in outlining the period of crisis between paradigms, it was the most respected voices in the field who were the loudest proponents of the need for a new paradigm to replace the one now viewed as no longer serviceable. And the *range* of critical responses within the American Catholic community to the 1968 Encyclical further confirms Kuhn's insight that the "period of crisis" between paradigms is not the work of just one "party" or group within the community of experts: Kuhn predicted that the widespread rejection of the older model would include practitioners with a spectrum of loyalties.

But before exploring the range of American models offered to fill in the paradigmatic void left by the nonreception of the 1968 encyclical, it might be well to look at the "Majority Report" of the commission appointed by John XXIII to consider the question of the Church's stance on contraception— a report that Paul VI seemed to have sidelined in promulgating *Humanae Vitae*. Neither that report nor its counterversion (the "Minority Report")— both of which were sent to the pope—purported to be full-fledged paradigms for the micro-tradition of natural law. But both limned issues and pathways that the full-scale paradigms that followed *Humanae Vitae* would explore.

B. *"The Magisterium Itself Is in Evolution": The Majority Report of the Pontifical Commission on Birth Control*

With the first appearance of oral contraceptives in 1960, a number of Catholic voices began calling for a reconsideration of the Church's absolute prohibition of contraceptive practice. The Boston physician who was one of the inventers of what would later become known as "the Pill," John Rock, was a devout Catholic who kept a crucifix in his office. A much-respected professor of obstetrics at Harvard Medical School for more than three decades, Rock was also a daily attendant at the 7:00 A.M. mass at St. Mary's parish in Brookline, Massachusetts. Immediately after US Food and Drug Administration

(FDA) approval for Rock's oral contraceptive device in 1960, Rock started appearing everywhere: in interviews on NBC and CBS; in articles in which he was quoted extensively in *Time, Newsweek, Life,* and the *Saturday Evening Post.* Part of the media scramble to interview him resulted from his widely discussed book, *The Time Has Come: A Catholic Doctor's Proposals to End the Battle over Birth Control,* which would, in time, be translated into French, German, and Dutch.[12]

Rock believed—precisely as a devout Catholic—that his church would embrace the Pill as morally acceptable simply because it was "natural" in a *specifically Catholic sense.* That is, precisely because the Pill made no use of what Catholic theology called a "barrier method"—*blocking* the female or male organic processes by intrauterine devices or prophylactics—Rock believed that the Church would approve his new approach to contraception as in accord with the "natural law." As Malcom Gladwell has observed in the most perceptive study of Rock's scientific and religious beliefs,

> Rock believed that the Pill was a "natural" method of birth control. By that he didn't mean that it *felt* natural, because it obviously didn't for many women, particularly in its earliest days, when the doses of hormone were many times as high as they are today. He meant that it worked by natural means. Women can get pregnant only during a certain interval each month, because after ovulation their bodies produced a surge of the hormone progesterone. Progesterone prepares the uterus for implantation and stops the ovaries from releasing new eggs. . . . When a woman is pregnant, her body produces a stream of [progesterone] so that another egg can't be released and threaten the pregnancy already under way. [Progesterone,] in other words, is "nature's" contraceptive.[13]

As Rock saw it, then, the Pill was simply progesterone in tablet form. When a woman took the new oral contraceptive, her body was receiving "nature's contraceptive" in a steady dose, so that ovulation was permanently shut down. But the key fact—from Rock's point of view, anyway—was that the Pill's ingredients simply duplicated what could already be found in the woman's body. And in precisely that "naturalness" he thought he saw important theological meaning. It was, for instance, for reasons of an analogous "naturalness" that Pope Pius XII had sanctioned the rhythm for Catholics in 1951—because he argued that such rhythm represented a "natural method" of regulating procreation: it didn't kill sperm (as did spermicides);

it didn't frustrate the normal process of fertilization (as did diaphragms); it didn't mutilate organs (as did sterilization). And Rock knew as much as anybody about the rhythm method: during the 1930s—at the Free Hospital for Women in Brookline, Massachusetts—Rock had founded the first "Rhythm Clinic" to educate Catholic couples in that Church-sanctioned form of "natural contraception." Thus Rock confidently believed that the new oral contraceptives might be characterized as a " 'pill-established' safe period and would seem to carry the *same moral implications' as the rhythm method.*" The Pill thus was, for John Rock, no more than an "adjunct to nature."[14]

But the Catholic version of the "story of the Pill" was considerably stranger than even this: while the Pill was still undergoing tests by the FDA before its appearance on the market, Pope Pius XII had approved its use as long as its contraceptive effects were *indirect* (i.e., as long as its effects occurred under what Catholic moral theology would call the "principle of double effect"). Thus, if a woman undertook the regimen of oral contraception to remedy especially painful menses or some "disease of the uterus," the Pill's "side effect"— its ability to prevent the woman from becoming pregnant—was morally permissible: the double (or side) effect of the prevention of contraception was allowed if the avoidance of pregnancy was not the *primary* purpose in the Pill's usage, at least according to the sometimes-arcane reasoning of Catholic moral theology. Thus, even before its appearance on the American market, the head of Rock's own beloved church had allowed use of "nature's contraceptive" under certain medical circumstances.[15]

But Pius XII's decision regarding the moral permissibility of the Pill under certain circumstances—however odd this entire argument may sound to non-Catholic, and even many Catholic, ears—seems to have confirmed John Rock's confidence that his church would appreciate the "naturalness" of his brand of oral contraception, and also seems to have encouraged him to go still further in making his medical version of a theological argument. He knew that short-term use of the Pill could regulate the menstruation cycles for women whose previous periods had been irregular or unpredictable. This realization led to Rock's argument in favor of the Pill as ancillary to the already-Church-approved rhythm method: if a regular menstrual cycle was absolutely necessary for the success of the rhythm method, and since the rhythm method had already received church sanction, couldn't one make a thoroughly orthodox moral argument that women who suffered irregular menstruation cycles should be allowed to use the Pill to ensure the success of the rhythm method?[16]

Thus it was that, even before the promulgation of *Humanae Vitae* in the summer of 1968, Roman Catholics not only had been actively involved in the discussion about contraceptive practice but also had actually played significant roles in its invention and successful production. Further, with the first appearance of John Rock's oral contraceptive device in 1960, Catholic voices in the United States and elsewhere began calling for the Church to reconsider its teaching regarding contraception—a call that grew so widespread that "Good Pope John" (John XXIII) formally established a commission of six European nontheologians (two physicians, a demographer, a diplomat, a sociologist, and an economist) in 1963 to study both the larger question of population growth (then emerging as a serious concern in developing nations where the Catholic Church was exponentially growing), and the more specific question of birth control within that larger challenge. That group of six, formally known as the "Pontifical Commission for the Study of Population, Family, and Births," began its meetings in the same year in which the Second Vatican Council met in its first session, in response to Pope John's call for *aggiornamento*—that is, in response to the pope's call to open the windows of the church to let in the air of the twentieth century. The timing, in other words, seemed to be propitious for a change in church teaching on the vexed question of contraception.[17]

But the original "blue-ribbon panel" of experts created by John XXIII quickly morphed into larger congeries of committees made up of more than seventy members by the time it completed its task in 1966. This growth in membership was affected by a number of factors, not the least of which was the death of John XXIII, and the sense of his successor (Paul VI) that a larger group was needed to reflect the range of opinions of the Catholic Church worldwide. Paul VI's "expanded commission" thus included biologists, theologians, married couples, physicians, and both bishops and cardinals. The leader of the Commission, Fr. Henri de Riedmatten, seemed to have realized early on the possibility of actually influencing church teaching on the vexed question of contraception, and so divided up the body to conduct studies in their respective areas of expertise, and offer reports to the entire group in order to gain as much insight as possible into the complex range of issues affecting church teaching regarding overpopulation and regulation of births.[18]

As it turned out, one of the most influential of these reports in shaping the Pontifical Commission's thinking on these matters was produced by Pat and Patty Crowley, a married couple from Chicago who at the time were the lay leaders of an international Catholic group called the Christian Family Movement (CFM). The Crowleys conducted three surveys in the United

States and in Europe among CFM members, asking the kinds of questions directly pertinent to "bedroom experience" of Catholic married couples: How effective, in fact, was the rhythm method in regulating pregnancy? How did the specific protocols of that method (e.g., vaginal temperature readings, abstention from sexual intercourse during certain times of the month) actually affect a couple's emotional and psychological relationship over the long haul? It was, arguably, the Crowley's final report on these extensive surveys—that "natural family planning" (i.e., the rhythm method) was detrimental to both conjugal relations and to the family life of the couples who practiced it—that had the biggest single influence on the Majority Report presented to the pope in 1966.[19]

Over this diverse group of seventy-two scholars, physicians, and lay people the pope set up an Executive Committee of sixteen bishops, which included seven cardinals without medical credentials. Cardinal Alfredo Ottaviani (a well-known archconservative who had opposed the calling of the Council in the first place) was appointed "President" of this executive committee, while Karol Wojtyla (then a rising star in the hierarchy who would eventually become Pope John Paul II) was named as one of the episcopal members. But Ottaviani's "wing" of the Commission was balanced by figures like Cardinal Leo Suenens of Belgium and John Dearden (soon to be Cardinal Dearden) of Detroit, who would emerge in the following decade as one of the most progressive episcopal voices in the American church. Thus what had begun as a rather modest "kitchen cabinet" established to advise the previous pope developed into a fairly large and highly visible committee of blue-ribbon "experts" of various kinds that—wittingly or not—would make history. This latter fact, also, would play an important role in the critical reception of the 1968 encyclical.[20]

The expanded commission duly produced a carefully argued document in 1966 popularly called the Majority Report, although its Latin (official) title was "Schema for a Document on Responsible Parenthood." That Report—which went to the pope with the strong support of nine of the bishops and cardinals on the (oversight) Executive Committee—took its title from a famous phrase ("responsible parenthood") that had generated a great deal of commentary when it had appeared in one of the Second Vatican Council's most important documents, "The Pastoral Constitution of the Church in the Modern World" (*Gaudium et Spes*). That document of Vatican II, the Majority Report noted, had "not explained the question of responsible parenthood under all its aspects." The first hint of the Report's approach to the vexed question of contraception thus appeared in the very title of the

proposed "Schema." But other hints followed in very short order, beginning
on the opening page of the document's Introduction:

> In response to the many problems posed by the changes occurring
> today in almost every field, the church in Vatican Council II has
> entered *into the way of dialogue.* . . . But since moral obligations can
> never be detailed in all their concrete particulars, *the personal respon-*
> *sibility of each individual must always be called into play.* This is even
> clearer today because of the complexity of modern life; [therefore] *the*
> *concrete moral norms to be followed must not be pushed to an extreme.*[21]

These important hints at new models of natural law that would be explored
in the decades after 1968—a model built on dialogue, personal responsibility,
a more robust understanding of "conscience" and of the rights of conscience,
and a different understanding of "concrete moral norms" (i.e., moral directives
that said, "this specifically must be done, and that specifically avoided")—
was confirmed in the first chapter of the document. That chapter argued that
Christian marriage must be understood "above all as a community of persons"
whose chief end was the "determined effort to perfect each other, [which]
can in a very real sense be said to be the chief reason and purpose of matrimony." And because that "perfection of the other" was understood to be the
telos of married love, the Report also argued that married couples instinctively
realized that they were only able "to perfect each other and establish a true
community if their love does not end in merely egotistic union"; rather, their
mutual perfection of each other "is made truly fruitful in the creation of new
life." Thus, by the end of the first chapter of the document, the spectrum of
voices represented in the Commission appeared to have spoken: while the
document argued that the ethical duties of married life required dialogue, respect for individual consciences, and a more complex and existential standard
of ethical living than simply measuring acts by holding up the yardstick of
concrete moral norms, it also quite specifically tied married sexual relations
to the "fruitful creation of new life."[22]

It was, however, in the second chapter of the Majority Report (entitled
"Responsible Parenthood and the Regulation of Conception") that other
possible approaches to natural law were limned: the first paragraph of that
chapter stated that

> to save, protect, and promote the good of the offspring, and thus of the
> family community and of human society, the married couple will take

care to consider all the values and seek to realize them harmoniously in the best way they can, with proper reverence toward each other as persons, and according to the concrete circumstances of their life. *They will make a judgement in conscience before God about the number of children to have and educate, according to the objective criteria indicated by Vatican II.* ("Constitution on the Church in the Modern World," II, chapter 1, paragraph 50).[23]

What was distinctive in laying out this argument regarding the regulation of conception was *not* that it referenced objective criteria established by the Church at its last ecumenical council (which, because its conciliar documents had been formally promulgated by the pope, represented the highest teaching authority in the Church): Catholic moral theology had consistently argued for such "objective criteria" for centuries, and neo-scholastic theology had certainly insisted on the objectivity of moral norms in judging the goodness and badness of human acts, as *Humanae Vitae* was to argue several years later. Rather, what was distinctive about the argument embedded in the Report— opening up the possibility of very different paradigms of natural law—was that it called married couples to make their own judgment before God *in light of* those objective criteria. Objective "rules," then, could not, in themselves, simply spell out which acts were virtuous and which were "intrinsically disordered," as the 1968 encyclical would come very close to arguing. It was, rather, the "judgement in conscience" that the couple would make before God that would determine the morality of their decision. And precisely because the "regulation of children appears necessary for many couples who wish to achieve a responsible, open, and reasonable parenthood" amidst the complexities of modern life, married couples must discern exactly what a "right ordering" of their common life should look like. Therefore (and this was something of an epochal "therefore," embedded in the ninth paragraph of the Report's second chapter) the morality of sexual acts in the context of married love

takes its meaning first of all and specifically from the ordering of their actions in a fruitful married life, one which is practiced with responsible, generous and prudent parenthood. *It does not then depend upon the fecundity of each and every particular act.* Moreover, the morality of every marital act *depends upon the requirements of mutual love in all its aspects. In a word, the morality of sexual actions is thus to be judged by the true exigencies of the nature of human sexuality.*[24]

It was that word "exigencies" that further opened a rather large door to the bedroom (to mix metaphors here). And it would be chapter 3 (entitled "On the Continuity of Doctrine and Its Deeper Meaning") that would spell out in dramatic detail exactly what the repercussions of that opened door might mean for married couples making their judgment before God. While not yet even having spelled out what its specific recommendations regarding contraceptive practice might be, chapter 3 opened by observing that the Report's recommendations regarding birth control in no way intended to "contradict the genuine sense of this tradition and the previous doctrinal condemnations" of that practice. Nonetheless,

> a further step in the doctrinal evolution, which it seems now should be developed, is founded less on these facts than on *a better, deeper, and more correct understanding of conjugal life and of the conjugal act when these changes occur. The doctrine on marriage and its essential values remains the same and whole, but is now applied differently out of a deeper understanding.*[25]

Further, chapter 2 of the Report announced that this doctrinal evolution was already underway because "the magisterium itself is in evolution." It referenced the teaching of both Pope Leo XIII and Pope Pius XI as having given a "fresh start to so many beginnings in a living conjugal spirituality." Therefore (again, something of an epochal "therefore" in the context of the events that were to follow) the notion of responsible parenthood implied in the phrase "prudent and generous regulation of conception" (the phrase that had been used in Vatican II's *Gaudium et Spes*) "had already been prepared by Pope Pius XII." The Majority Report, ostensibly resting its arguments on the teachings of Popes Leo XIII, Pius XI, and Pius XII, no less—distinguished the "contraceptive intention" from the sheer physical separation of the unitive and procreative aspects of the act:

> The tradition has always rejected seeking this separation with a contraceptive intention for *motives spoiled by egoism and hedonism,* and such seeking can never be admitted. The true opposition is not to be sought between some material conformity to the physiological processes of nature and some artificial intervention. For it is natural in man [*sic*] to use his skill in order to put under human control what is given in physical nature. *The opposition is really to be sought between one way of acting which is contraceptive and opposed to a prudent and generous fruitfulness,*

and another which is in an ordered relationship to responsible fruitfulness and which has a concern for education and all the essential, human and Christian, values.[26]

"Of course," the Majority Report declared perhaps one too many times, its members recognized the importance of objective moral norms in constructing the ethical life of Christian discipleship. Of course, it averred, sexual relations between married Christians needed to remain open to the transmission of new life, and avoid what the Church had correctly identified as a "contraceptive mentality" focused on selfish concerns. Of course, Christian couples, committed to the values of responsible parenthood and the good of the human family, must order their relationships in light of the (larger) horizon of meaning that defined the ways in which the Christian sacrament of marriage differed in type and in lived reality from a merely secular, atomized, understanding of marriage focused just on the rights and needs of two individuals. Nonetheless—again, a rather epochal "nonetheless" given its formal status as a standing body authorized by the Supreme Pontiff—the commission's Majority Report argued that these values did not exhaust, or even define, what Christian marriage was primarily about. *That* was a singular—indeed a revolutionary—"nonetheless." And that "nonetheless" was the key to understanding the revolutionary purpose of the Report's third chapter, which was entitled (ironically enough) "On the Continuity of Doctrine and Its Deeper Meaning." For the spin put on that fraught question of "continuity of doctrine"—the same question on which the pope would make his historic decision regarding the acceptance or rejection of the Majority Report— adumbrated a very different future from the neo-scholastic past:

> The large amount of knowledge and facts which throw light on today's world suggest that *it is not to contradict the genuine sense of this tradition and the purpose of the previous doctrinal condemnations* if we speak of the regulation of conception by using means, human and decent, *ordered to favoring fecundity in the totality of married life and toward the realization of the authentic values of a fruitful matrimonial community.*[27]

Read in the light of Kuhn's theory regarding paradigm revolutions, how—or perhaps better, in what ways—can we read the Majority Report delivered to Pope Paul VI in 1966 as opening the possibility of exploring very different models of natural law, and not just a revised version of the older neo-scholastic model (as many of that Report's supporters claimed)? Perhaps the easiest way of answering that important question is by focusing on four features of the overall argument of "Responsible Parenthood" that elucidated a very model of what natural law was about.

First: "Responsible Parenthood" presumes that natural law is marked by evolutionary development, and not by immutable laws that could be found in "Nature." And it was not just natural law that was evolving: "the magisterium [the official teaching of the Church] itself is in evolution" the report observed, matter-of-factly, without any apparent need to defend such a statement. Bernard Lonergan would have said that the model of reality informing the Report had already made the turn from a classicist to a historicist universe. And having made that turn, the teaching office of the Church could *not* just assume that moral norms always remained the same, or that natural law undergirding those norms was necessarily marked by a static, ahistorical unchangeableness. With that one simple phrase—"the magisterium itself is in evolution"—the Commission constituted by the pope announced that the older paradigm of natural law, defined by a propositional, unchanging set of norms that transcended history, was recognized as dated and—more to the point—no longer useful in undergirding church teaching. Thus the authors of the Majority Report claimed to be writing from the standpoint of an "evolved" insight into marriage—a "better, deeper, and more correct understanding of conjugal life and the conjugal act," in the words of the Report.

Second: the Report presumed that theology was obliged to both recognize and attempt to answer anomalies that arose from the application of moral teaching to the actual experience of believers. This second feature derived from a very different understanding of how theology was "the queen of the sciences," or at least a valid science—that is, a human undertaking that studied and built on actual *data.* The older neo-scholastic understanding of both "nature" and "law" was thus neither parried nor denigrated: it was simply ignored in adumbrating how moral theology was to proceed *scientifically.* Before anything else, the argument presented here simply presumed that one had to begin with a careful study of the "many problems posed by the changes occurring today in almost every field"—changes which themselves represented part of the *data* of natural law. From the point of view of the Majority Report, these changes didn't represent challenges to natural law; they were *part* of the structure of natural law. And precisely because of the "complexity of modern life," concrete moral norms (the very manner in which the older paradigm presented its understanding of natural law) needed to be *rethought.*

Thus, building on the three surveys that had been conducted by the Crowleys among CFM members in both Europe and the United States, the Majority Report sought to integrate the "science" of theology with the best data provided by other physical and social sciences, as well as by demographic reports from married people. The Report built on the sound Catholic understanding that the Church's purchase on natural law—while not "rational" in a strict sense—nonetheless *had* to be at least reasonable, in the sense of being understandable to nonspecialists in moral theology. That is, it had to be in accord with data that confirmed the reasonableness of its application of natural law principles to the actual, lived experience of believers. That seemed a minimum bar for understanding the discipline of theology as in any sense a "science." Whatever intellectual elegance the older church teaching about the rhythm method may have embodied according to the model it built on, the reported experience of married couples seemed to belie its status as "ordained by God." How could such sexual practice be understood to have been "ordained by God" if it could only work by virtue of something approaching heroic charity? Further, how could God have "ordained" a practice—like the rhythm method—which in fact strained marital relations between couples dedicated to living in conformity to church teaching? Even by the arcane standards of Catholic theology, church teaching regarding the rhythm method thus seemed (at best) unreasonable and *unscientific:* it flew in the face of the experience of the couples who practiced it.

Third: The Majority Report simply presumed that a lucid application of the principles of any viable model of natural law could only be arrived at *dialogically*—that is, in conversation with *data* produced by the physical and social sciences, and from the free exchange of ideas with all parties involved. In this third (dialogical) sense, the Report represented a rather dramatic break with the neo-scholastic approach to arriving at moral teaching ostensibly based on natural law. That older approach had favored a "top down" process that was altogether too dependent on what Aristotle had termed the "argument from authority"—that is, the argument that ended discussion by saying "do this because I told you to." As Aristotle had reminded his own students millennia before, this was the weakest form of argument, and (as it would turn out) was no more compelling in the twentieth century than it had been in the fourth century B.C. And the events of 1968 would certainly bear witness that such an argument was less than compelling for adult believers attempting to order their faith lives in light of the best data available. In the Majority Report's micro-paradigm of natural law, a central component of nature "out there" that had to be taken into account in understanding natural law was the lived experience of believers. This model turned the entire paradigm of neo-scholasticism on its head: "human nature" (the nature that represented the focus of natural law) could not be simply derived intellectually from first principles by theologians and Vatican officials. Human nature had to be observed, discussed, and formulated in light of the actual experience of human persons. One did not begin with propositions; one finally arrived at knowledge *after* dialogue, debate, and the application of theory to experience.

And the Second Vatican Council had limned and embodied precisely such a dialogical method for arriving at valid ecclesiastical teaching. As the first paragraph in chapter 4 of the Majority Report had put it: "In resolving the problem of responsible parenthood and the appropriate determination of the size of the family, Vatican Council II has shown the way." And it had shown the way precisely by arriving at a clearer understanding of the contemporary meaning of church teaching through the processes of conversation (and sometimes even fierce debate), the free exchange of ideas, and—finally—through the democratic medium of voting. The authors of the Majority Report, we can validly assume, undoubtedly seconded the wry observation made by the signers of the Mayflower Document still two years in the future: that it was, "to say the least, surprising that what was alleged to be the design of God could only be discovered in the utmost secrecy." Natural law could neither be "discovered" nor elucidated behind closed doors: it was much more reliably discerned in open debate, utilizing the messy (but effective) processes of democracy. Just as physical scientists had long been accustomed to doing in their day-to-day undertakings in normal science, the Majority Report now enjoined students of natural law to pay careful attention to anomalies that arose in their application of ecclesiastical teaching to human behavior, to debate—freely and openly—the possible meanings of those anomalies with both Christian ethicists and social and physical scientists, and to attempt to arrive at a more concise and intellectually satisfying model of the moral meaning of both church teaching and the human behavior it addressed. Thus one did not begin with principles purportedly derived from natural law to be applied to moral cases, as the neo-scholastic paradigm presupposed. One rather *arrived at principles* after studying both the data available and the anomalies produced by other paradigms. However "true" a model of natural law might be derived from supposedly "orthodox" first principles (whatever the authority proposing such a model), the Majority Report's paradigm simply dismissed such an anomalous model as irrelevant to the task at hand.

Fourth: The Majority Report assumed that an important component of "nature" was the advances of human science. As chapter 3 of the Report observed," it is *natural* in man to use his skill in order to put under human control what is given in physical nature." This simple observation represented, in itself, a revolution, and not an evolution, in the Catholic understanding of natural law. The "nature" referenced here included both human nature and physical nature (the "out there" givenness of what humans discovered in the physical universe). But it also now included the advances of physical science; those advances ineluctably informed the "natural" impulse among *homo sapiens* to "put under human control what is given in physical nature." Those very advances—like John Rock's "natural" method for regulating births— were now presented less as challenges to natural law than as invitations to consider how natural law had evolved in tandem with the evolution of the natural and social sciences. Such an understanding of nature, the Report observed, represented the *true* understanding of the trajectory of natural law thinking.

While these four aspects of the Majority Report's model of natural law might seem obvious to any careful reader of that remarkable document, it is nonetheless important to highlight them because so much of the language of the Report used the same words and phrases that all moral theologians had used for centuries, perhaps obscuring how revolutionary the path it was advocating actually was. Building on the important work of ethical revisionists like Bernard Haring, Joseph Fuchs, and others who had been reshaping the Catholic moral tradition in faculty offices and Jesuit rec rooms but on the margins of Catholic "public culture," the Report nonetheless offered its arguments in language that was reassuringly familiar, if now applied in revolutionary ways: "the proper ends of marriage and the marriage act"; "a firm rejection of the contraceptive mentality"; "the central role of objective moral norms in guiding the formation of individual consciences"; "teaching based on the solid foundations elucidated by Pius XI in *Casti Canubii* [*sic*]"; "a proper willingness to raise a family with full acceptance of Christian responsibilities."

Such reassuringly familiar phrases, offered in service of adumbrating revolutionary new paths for exploring what natural law was, and how it was to be utilized in Catholic moral theology, might have led a less astute reader of the Majority Report to read it as being in seamless continuity with neo-scholasticism. But theologians would do well to remember Kuhn's famous observation that "progress" is a word that physical scientists used with scare quotes around it because science didn't "advance" from Galileo to Newton, and then to Einstein. Rather, each of those names represented the scuttling of an older model of science for a totally new one. The scientific terminology remained the same (e.g., the velocity of falling bodies), but the entire field against which those terms were used had changed dramatically.

Whatever else one might say about him, Pope Paul VI was nothing if not an extremely astute church politician, as well as a thoughtful student of the history of Catholic theology. The pope clearly recognized the Majority Report's replacement of the older neo-scholastic paradigm with one that operated from totally different principles. It was thus less than surprising that Paul decided against acting on that Report—with dramatic results in the decades that followed. He was widely perceived, both in and outside the Church, as having rejected the Report's conclusions when he issued *Humanae Vitae* in 1968 in favor of the same Pontifical Commission's Minority Report, which appeared to build more deliberately on the nineteenth-century neo-scholastic paradigm of a manualist approach to natural law. Indeed, no less an insider than Fr. Gregory Baum—who had served as a *peritus* at Vatican II—stated baldly in a *National Catholic Reporter* article in 1968 that precisely this was the case. But as historians are so anxious to remind us, the truth is rather more complicated than such a simple binary implied. And it is here that another American Jesuit played a central role in setting the stage for the events of 1968.[28]

C. *The Minority Report: John Ford and the "Credible Manualists"*

If one decided to write a "binary history" of American Catholicism during the 1960s—facing off theological "liberals" versus "conservatives" in the various battles roiling the Catholic community during that fractious decade—one could do far worse than pitting American Jesuit Richard McCormick (he of the famous *Theological Studies* article critiquing the 1968 encyclical) against John Ford, another American Jesuit who had served on the Papal Commission between 1963 and 1966. Ford, a theologian teaching at the Jesuits' seminary in Weston, Massachusetts, was what moralist James Keenan has termed a "credible manualist," having gained international notice in the Catholic community in 1944, when he published an

> electrifying essay against obliteration bombing, right in the crucible of the Second World War. Ford did what his European colleagues on either side of the war did not do: criticize and condemn the saturation bombing of cities.[29]

With his fellow Jesuit Gerald Kelly (who taught moral theology at the Jesuits' seminary in St. Mary's, Kansas), Ford edited the famed "Notes in Moral Theology" section of the periodical *Theological Studies*, in order to do which meant that he read almost every book and article published in the Catholic theological world. Ford was thus a kind of "mirror image" of McCormick—a moral theologian widely considered to offer an "authoritatively sound" interpretation of official Catholic moral teaching, especially in the areas of sexual and medical ethics. In contrast to McCormick's revisionist reading of the Catholic moral tradition, Ford was considered a "rigorist" because of his strict interpretation of church teaching. In the in-house argot of moral theology, this meant that Ford was considered one of the foremost voices in the "*tutiorist*" tradition (from the Latin *tutior*, meaning "safest"). Thus, for Ford and Kelly, in any question relating to moral theology, it was always better to follow the strictest or "safest" opinion on the subject.[30]

Ford believed that the older "classicist" tradition of Catholic moral theology—embodied in the manualist school dedicated to training priests to hear "cases of conscience" in the confessional—was the safest and most reliable form for handing on the revered tradition of Catholic moral theology to clergy-in-training. It is, then, not exactly surprising that he set his face against the kind of moral revisionism being explored by Haring, Fuchs, and others. But it is important to remember that the "classicism" that provided the framework for Ford's theology could produce quite prophetic and even radical stances, like that of Ford's strong condemnation of obliteration bombing during the tense final months of the century's bloodiest war. "Classicist" he might be (to utilize Bernard Lonergan's famous definition); intellectually timid Ford was not.[31]

Thus, by 1963—when he was appointed to the Pontifical Commission for the Study of Population, Family, and Births—Ford and fellow "respectable manualists" like Gerald Kelly had already fought in a number of skirmishes with younger revisionist moralists (many of them fellow Jesuits); indeed, Ford and Kelly would produce a two-volume work in 1964—*Contemporary Moral Theology*—that might be taken as one of the last widely read works defending the manualist tradition as the only true Catholic approach to moral questions, precisely against the revisionist theologians then storming the field. That work proved (if proving was needed) that Ford well understood the newer (historicist) "takes" on natural law; he just thought they were wrong, and believed that they operated out of a completely different model of natural law that bore little or no resemblance to the moral tradition that had emerged out of the nineteenth-century neo-scholastic revival. And read through the lens of Kuhn's theory of paradigms, Ford was (of course) exactly right.[32]

Catholic theology as a discipline had been marked during the Middle Ages by decentralized debates between various "schools"—between, for instance, the theology faculties at the University of Paris and Oxford. Those various schools had certainly appealed certain theological questions to Rome for clarification, and occasionally even for a definitive answer: thus the famous Catholic adage *Roma locuta; causa finita est* ("Rome has spoken; the case is closed"). That tendency of seeking papal pronouncements on disputed theological questions had quickened in the centuries after the Protestant Reformation—when centripetal forces seemed to be tearing the Church apart—and had reached flood tide during the nineteenth and early twentieth centuries, when Rome was battling modern culture on a number of fronts. But Ford and Kelly took that centripetal *tendency* and systematized it into something else again, something that had been unformulated, and marked by irregular practice, in earlier centuries—something that represented a singular departure even from the nineteenth-century neo-scholastic dedication to ultramontanism. To that extent, anyway, Ford and Kelly's *systematization* of the appeal to ecclesial authority as part and parcel of the task of moral theology represented a new paradigm for the discipline, if hidden under the ancient tradition of occasionally undertaking such appeals.[33]

Ford and Kelly developed a theology centered on, and dedicated to, the appeal to papal authority. From John Ford's viewpoint, moral theology was not a discipline undertaken by scholars to elucidate church teaching by using natural law (i.e., "reasonable") arguments in order to show how that teaching accorded with human experience, in the process elucidating the famous adage of Aquinas—that "grace built on nature." On the contrary, for Ford and Kelly, the place to *start* the discipline of moral theology was by appealing directly to Authority, in this case, to the authority of the Supreme Pontiff as the infallible teacher in the Church. Ford and Kelly thus developed an entire system built on the proposition that their discipline was *not* about the disciplined *search* for moral truth—as though the end of that search could ever be in doubt; rather, their paradigm was built on the belief that the place to start was the *reception* of moral truth from Rome. In the search for moral truth, then, all any moral theologian had to do was to study statements promulgated by the pope or someone delegated by him (statements usually presented in propositional form), and then explain them.[34]

Such a model for moral theology represented a "take" on the old *Roma locuta, causa finita est* adage that was quite new: indeed, it was, to use Kuhnian categories, the elucidation of an entirely new micro-paradigm of natural law. Thus, for Ford and Kelly, "the principal *approach* to any theological treatise should be the teaching of the magisterium, especially of the Holy See itself, when such teaching is available." And this argument rested on a watertight syllogism—watertight at least if you granted them their first principles. As "Rome" was the only authentic interpreter of divine law, "it was only through conformity to [papal teaching] that the individual conscience can have security from error." And while Ford believed that when Rome had not yet decided a question moralists were free to offer their opinions, once Rome *had* spoken the theologian's duty was clear: "to fulfill his acknowledged duty of explaining papal teaching, a theologian must in some measure interpret it."[35]

Ford and Kelly thus elucidated something like a "regressivist" theory of moral theology, in the process radically recentering the nineteenth-century neo-scholastic understanding of the role of natural law in arriving at moral truth. That is, they sought to find "proof" of the validity of contemporary church teaching by looking backward to the "constant teaching" of popes, council, and older theologians. Thus, in the first volume of their 1964 work, *Contemporary Moral Theology,* they argued that moral theology was called to study

> man [*sic*] in the supernatural order, possessed of a supernatural destiny; it is *a science based not only on reason—nor [even] principally on reason*—but especially on revelation and on the teaching of the church. Reason is the supreme argument in ethics; *authority is the sovereign guide of the theologian.*[36]

As James Keenan has further noted, in so defining the field of moral theology Ford and Kelly *inverted* the manner in which most Catholic thinkers had proceeded in constructing moral arguments: rather than beginning by applying propositions about human nature in order to arrive at church teaching, Ford and Kelly *began* their task of stating moral opinions by invoking the authority of papal teaching. In so doing, they had outlined a radically new model of doing moral theology, one in which they stated moral teaching

> *before, and sometimes without* considering the internal [coherence] of the argument. They used no critical reason vis-à-vis a magisterial utterance. That a claim was "magisterial" was, for Ford and Kelly, itself the guarantor of its truthfulness.[37]

And the radical core of their approach was their belief that moral theologians could practice their discipline without recourse to the kind of critical analysis that moral theology had utilized since Aquinas. If there was no need for critical analysis when magisterial authority had already pronounced its judgment, then the traditional place of reason in moral theology lost its independent status: natural law was whatever the Church pronounced it to be. How such a conception of natural law could be conceived of as "natural"—as distinct from "revealed"—was, as Keenan and others have observed, something of a problem that perplexed their colleagues in the guild of moral theology. What was the utility of the concept of a "natural" law if it could only be discerned and elucidated by church officials? How was its "naturalness" apparent to non-Christians or non-Catholics, except as a component of divine wrath?[38]

In terms of the history of Catholic theology in the United States, it is important to note how Ford and Kelly's approach, which obviated any need to examine the intellectual coherence of a moral position if some external authority proposed it, drew a new and dramatic distinction between "ethics" and "moral theology," the former purportedly being grounded in reason (and therefore in natural law), and the latter glossing over reason in favor of authority. This was an audacious new articulation of the Catholic tradition, and therefore warrants notice as a somewhat singular "take" on Catholic notions of the concept of natural law. But for the purposes of this study, their newly articulated approach, mapped out in the 1964 two-volume *Contemporary Moral Theology*, is especially pertinent for understanding the events around the 1968 encyclical and its lengthy if contentious afterlife. And this is so because Ford (with advice from another American theologian, Germain Grisez) was the principal author of the Minority Report of the Pontifical Commission, which also went to the pope in 1966.

While Ford and Kelly maintained that their model of Catholic moral theology represented simply an articulation and elucidation of the centuries-old manualist, neo-scholastic tradition of natural law, we might now recognize—with the benefit of lens provided by Kuhn—that theirs was actually a revolutionary approach that offered a significantly different way of addressing the anomalies uncovered by revisionist moralists like McCormick. And Paul VI, being a careful reader of ecclesial documents, undoubtedly recognized precisely that fact in rejecting it as a basis for his 1968 encyclical.

The Minority Report delivered to Paul VI in 1966—actually more like a working paper than a final document—was signed by Ford and three other priests who had sat on the Pontifical Commission. Although intended by

Ford and fellow signatories to be read only by the pope, its text was "leaked" to the press in 1967—that is, a year before Paul VI promulgated the 1968 encyclical that was purportedly aimed to end the internal debates within the Commission to which both reports witnessed. Thus what was intended as a secret vote of "no confidence"—offered in rejoinder to the Pontifical Commission's Majority Report—quickly made its way into newspapers in both Europe and America. What the readers of those newspaper stories quickly learned was that Ford's Minority Report voiced a number of significant reservations regarding the positions advanced in the majority's document; what they may have failed to notice, but what we can now appreciate with the twenty-twenty vision of hindsight, was that two such concerns stood out as of overriding importance, garnering the most space in the document delivered to Paul VI. The first was the concern about the Majority Report's understanding of natural law.[39]

In a section entitled "Philosophical Foundations and Arguments of Others and Critique" (the "Others" of the title presumably being the signatories of the Majority Report), Ford argued that the latter report's

> notion of natural law remains uncertain, changeable, [and] withdrawn from the magisterium. . . . This view does not do justice to protect either the competence which the Church has so many times vindicated for herself for the interpretation of the natural law, nor the Church's effective capacity of discerning the moral order established by God, which is so often obscure to fallen man. Nature [in the Majority Report] seems to have . . . granted the dominion to man, so that he can experiment with them, foster change, or frustrate them for his own earthly convenience.[40]

In light of Kuhn's construct of the "period of crisis," we can now appreciate the absolute truth of Ford's accusation that the Majority Report offered a revolutionary different understanding than the one proffered by nineteenth-century neo-scholastic theology; but what Ford seemed unaware of was how different his *own* model of natural law was from that nineteenth-century model as well. But what clearly alarmed Ford was his (correct) perception that the Majority Report's model of natural law simply presupposed "the mutability of nature in the human person according to the evolution of history." Such an evolutionary understanding of human nature strongly implied that different cultural conditions "may permit or require contradictory moral actions in diverse situations, though under the same principle." In any such application of the idea of evolution to moral teaching, Ford averred, "the authenticity of the magisterium seems to be substantially violated."[41]

And it was here that Ford made the most transparent appeal to the political considerations involved in any Vatican statement regarding contraception. Precisely because it had been promised the inerrant guidance of the Holy Spirit in interpreting a natural law established by God,

> the Church cannot change her answer because this answer is true. It is true because the Catholic Church, instituted by Christ to show men a secure way to eternal life, could not have so wrongly erred during all those centuries of history. The Church cannot substantially err in teaching doctrine which is most serious in import for faith and morals, throughout all centuries or even one century.[42]

It was precisely the univocacy and undoubted reliability of the Church's understanding of natural law that, in Ford's eyes, the Majority Report seemed to undermine. By stating that the Magisterium—the Church's official teaching office—had to reform or even change previous positions based on what Ford took to be an unchanging natural law was to undermine the reliability of that teaching office. And it was this question of the absolutely unchanging nature of the Magisterium that constituted the kernel of Ford's second concern: if, after so many centuries of teaching only one view of the morality of contraception (the nonobservance of which constituted the kind of "intrinsically disordered act" that cut one off from God's grace), the Church was now to change that teaching,

> it must be greatly feared that its authority in almost all moral and dogmatic matters will be greatly harmed. For there are few moral truths so constantly, solemnly, and—as it has appeared—definitely stated as this one, for which it is now so quickly proposed that it be changed to the contrary.[43]

And an important component motivating this second concern was how the Church might be seen with other Christian bodies. As Ford knew well, and strenuously argued in his Minority Report, the teaching of Pius XI in *Casti Connubii* in 1930, which had strongly condemned contraception as a violation of both natural law and the consistent teaching of the Church, had been solemnly proposed in conscious opposition to the new teaching of the Anglican Communion, which elucidated by its Lambeth Conference of that year, the permissibility of contraception in certain situations. If it were *now* admitted that the Catholic Church, "to whom God has entrusted the defense of the integrity and purity of morals," was changing its position on precisely this controverted issue, it would now have "to be admitted that the Church erred [on this topic], and that the Holy Spirit rather assists the Anglican Church." And it was *precisely* the Majority Report's argument that while such a condemnation might have been right "for those times," new historical circumstances now demanded changed teaching that had to be strenuously rejected:

> This seems to be something that one cannot propose, for the Anglican Church was teaching precisely that, and for the very reasons which the Catholic Church solemnly denied, but which it would now admit. Certainly such a manner of speaking would be unintelligible to the people, and would seem to be a specious pretext.[44]

While Paul VI clearly chose not to act on the recommendation offered in the Pontifical Commission's Majority Report, Gregory Baum was just as clearly mistaken in asserting that the pope decided in favor of Ford's Minority Report in writing *Humanae Vitae*. For while Ford's final recommendation—that the Church stand by its previous teaching regarding the profound sinfulness of contraception—undoubtedly resonated with leading figures in the Vatican (and most probably with the pope himself), they just as clearly recognized that Ford's approach represented a striking departure from how moral theologians had practiced their craft, especially with his singular folding of the entire tradition of natural law into revealed teaching.

The result was something like a catch-22 situation: rejecting the paths outlined by both the Majority and Minority Reports of the papal commission constituted by his own beloved predecessor, Paul VI promulgated an encyclical that reflected both and neither, but rather an effort to craft a third way in condemning the practice of contraception as "intrinsically disordered." The resulting problem, of course, was that the vast majority of practicing Catholics in the United States rejected both the arguments and the conclusions of *Humanae Vitae*. And just like Mother Nature, Mother Church seemed to abhor a vacuum: the result of the vacuum left by the 1968 encyclical—at least for Catholic moral theologians—was a lush growth of new paradigms of natural law. Just as Kuhn had predicted, the "period of crisis" set off by the anomalies in the older paradigm opened up three decades that witnessed a proliferation of new ones.

PART III

Other Voices, Other Paradigms

4

Charles Curran and "Loyal Dissent"

THE FIRST POSTCLASSICIST NATURAL LAW PARADIGM

A. Between "The Rock" and a Hard Place

It is a safe conjecture that none of the signatories of the "Mayflower Statement" presented to the press on July 30, 1968, considered their undertaking to be anything like an open revolt against the right of the Church to offer moral guidance on important questions of the Christian life. Composed as it was of Roman Catholic priests in good standing with their respective bishops and religious superiors—all of whom had been trained in Catholic moral theology in seminaries and pontifical institutions like the Gregorian University in Rome—it would undoubtedly be much closer to their self-perception to see them as "loyal dissenters" from the pope's 1968 encyclical—dissenters yes, but loyal nonetheless to the Catholic tradition of faith and practice, and indeed to the pope. And none of those present on that fateful (and humid) July day during the "Summer of Love" would earn that label of loyal dissenter more validly than Fr. Charles Curran, a priest of the Rochester, New York diocese.[1]

But if the Mayflower Statement was an unlikely document to begin a micro-tradition revolution, the fact that Curran would soon emerge as one of the leaders in the construction of a new paradigm in moral theology was somewhat less surprising. At the tender age of thirteen, Curran had entered a high school seminary, from which he graduated (not surprisingly) as valedictorian. From there he had entered St. Bernard's Seminary in Rochester, often referred to by its alumni—not always affectionately—as "The Rock." His description of the daily rigorous—even monastic—regimen in that place was surprisingly positive and even complementary.[2]

As was common for Catholic dioceses in the United States, Rochester sent two of its most promising seminarians to the North American College in Rome (the "NAC" as it was familiarly known to its alumni) to study at the "home office." Perched high above the Vatican, the NAC had the (well-deserved) reputation among American priests as an ecclesiastical hot house for budding bishops and seminary professors; it was thus hardly surprising that Charlie Curran—the brilliant student who had carried away most of the academic prizes in both high school and his college seminary classes—was chosen as one of the two sent to Rome. Curran spent the years 1955 to 1961 living at the NAC (itself a seminary residence and not an academic institution) while taking courses at the Gregorian University, run by the Jesuits and founded in the sixteenth century. Classes at the Gregorian were taught in Latin to an international student body, many of whom were destined to be bishops, diocesan chancellors, and seminary professors when they returned to their home country.[3]

Arguably the most important intellectual influence on Curran at the Gregorian University was German Jesuit Josef Fuchs, who taught Curran's course on sexual morality. Although something of a traditionalist regarding the Church's teaching on sexual issues, Fuchs nonetheless was (correctly) perceived to be one of the stars of the revisionist school in moral theology; that is, Fuchs had moved a considerable distance from the older "propositional" model of manualist moral theology to emphasize the intrinsic relationship of sexuality to a holistic understanding of the life of Christian discipleship. In his courses Fuchs situated sexuality as an important—but not necessarily determinative—component in the whole of Christian life, and not just a potential area of sinful acts that had to be confessed to a priest (as the manualists tended to do). Curran came to respect Fuchs as both a scholar and person. Nonetheless, years later—in 1968—when Fuchs visited the Catholic University of America (CUA) to give a lecture, Fuchs confessed that he was happy to see that the younger priest had matured in his theological views, telling Curran, "I can remember when you were as rigid as a telephone pole."[4]

Curran was ordained a priest in Rome in July 1958, after which he was informed by his bishop that he would remain in Rome to study for a doctorate in moral theology, eventually to return to The Rock to teach seminarians. As it happened, Curran got word about his future just as he had finished reading an Italian translation of Bernard Haring's two-volume work on moral theology, which in retrospect might be seen as one of the most important intellectual influences on Curran's subsequent career. *The Law of Christ*, Haring's landmark work, proposed a "person-centered" approach to moral theology, rather than the older (manualist) "act-centered" one. That is, in his book Haring proposed a more historicist, teleological approach to Christian morality that brought together spirituality, scripture, and the sacramental life of the Church to talk about the "ends" of Christian living: What kind of *person*—considered holistically—did moral theology seek to shape? What kinds of values and virtues did Christian morality seek to instill in believers? Such a person-centered approach to moral theology represented a marked departure from the older, manualist, approach to understanding moral theology, which had focused on the morality of specific acts in an individual's life. For Haring, Christian morality was less about specific *acts* than about the kind of *believer* who performed those acts: a person's moral status before God could not be determined by a simplistic cataloguing of "good" acts from "bad" ones in a person's life ("laundry list" style); rather, evaluating the moral health of a person could only be evaluated by considering how specific acts were emblematic of the believer's faith life. How well (or badly) did a person's actions embody the virtues of a life of discipleship?[5]

The influence of both Josef Fuchs in the classroom and his encounter with the scholarship of Bernard Haring while still a student in Rome would have a deep effect on Curran's career as one of Catholic America's most esteemed moral theologians. As Curran would later remember this time,

> I had already begun to move beyond the pre-Vatican II neoscholastic approaches to Catholicism. As a seminarian in Rome I had become quite conscious of the human side of the church, and had begun to recognize the significance of historical development in both theology and the life of the church. Pious Catholics visiting Rome would occasionally comment that it must be a great privilege to study in Rome and have such an opportunity to grow in faith.... But by the time I left Rome in 1961, I was conscious that the church was not only human but sinful. I was still a very committed Catholic, but I recognized the pilgrim nature of the church—that it is always in need of reform, an important concept which Vatican II brought to the fore.[6]

Unsurprisingly, Curran (ever the outstanding student) wrote not one but two doctoral dissertations in Rome. But it was his doctoral dissertation at the Alfonsiana Academy (on the seemingly arcane topic of "The Concept of Invincible Ignorance of the Natural Law in the Thought of St. Alphonsus Liguori") that was most pertinent to understanding his subsequent distinguished career. More to the point, the theological implications of what he found in researching that topic were anything but arcane; indeed, one can construct a compelling argument that his research for that dissertation profoundly influenced his later role as the leader of the loyal opposition to *Humanae Vitae* in 1968.[7]

In the course of his research for the dissertation Curran discovered that there had been sharp disagreements when St. Alphonsus was writing in the eighteenth century (as there was in the 1960s) between reliable Catholic authorities about the gravity and even moral meaning of specific acts: what some Catholic moralists in the eighteenth century had declared to be intrinsically disordered and deeply sinful acts, other—equally "sound"—Catholic authorities had declared morally neutral. As Curran came to realize in writing his dissertation, then, the static "classicist" understanding of moral theology—in which certain acts were sinful everywhere, all the time, regardless of context—was not borne out by the historical record. Studying Liguori (whom the Catholic tradition had labeled the best confessor of his time) led Curran to believe that the *subjective* aspect of human acts could be just as important—indeed, more important in certain situations—as the objective facts in judging the morality of human activity. Thus began a paradigm revolution in Curran's understanding of natural law.

In September 1961 Curran returned to The Rock in Rochester to teach moral theology to the seminarians studying there, but he returned a very different person than who he was when he left that very institution. Curran had come to reject the narrow manualist approach to understanding the Christian life that he had been taught in Rochester as a seminarian:

> Moral theology had to deal with the whole of the Christian life, especially the call to continual conversion, as Bernard Haring insisted. I had also become aware of historical consciousness, with its recognition of the importance of the particular, and the recognition of the historical embeddedness of every human thinker and knower.[8]

To his own surprise (given the static understanding of moral theology that prevailed in those years just before the Second Vatican Council) the other priests on the Seminary faculty both welcomed their young colleague and even encouraged him to write about the new approach to Christian morality that he had learned from Fuchs and Haring. And Curran did just that, producing (unsurprisingly) lucid and well-argued articles that led to an ever-growing list of speaking engagements; among which was an invitation to speak at an ecumenical gathering of Catholic and Protestant theologians (the first of its kind) at Harvard University in 1963. That event, in turn, led to an invitation in 1964 to address the Catholic Club at Harvard, in which he argued (to the astonishment of his own auxiliary bishop) that a more historically inflected understanding of natural law would allow the Church to reverse its official teaching banning contraceptive practice. One would be on very safe ground in asserting that no faculty member at St. Bernard's Seminary had ever—either overtly or covertly—declared such a thing in public (or perhaps even in private).[9]

Curran's rise to prominence as a speaker of some renown in the early sixties was thus not greeted by everyone as an unalloyed good thing. Lawrence Casey, the auxiliary (assistant) bishop of Curran's own diocese, reportedly became increasingly uncomfortable with Curran's career path—both the reports that came back from speaking engagements (like those at Harvard) and the lecture series that Curran coordinated at the seminary. After bringing in luminaries like Bernard Haring and Gustav Weigel—prominent if progressive theologians and scripture scholars who were elucidating what would become the distinctive post–Vatican II style of Roman Catholicism—Casey informed Curran that the lecture series had to be discontinued because of concerns that had been voiced. Further, in early 1965 Curran was "called on the carpet" (in this case literally) in seminary rector's office, where he was warned that some of the positions he was teaching the seminarians—like his observations that the Church would have to change its position on contraception—had caused disquiet (although to whom remained both unclear and unspecified). At the end of that interchange, Curran was further informed that "it would be better if [he] did not give talks in parishes." By July 1965, tensions between Curran and his diocesan superiors had reached the point at which he was informed that he could no longer teach at the seminary.[10]

But Bishop Casey also offered to write to the rector (president) of the Catholic University of America in Washington, DC, offering Curran's services there: within a week CUA's rector wrote to Curran, welcoming him to his new position on the faculty that coming fall. The "firing" from The Rock turned out to be a happy fault, as Curran immediately took to the more academic and research atmosphere of CUA, which allowed him much more time for research and publication. And how he used that seemingly "ivory tower" atmosphere to study quite concrete issues touching the lives of millions of Catholics can be easily illustrated by how he utilized his doctoral seminar during the Spring 1966 academic term: using the occasion of the seminar discussions with advanced doctoral students that term, Curran penned a paper to be presented at the annual meeting of the Catholic Theological Society of America (CTSA) later that spring on the topic of masturbation. [11]

The nineteenth-century (manualist) neo-scholastics had taught that masturbation *always* involved "objectively grave matter"; that is, masturbation was a mortal sin that, under normal circumstances, cut off a person from God's grace. Curran, utilizing contemporary psychological and scientific data about the psychosexual development of individuals, as well as St. Thomas Aquinas' nuanced position on what exactly constituted "gravely sinful matter," offered his own nuanced position built on the important distinction between "objectively grave matter" (actions that are in themselves very sinful) and "subjective culpability" (the degree of guilt on the part of the person doing the action). In light of that important distinction—itself built on the most respected authority in Catholic theology, Aquinas—Curran argued that masturbation did not always involve serious sin, as one had to take into account the context of the act, the intention of the person involved in the act, and that person's psychological maturity. In the event, Curran's CTSA paper was very well received by his (largely clerical) audience that June; but his paper also served notice—well beyond the CTSA—that those who conceived of Catholic moral theology as a set of universally true "correct answers" applicable in all situations would now have to contend with a new (and brilliant) voice in the field, teaching at the US bishops' own university. [12]

Curran's CTSA paper from June 1965 in fact adumbrated his future trajectory in writing about natural law over the course of the next several decades: Curran set about producing articles and talks that seriously examined the neo-scholastic approaches to natural law in light of the insights he had gained from both Josef Fuchs and Bernard Haring, as well as from his own reading and research in the field. Basic to his ongoing study was his growing sense of the serious intellectual inadequacy of the nineteenth-century understanding of natural law by the neo-scholastics—precisely the approach he had learned before going to Rome. And close to the core of his critique of that older tradition was its static, ahistorical understanding of both human nature and the "natural law" embedded in that nature. Curran became increasingly impatient with the way in which Catholic teaching had "absolutized" the biological and physiological aspects of human sexuality (well before the appearance of the 1968 encyclical): why, he increasingly came to ask, does *every* physical act have to embody the vast range of meanings that all human acts might embody? How could finite and contingent human acts—undertaken in the midst of history—be read through the lens of such absolute values? This seemed—at best—a highly improbable basis for handing on a Christian understanding of ethical behavior, and at worst a classic example of what John Noonan had warned against in his magnum opus on contraception: a misguided attempt to hold on to past answers simply because they were old.[13]

Equally damming in Curran's view was the fact that the neo-scholastics had naively believed that they had actually proved their case; it was, he believed, both embarrassing and risible as a fellow moral theologian to see how the ostensibly sophisticated arguments offered to "prove" the grave moral evil of issues like contraception and masturbation were shot through with outdated understandings of philosophical causality and embarrassingly dated scientific reasoning. As Haring had so brilliantly argued a decade earlier, even Aquinas' magisterial synthesis of natural law in the thirteenth century—the supposedly unimpeachable authority to which neo-scholastics appealed—was a historically conditioned end product of generations of scholarly debate. Aquinas' appeal to Aristotle to frame the medieval Church's teaching on morality was simply an appeal to the best science of the day—the newly discovered corpus of Aristotle's work by Muslim scholars in North Africa and Spain. But by the middle of the twentieth century neither scientists nor the Christian faithful found such scientific reasoning plausible—or even understandable. Indeed, Curran came to believe that any moral teaching that ignored the actual experience of the Christian faithful—or, conversely, that offered moral teaching that appeared implausible or unreasonable on the face of it—flew in the face of the Catholic tradition of moral reasoning. That tradition, Curran noted, had certainly allowed that the

> experience of individuals and groups, and perhaps even of the whole community, can be wrong (consider, for example, the former Christian position on slavery). But [it also taught that] the experience of the Christian community is an important source of moral wisdom and knowledge. In a sense, Catholic theology has always recognized this reality in its acceptance of the role of the *sensus fidelium*—the sense of the faithful. The church must always value the experience of people, even though sometimes that experience can be wrong.[14]

Curran's growing sense of the need to radically redefine the older neo-scholastic paradigm of natural law thus predated the appearance of *Humanae Vitae* in 1968 by a number of years; but that growing sense also positioned him to take a leading role in crafting the Mayflower Document in response to the encyclical when it did appear.

Thus, well before the events of July 1968, Curran had emerged as a progressive theological voice at CUA. After only one year on CUA's faculty, Curran had been called in by CUA's Rector to voice concern about Curran's membership on the board of directors of the (ominously named) Institute for Freedom in the Church. At the meeting the Rector had also voiced the anxiety of a number of members on the university's board of trustees (all of whom were bishops) about Curran's increasing prominence in "liberal" periodicals like the recently founded *National Catholic Reporter*: that periodical had portrayed Curran as something like the "ringleader" of a group of younger Catholic revisionist moralists challenging the traditional classicist approach to moral theology. In recounting his interchange, Curran (unfailingly charitable to his critics) simply observed that those anxieties had been duly voiced and duly noted. But in the event, the revisionist Curran would go considerably further in elucidating a new paradigm of natural law than any previous Catholic theologian in the United States.[15]

Viewed from half a century later, of course, it now appears inevitable (or providential, depending on one's viewpoint) that the centerpiece of Curran's battles with institutional church officials during the "Catholic sixties"—his firing by CUA in 1967—would take place at the American institution most formally tied to the Catholic Church. In February 1967—backed by the unanimous vote of both his department and of the University Senate (the faculty-wide body set up to guarantee that "deals" were not struck in departmental personnel issues), Curran applied for promotion to the rank of associate professor. Curran, like his faculty colleagues, presumed that this would be a purely *pro forma* exercise in academic hoop-jumping. But on April 7, 1967, Curran was called into office of CUA's Rector (who had hired him just two years previously) to be informed that university's (episcopal) Board of Trustees had voted *not* to renew his contract. Two of the most prominent bishops on the Board (Washington DC's Archbishop Patrick O'Boyle and Philadelphia's Cardinal John Krol), had colluded with no less a personage than Apostolic Delegate Egidio Vagnozzi (the pope's own representative to the United States) to affect the Board vote. Indeed, Vagnozzi would later boast to journalist Roy Meacham that he had been instrumental in Curran's firing. But Curran's response to this announcement in the University Rector's office was hardly one of a cowed or intimidated cleric: he announced that he found the entire process both secretive and dishonest, and "dishonesty in the church had to stop." Curran further informed the rector that perhaps the best response was to make the action of the Board public—a threat that made CUA's president "so flustered that he never gave [Curran] the letter that he had prepared." As Curran would later write about that fateful conversation, "the Vatican wanted to make an example of a liberal priest, and I was to be the one."[16]

Things unraveled shortly thereafter: two days after Curran's meeting with the university president, two thousand students—many of them seminarians from the various religious order houses of study that bordered Catholic University's campus—gathered in front of the Rector's office to demand a hearing, while the entire theology department convened at a hastily called emergency meeting. The unanimous resolution passed at the meeting declared that "under these circumstances we cannot and will not function unless and until Fr. Curran is reinstated. We invite our colleagues in other schools of the university to join us in our protest." The faculty of every division of the university—save for the small School of Education—responded by joining in the protest, so that the very next day something literally unimaginable to the institution's (episcopal) founders eighty years earlier happened: the Catholic University of America went on strike.[17]

Much to the chagrin of both the Rector and most of CUA's Board, the strike immediately became national news, in some cases (particularly in New York and Washington) being featured on the front pages of newspapers of record. Two of the most powerful cardinals in the US hierarchy—Lawrence Sheehan of Baltimore and Richard Cushing of Boston—publicly denounced the Board's action against Curran as both intemperate and not in keeping with the character of a university—statements undoubtedly confirming the worst fears of Apostolic Delegate Vagnozzi (and of the Vatican officials in Rome who had jockeyed for his appointment to the United States) that the American Catholic community had become so devoted to personal freedom and self-determination that it needed serious disciplining. In some respects the strike at CUA partook as much of the sixties' genre of a "happening" as a serious academic event: students were photographed carrying signs on campus that read "Even my mother supports Father Curran," while pictures of nuns in full habit attending strike meetings appeared in newspapers and Catholic periodicals. One could easily argue that the CUA strike was the closest Catholic analogue to the "free speech" protests happening that very year at Columbia University in New York and at the University of California at Berkeley. But it is safe to say that America Catholics had never seen anything like it at any of the other 200 or so Catholic universities and colleges in the United States.[18]

On Monday of the following week—after a weekend of hurried phone calls among Catholic bishops and academic administrators—Cardinal

O'Boyle (who as Archbishop of Washington served as *ex officio* chancellor of CUA) and Rector McDonald emerged from yet another hastily called meeting looking weary—this time from a joint meeting of members of the Board of Trustees and the Theology Department—to address the large crowd that had gathered in front of the university library. O'Boyle announced—to a cheering crowd—that the Board had voted to reverse its decision from the previous week, and that Curran's promotion to associate professor would become effective the following September.[19]

Thus it was that when Catholic historians later began to refer to the "Curran Affair," they were *not* referring simply (or even primarily) to the famous news conference that would occur the following summer at the Mayflower Hotel, but rather to an entire series of events that began more than a year earlier at the Catholic University of America, and would eventuate in Curran's ultimate dismissal from CUA a year after the Mayflower News Conference. This historical focus on the rollicking events at CUA and in Cardinal O'Boyle's chancery office is perhaps not surprising because it supplied "good copy" for those interested in the distinctively Catholic role in the historical epoch known as "the sixties." But in another sense that focus on the happenings at CUA has shifted attention away from what is Curran's more important gift to the history of American Catholicism: a new paradigm of natural law that would open up a trajectory of genuine creativity and brilliance in American Catholic thought in the half century after the Summer of Love.

B. *"There is No Monolithic Philosophical Tradition called the Natural Law"*

The crucial role of Curran in hammering out what subsequently became known as the Mayflower Statement presented just days after the promulgation of *Humanae Vitae* offers compelling proof—if proof was needed—that the intellectual revolution that had begun in Rome and continued back in Rochester and Washington had borne considerable fruit in Curran's theology well before the summer of 1968. The astonishingly quick turnaround that Curran orchestrated—overseeing and coordinating the efforts of several dozen Catholic theologians before the age of social media—bore witness to the ways in which Curran's growing dissatisfaction with the older nineteenth-century neo-scholastic paradigm of natural law had matured into what Kuhn would have termed the early stages of "paradigm production" to replace it. While the Mayflower document thus offered a thoughtful rejoinder to the anomalies that some of America's most distinguished theologians—under

Curran's leadership—discovered in the arguments offered in Paul VI's encyclical, Curran's subsequent work brilliantly elaborated that critique into a new "postclassicist" paradigm that adumbrated the way for several new generations of Catholic scholars.

In a thought-provoking article published after the "event" at Washington's Mayflower Hotel, Curran laid out a number of postclassicist paradigms of natural law that rejected what some of his colleagues saw as the fatal anomalies of neo-scholasticism, while also addressing the modern concern to engage both religious pluralism and the insights of the modern physical sciences. Curran began his overview of the several possible paradigms that moral theology might utilize—in good revisionist fashion—with the acknowledgement of the historically contextualized nature of all human knowledge, including knowledge of natural law:

The natural law theory employed in the [1968] encyclical thus identifies the moral and human action with the physical structure of the conjugal act itself. *Humanae Vitae* in its methodology well illustrates a classicist approach. The papal letter admits that "changes which have taken place are in fact noteworthy and of varied kinds (*HV*, no. 2), [and that] these changes give rise to new questions. However, the changing historical circumstances have not affected the answer or the method employed in arriving at [the encyclical's] concrete conclusions. . . . The encyclical specifically acknowledges that there are new signs of the times, but one wonders if sufficient attention has really been paid to such changes. The footnote references contain no indication of any type of dialogue with other Christians, non-Christians, or with the modern sciences. . . . The encyclical thus betrays an epistemology that has been rejected by many Catholic theologians and philosophers today.[20]

Curran further noted that the natural law tradition of Catholic theology had consistently upheld two values that were crucially important for any attempt to elucidate an alternative model. First, he noted that the ancient Catholic tradition of natural law had insisted that Christians shared with everyone (believers or not) a source of ethical knowledge and wisdom that could be utilized in constructing ethical systems regardless of cultural, religious, or political context. This "universalist" aspect of the natural law tradition was rooted in the Greek philosophy of Aristotle, but Aquinas had insisted that all genuine natural law approaches to morality—including his own—recognize this "universalist" aspect of Aristotle's understanding of what natural law was. And second, Curran observed that such an insistence on universality was crucially important in considering ethical matters because morality had to rest on more than merely the subjective whims of individuals or groups. Those two values—the emphasis on both universality and on what Catholic moralists had termed the "realist" foundations of morality—had to define the foundations of any new model of natural law. But that being said, Curran also noted that those values *could* continue to define newer models without necessarily endorsing what he called "the particular understanding of natural law *presupposed* in the encyclical."[21]

In fact, Curran observed, a number of Catholic moralists had already been developing and experimenting with "alternative" approaches to understanding both natural law and its implications for the moral life while retaining the two core values that ethicists had inherited from the Angelic Doctor. Some of these revisionist moralists understood their experiments as simply "modifications" of the older scholastic tradition; others, engaged in a more radical enterprise, actually preferred to abandon the term "natural law" altogether, as the very concept of such a law in "nature" appeared ambiguous, or even naive. But driving both groups was the (historicist) realization that "*there is no monolithic philosophical system called the natural law, and the term itself has been somewhat discredited because of the tendency among some to understand 'natural' in terms of the physical structure of acts.*"[22]

That latter realization—that there was, in fact, "no monolithic philosophical system called the natural law" (in itself a revolutionary, and not an evolutionary, insight) freed Curran to propose an entirely different kind of approach to the micro-tradition. Curran listed three "alternative approaches" to understanding how natural law worked that were being explored by his colleagues to replace the older classicist model focused on physical acts: the "personalist" approach, which understood the meaning of moral acts in terms of the person doing the act (an approach that had been explored by Bernard Haring in *The Law of Christ*—a work that had deeply influenced Curran's own understanding of moral theology). Personalism, Curran noted, took both history and cultural context seriously in understanding how the life of discipleship was actually *lived* in the world, and how moral actors appropriated a natural law understanding of ethical life in a quite specific personal context. Second, Curran outlined what he called the "relational/communitarian" approach, in which moral acts could only be understood by contextualizing them within the larger picture of what those acts revealed about the quality of personal interaction between the actor and other persons, as well as between the actor and the wider community. Curran pointed to the scholarship of both Robert Johann and William van der Marck as examples of the rigorous application of that approach to understanding what natural law offered as the goal of human living. Curran then listed the "transcendental method" found in the scholarship of Karl Rahner and Bernard Lonergan as a third fruitful approach to understanding the role of natural law in moral theology. In this third approach, moral living was not an intrinsic property of external acts or objects, but was rather an aspect of consciously free acts done in relation to what observed reality revealed about the nature of knowing and deciding. "Moral value" in this third approach could only be evaluated in light of the "horizon" of meaning that called human persons to move beyond inauthenticity, unreasonableness, and "the surd of sin."[23]

What at first glance might appear as simply a free-wheeling catalogue of then-current paths being explored to replace the kind of neo-scholasticism offered in the 1968 encyclical in fact outlines an understanding of moral theology in almost perfect alignment with Kuhn's arguments about the strengths—and weaknesses—of both "normal science" and the need for paradigm change when normal science can no longer function in light of the accumulation of anomalies in an older paradigm, so it might be well to pause and highlight those alignments.

First: Curran both understood and appreciated why the "normal science" that defined the regular work of moral theologians (like their physical scientific cousins) was *both* an absolutely necessary *and* a somewhat arbitrary, intellectual construct. The day-to-day work of moral theologians—what Kuhn had labeled the "normal science" of physical scientists—rested on an agreement reached among a majority of practitioners that the overarching model defining the "reality" they studied was both helpful and necessary in explaining how the real world *actually operated.* That agreement had elucidated a working paradigm that was absolutely necessary for their day-to-day work as scholars. And it was absolutely necessary because (*second*) they understood that the working paradigm they utilized was both arbitrary and humanly constructed (or, as Curran put this understanding of human construction with regard to *Humanae Vitae*, "the *particular understanding* of natural law presupposed in the encyclical"), therewith implying that there were a number of other valid "particular understandings" that were also theoretically possible.

Curran seemed to have intuitively grasped the truth of Kuhn's famous argument regarding the all-important distinction between "reality," on the one hand, and the working paradigm scholars utilized to describe it, on the other. As Kuhn had argued, it was (literally) impossible to test the truth of any working paradigm by comparing it firsthand with some ostensibly real world "out there"—simply because that real world was a welter of myriad possible relationships, interactions, and pieces of data that yielded different answers, depending on cultural and religious location, gender, race, educational background, and socioeconomic reach. In light of the sheer "manyness" of human experience, then, the only possible way of arriving at a working understanding of what experience revealed about human flourishing was to approach it armed with hypotheses that sought to make the most sense of the most data and the widest range of human experience. No hypothesis or set of hypotheses—however supple, perceptive, or capacious—could make sense of *all* the data or all the possible sets of relationships one might find. "Anomalies" (in Kuhn's technical sense) would always exist that eluded an easy fit into any paradigm: that was as true in moral theology as it was in the study of subatomic particles. But the *working* paradigm —however admittedly arbitrary and provisional—nonetheless *did* allow for a clearer understanding of the data at hand (even if not of all the data). Such paradigms could be thus understood as both "arbitrary" (in the sense of being humanly constructed) and "provisional" (in the sense of being "good enough for now," if not for all places in all times).

But implicit in Curran's adumbration of the three *possible* paradigms on offer to moral theology was the realization that the best way to approach the question of a more workable paradigm was the same as the approach to talking about the Church offered in Second Vatican Council's most important theological document, *Lumen Gentium* ("The Dogmatic Constitution on the Church"). In that epochal document the Council Fathers had replaced the older, ahistorical, classicist paradigm informing how Catholics understood the Church (the *Societas Perfecta*—the "perfect society" that never changed precisely because it was perfect from the get-go) with a *plurality* of models: the Church as the Body of Christ, the Church as communion, the Church as the servant of the world, etc.. But it had also privileged as its controlling model a more biblical, less triumphalist understanding of the Church as the "People of God." These newer models—especially the last—were more inclusive, less hierarchical, and more plastic: they witnessed to the realization that the Church changes as it makes its pilgrimage through history. No one metaphor could capture the entire truth of what the Church was, precisely because the metaphors were just that: humanly constructed models to explain a reality that was partially captured in all of them, but which also transcended all of them. Therefore (as Aquinas had argued) the more metaphors, the better, because they were all true; but they all failed to completely capture a reality that transcended metaphor. *Lumen Gentium* had thus offered a "pilgrim theology"—a theology on journey, changing and adapting as best it could, sometimes stumbling, but always aware of its duty to bear witness to something greater than itself. But the awareness of the arbitrary, provisional nature of its controlling metaphors in no way compromised the promise of its Founder to be with it always. It was simply the confession that the divine reality at the heart of the Church, and the human ways that were constructed to talk about it, were two very different things, and it was always better—and truer—not to confuse the two.[24]

In an exactly analogous way, Curran—like Kuhn—presumed (*third*) that his readers understood that the "natural law" wasn't nature's—or even God's—law in the sense of a set of ready-made propositions that existed "out there" somewhere in the physical universe, that only had to be mined in order to be utilized. Natural law wasn't "found," like one found and mined ore in some physical landscape; it was rather *constructed* utilizing the best tools at hand. Thus the phrase "natural law" was directly analogous to the phrase "laws of science" as Kuhn had utilized it: the laws of science weren't *nature's* laws as discovered by scientific inquiry; they were rather *human laws* constructed to explain (and more important, to predict) what might happen when scientists studied "nature."

Such laws were humanly constructed, provisional, and admittedly incomplete (in the sense of being unable to explain all the observed data all the time); but they did offer something *like* reliable knowledge on which to build models of scientific prediction, even if only for now. Thus, if a skeptic had asked Curran which of the three "alternative paradigms" he had outlined in his 1969 article—the personalist, the relational/communitarian, or the transcendental—offered the *real* natural law, one might reasonably conjecture that Curran would have answered, "all of them, and none of them." *Each* of them pointed to certain important aspects of how the real world operated, and what that real world taught about human flourishing and "the good life." *None* of them exhausted what human nature revealed about how humans were called to live "the good life," or to construct "the good society."

Given that hypothetical answer (that all and none of them were true) one might reasonably ask if Curran was a "realist" in the Catholic sense—that is, did Curran believe that theological categories and constructs referred to how the real world actually operated, or were such categories human constructs with no anchor in objective reality? Perhaps the truest answer was "yes and no." Yes, human beings (and especially Christians) had a moral obligation to try to understand the kinds of activity that sponsored the flourishing of both individuals and communities, and explain why it was important to do so. There were, in fact, certain kinds of ethical action that furthered that end, and other kinds of actions that hindered such flourishing. But no—there was no set formula or model that perfectly captured the "real world" without remainder: multiple models may be true (in part), and also incomplete (in part). It finally came down to how one defined "realist" in a moral sense. The answer to that question, in other words, had a great deal to do with optics and perspective.

Fourth: Curran understood from his own study of the history of moral theology, beginning with his doctoral dissertation on St. Alphonsus Liguori in Rome, that there had been (and would always be) "anomalies" in any working model of natural law. Precisely because "reality is more complex than any model we can construct to explain it," no model of natural law could be "totalistic" in an absolute sense. Thus "moral realism" couldn't be taken to mean a "one-to-one correlation" of moral-specific models of discourse with reality. As Curran discovered in writing his dissertation on Liguori, some reliable and "safe" theologians had argued for one model of the Catholic moral code, while others—equally reliable and "safe" authorities—questioned not only the gravity but also the very sinfulness of actions that their "reliable" colleagues had labeled as "extremely grave sins." And if that had been the case in the eighteenth century, why should theologians expect a less complex picture in the twentieth?

From Curran's point of view, then, the question of "outliers" in the field of Christian ethics was hardly a theoretical one: a simple study of the history of Catholic moral theology illustrated the solid reality of such debates between peers who had been considered in their time to be faithful and well-educated Catholic scholars. As Kuhn had predicted—and as Curran had discovered in his own dissertation research—the "winning" paradigm that Liguori offered seemed to have elicited a majority, or at least a significant number, of "reliable" moral theologians. But this implied that there would always be outliers in the discipline who questioned the ability of the reigning paradigm—even one as smart as that of St. Alphonsus Liguori—to explain how the Catholic tradition did or should interpret the moral meaning of human experience in light of the Gospel. Again, this last point seems minor, but it is in fact *key* to both Kuhn's—and Curran's—larger argument.

And this last point is key because the sheer fact of outliers in the discipline points to the awareness of both Kuhn and Curran that no model of science or moral theology can ever claim to be the definitive and *final* model of a reality that transcends paradigms. Rather than aiming at the "perfect" model, both

Kuhn and Curran understood that a far better plan of action was to proceed on the basis of a humanly constructed *predictive* model that could explain more of the data than the previous reigning paradigm could. Such a model— or to use Kuhn's word, "paradigm"—was never totalistic or complete: there would always be data and observed behavior that eluded the explanatory powers of the reigning paradigm. Indeed, Kuhn had been at pains to point out that there would *always* be data encountered in scientific research that implied not only that the proposed paradigm was incomplete but also that it might be *wrong*. Thus it was not only realistic but also probably a good thing to have "others" in the field who pressed the question of what the anomalies encountered in the application of the paradigm implied about the veracity of the reigning paradigm. If nothing else, it kept everyone engaged in the research honest and on their toes. And the sheer fact of being an outlier hardly implied anything about one's scientific, moral, or theological probity.[25]

Yet again, this last point is important for understanding Curran's career after 1968: what Curran and his colleagues who hosted the news conference at the Mayflower Hotel discovered was *not that* they were they were outliers to the reigning (neo-scholastic) paradigm of moral theology that had defined the "Long Nineteenth Century" (roughly from the French Revolution in 1789 to the end of World War II in 1945). As revisionist students of distinguished revisionists scholars like Josef Fuchs and Bernard Haring, moral theologians like Curran and Richard McCormick were fully aware long before 1968 that the nineteenth-century paradigm that had "carried the day" for so long had failed to explain in a completely convincing way what the following of the Lord Jesus meant in terms of ethical living—or at least it failed to completely convince *them*. Being outliers was something that they had recognized about themselves considerably before 1968: as early as the 1950s, many of them (like Curran) had already realized that the anomalies encountered in the older paradigm were such that important parts of it needed to be revised, or rethought, or perhaps totally jettisoned in favor of grafting onto the older model newer ideas that might make it "fit" better in explaining the real, practical world of Christian ethics.

Rather, what the events surrounding their "nonreception" of *Humanae Vitae*—and most especially the very *public* nonreception of the encyclical at the Mayflower Hotel—revealed was that the time had at long last arrived to exchange their "negative" outlier status for a more proactive, positive one: that of paradigm producers. Read in the light of Kuhn's theories of the stages of paradigm revolutions, the Mayflower news conference announced—in the most public way imaginable for Catholic priests to say "no thank you" to the

Supreme Pontiff of the Roman Church—that what Kuhn had identified as the "period of perceived anomalies" was now over, and that the "period of crisis" had already begun.

The early stages of their recognition of anomalies in the nineteenth-century paradigm of moral theology—the intellectually troubling and existentially inaccessible arguments about the propositional nature of Christian morality; the reduction of human sexuality to "things that had to be confessed on Saturday afternoons to a priest"; the static and ahistorical approach to the study of physical acts as somehow bearing in themselves the ethical meanings of the Christian life—all of these critical responses *had* (just as Kuhn had predicted) initially been accompanied by a continued (if now qualified) support of the reigning paradigm. In the earliest stages of their perception of the anomalies, they continued something like a "guarded" assent to the older paradigm: perhaps, they thought, the paradigm simply needed to be "revised," or stretched, or rethought in certain parts. One might reasonably conceive of at least part of the "revisionist movement" in twentieth-century moral theology along the lines that Kuhn had outlined in describing the precrisis stage of paradigm production: "yes, there are these troubling parts of the model that seem problematic, or even unbelievable, but it could just be that we haven't stretched the paradigm enough, or considered other ways of revising the system to make the exceptions disappear." The anomalies had been recognized as eliciting critical questions, if not yet a full-scale *crisis*.

But by July 1968, the anomalies encountered in the use of the older neoscholastic paradigm were now so many, and so serious, and caused such intellectual scandal (and even dismissal) by both the Catholic faithful and those moral theologians tasked with passing on the tradition that a new paradigm was called for. What the Mayflower Hotel conference actually announced, then, was that the period of even qualified support for the older paradigm was now over, and that an entirely new paradigm of natural law on which to build a faithful but *believable* science of Christian ethics was now called for. And Curran was to be among the first distinguished practitioners of the craft of moral theology to attempt that.

C. An Evolutionary, Historicist Paradigm of Natural Law

In an important essay published within months of the Mayflower Hotel news conference, Curran put all of his cards regarding the rethinking of natural law theory on the theological table. He opened his essay by noting that among other forces fueling that rethinking were the ecumenical dialogues that had become a staple of American Catholic life in the years after Vatican II. In the new-found transdenominational discussions taking place in the United States, Curran had emerged as an important voice on the Catholic "side" shortly after his arrival back in Rochester after his doctoral studies in Rome. But one result of those ecumenical discussions was that Catholic theologians had become more conscious of how natural law theory had failed in one of its most vaunted claims: providing a "denominationally neutral" discourse in which people from different religious backgrounds might discuss important ethical issues. But Curran observed that

> many Protestant theologians point out that the natural law concept constitutes a primary source of *disagreement* between Protestant and Catholic theologians. The ongoing dialogue with our world has shown Catholic theologians a world and a reality that differs considerably from the view of the world and reality enshrined in the traditional [Catholic] textbook understanding of natural law. [Thus] the *entire process of renewal within the Church demands a critical reappraisal of natural law theory.*[26]

And Curran began his own critical reappraisal in light of both the new approach to Catholic Christianity undertaken by the Second Vatican Council and the ecumenical and interreligious dialogues that defined the post–Vatican II era: if natural law *were* to remain the basis (or one of the bases) for Catholic moral theology—just then a very lively topic among ethicists, and by no means a foregone conclusion that it *would* remain the basis for Catholic ethical discussions—then the newer paradigms offered to replace the older classicist models would need to be compelling to modern believers, including non-Catholic and non-Christian believers, who found the neo-scholastic paradigm unbelievable (in a literal as well as metaphorical sense). This concern to construct a newer paradigm built on the need for dialogue with non-Catholic and even non-Christian believers constituted the first "move" that Curran's paradigm sought to address.

Second, Curran sought to address the deeply problematic vacillation in Thomistic theory between contextualizing human action in either the "order of nature" or the "order of reason"—that is, between "seeing man [*sic*] in perfect continuity with nature" (on the one hand), and viewing "man completely apart from nature, and as completely surpassing nature" (on the other). While

in general Curran argued that the main thrust of Thomistic ethical theory
was toward the predominance of *reason* in natural law theory,

> however, there is in Thomas a *definite* tendency to identify the demands
> of natural law with physical and biological processes. [But] *Thomas too*
> *is a historical person conditioned by the circumstances and influences of*
> *his own time.* These influences help to explain the tendency (even if not
> the predominant tendency) in Thomas to identify the human action
> with the physical and biological structure of the human act.[27]

Thus it was that manualist textbooks in moral theology had divided sins
against the Sixth Commandment (the rather large "catch-all" commandment
dealing with sexual sins) into two subcategories: *peccata contra naturam* (sins
"against nature") and *peccata secundum naturam* (sins "in accord" with nature). The "contra" sins in the first category were human acts in which ostensibly "natural" rules that human beings were expected to observe as "members
of the animal kingdom" (at least with regard to their bodies) had been
violated, acts which included masturbation, homosexual relations, bestiality,
and contraception. The second "secundum" category of sinful activity referred
to those acts "in which the proper biological process *had* been observed [*sic*],"
but something had been "lacking in the sphere which belongs only to rational
men" (i.e., human beings had not followed their rational faculties toward the
"end" laid out by reason). In this second category were included fornication,
adultery, incest, rape, and (strangely enough) sacrilege.[28]

But Curran observed that this very subdivision of sins "against" or "in
accord with" nature seemed to presuppose that the physical "meanings" of
human sexual intercourse were directly analogous to the meanings of animal
sexual reproduction, and that the "meanings" had somehow been spelled
out in a "law of nature" morally (as well as physically) applicable to both.
Further—and far more disastrously from Curran's point of view—such an
approach to understanding what natural law ostensibly "taught" resulted in
what he called a" two-layer anthropology" that had informed, and fatally
undercut the usefulness of, the neo-scholastic model of natural law. In this
two-tiered anthropology, a "top layer" of rationality was added to an already
constituted (and independent) "bottom layer" of animality."[29]

But such a two-layered anthropology, Curran argued, was both extremely
problematic in light of what modern science had garnered from evolutionary theory, and psychologically simplistic for understanding the complexity of human acts. In this model of how of human beings operated, the

union between the "two layers" of human identity was merely extrinsic—one layer "resting" on top of another—while finally remaining separate and distinct from each other. The "animal layer" retained its own "finalities" and tendencies, independently of the demands of rationality. Further—and far more troubling in Curran's view—human reason (the "top layer") could never change or nuance the meanings of the animal processes and tendencies, precisely because those processes and tendencies had been implanted in "nature" by God, itself constituting an intrinsic part of "natural law." And Aquinas had seemingly preferred—and followed—this definition, borrowed from the third-century Roman lawyer Ulpian: natural law, as Ulpian and Aquinas defined it, was "that which nature teaches all the animals." Human reason, then—ostensibly the "distinguishing mark" of human beings in the animal kingdom—was not able to control or order the ends of acts whose *actors* were ostensibly rational creatures. Human physical acts—especially human sexual acts—possessed meanings ("finalities," in the language of neo-scholasticism) that were prior to, and independent of, reasoned application: thus the singular language of manualist moral theology about "acts achieving their ends," and "intrinsically disordered acts"—as though there existed an external yardstick to measure what the "meaning" of human acts was *really* about, regardless of the intentions of the human actors involved, precisely because it was a "law that nature teaches all animals [including human ones]."[30]

But Curran observed that such a model of human nature and human action was both naive and extremely dated, as well as being unbelievable to modern persons. This model rested on older (Aristotelian and medieval) models of faculty psychology and human behavior, as well as on a classicist and ahistorical understanding of how science understood "nature." The modern fields of social psychology, anthropology, and evolutionary biology had dismissed the very idea that rationality (itself a slippery term) somehow rested "on top of" animality, as though human evolution had somehow shaped the one and not the other. If nothing else, evolutionary theory after Charles Darwin had adumbrated a model of human nature in which rationality was an intrinsic *part of* the evolutionary processes of nature: so understood, rationality conceivably shaped the "ends" and purposes of human sexual activity no less than human thought, and thus contributed toward ordering the "ends" of those acts. Those ends were no more fixed and immovable than human culture itself. Indeed, even Catholic thinkers like the Jesuit Pierre Teilhard de Chardin had come to see in the discoveries of evolutionary biology the profound theological possibility that the human "vocation" might be to *bring* order and intelligence into the world, not to mine for realities already "implanted" there.

As Curran characterized this newer understanding of human nature (and thus of natural law):

> a proper understanding of man should start with that which is proper to man. Rationality does not just lie on top of animality, *but rationality characterizes and guides the whole person.* Animal processes and finalities are not untouchable. Man's whole vocation, we have come to see, is to bring order and intelligence into the world, and to *shape animal and biological finalities toward a truly human purpose.* Ulpian's concept of natural law *logically falsifies the understanding of man, and tends to canonize the finalities and processes which man shares with the animal world.*[31]

Curran believed that a far better model of natural law should start with an anthropology that posited that rationality was an intrinsic component of human life, rather than just one part.

Rationality was a component in human sexual activity no less than in human thought. Curran therefore rejected the notion of the human person "that sees animality existing in man, retaining animal finalities and tendencies without any intervention of the specifically human [rational] part of men." In the *unified* anthropology of Curran's paradigm, human persons were not to be conceived as "part" animal and "part" rational, but rather as rational beings in which rationality played a determinative role in all distinctively human acts, including sexual relations. In thus beginning his paradigm by targeting the "two-layer" anthropology of neo-scholasticism, Curran also targeted the kind of "physicalist" argument that had informed *Humanae Vitae.* In this, Curran was simply expanding the critique of the encyclical offered in the Mayflower Statement: the encyclical, Curran had argued, had identified the words "nature" and "natural" with animal processes, and also with the mere physical structure of human acts. Such a facile identification had led to a model of "natural" law in which the meanings of human acts could be determined independently of any consideration of human intentionality, interpersonal relations, or the needs of the larger community. As Curran would have it, precisely *that* approach (evinced in the 1968 encyclical) was "irrational."[32]

In this one historical move—rejecting neo-scholasticism's overreliance on a classicist, ahistorical understanding of natural law in favor of retrieving a more plastic and supple understanding of anthropology that he believed opened up possibilities for fruitful rethinking of the Thomistic approach to

Christian ethics—Curran was carving out a historicist pathway that almost everyone involved in paradigm production in the decades after him would follow.

Third, Curran's paradigm focused quite specifically on what Catholic moralists had previously termed "the ends of marriage." There had been, he argued, a "deleterious" tendency in Catholic moral theology of speaking of the "primary" and "secondary" ends of marriage—a tendency that *Gaudium et Spes* (Vatican II's famous "Pastoral Constitution on the Church in the Modern World") had happily avoided. And Curran argued that Catholic moral theologians should follow the example of the Council in this. The previous approach to natural law had understood

> "primary" [as] that which is common to man and all the animals. Ulpian, and Thomas in citing Ulpian, use the union of the sexes, and the procreation and education of offspring, as examples of that which is common to man and all the animals. "Secondary" is that which is proper to man. Since only man—and not animals—have sexual intercourse as a sign and expression of love, the love union aspect of sexuality remains proper to man, and therefore secondary. [Previous church] teaching on the "ends of marriage" is logically connected with Ulpian's understanding of man and natural law. Thus the teaching of Ulpian on natural law has a logical connection with the *inadequate understanding of a human action as identified with an animal process.*[33]

Curran's third move in constructing a new paradigm to replace the older neo-scholastic one—replacing the "two-layered" anthropology that had conceived of humans as "part" animal and "part" rational, as well as building in an absolutely dialogical aspect of understanding what that "law" might mean—offered a revolutionary understanding of the relation of human beings to "nature":

> We who live in a scientific and technological society will have a different view of man and his happiness. Modern man does not find his happiness in conforming to nature. The whole ethos and genius of modern society is different. *Modern man makes nature conform to him, rather than vice-versa.* Through electricity man can change night into day. Nature did not provide man with wings to fly; in fact, the law of gravity seems to forbid man to fly . . . [Thus] modern man could never tolerate a theory which equates human happiness with conformity

to nature. *Contemporary man interferes with the processes of nature, to make nature conform to man.*[34]

Indeed, Curran explicitly identified the very process of "measuring" human activity by its conformity to nature as one of the hallmarks of primitive societies: primitive societies tended to measure the meaning of things "in terms of the physical and the sensible." And here Curran turned to one of his earliest professional papers delivered shortly after his return to Rochester from his studies in Rome to make his point: "for example, the importance that Catholic theology has attached to masturbatory activity, especially the overemphasis since the sixteenth century, seems to come from viewing it purely in terms of the physiological and biological aspects of the act." But many moral theologians (Curran among them) had already turned to the findings of modern psychology and developmental biology to arrive at a very different moral evaluation of what the older tradition had labeled as "gravely sinful matter." That very phrase, in fact, now appeared extremely problematic when applied to human physical acts without recourse to context or human development. "Nature," in this third component of Curran's paradigm, no longer existed as the "ground" for measuring human action: on the contrary, "contemporary man *interferes with nature, to make nature conform to man.*"

This third move in constructing a new paradigm was a revolutionary one, and it is important to note it as such: Curran argued that far from being simply—or even primarily—the "product" of nature or of evolution, human nature had reached a stage of the evolutionary process where human intelligence actually *shaped* nature. Curran thus proposed that human nature and the meanings of human acts could not be simply *derived* from studying physical processes, whose ostensible meanings were somehow embedded in "nature," as though the latter were a reality completely separate and exterior to human culture. Rather, just the opposite defined modern culture: "modern man interferes with the processes of nature, to make nature conform to man." In Curran's model, the evolutionary process should be conceived of less as a set of rules and processes that determined human nature than as a set of processes part of whose direction and outcomes were now directly under human control. Curran's construal of the place of human beings in the natural world turned the traditional neo-scholastic paradigm of natural law on its head: God had made human beings "co-creators" in a new (and almost literal) way. Human beings "co-created" the meanings of the physical order in a way that neo-scholasticism's model could not incorporate, much less approve. From the standpoint of Curran's paradigm, studying "nature" to determine the meanings of physical acts was, in an important sense, oxymoronic, because human intelligence was evolving in a direction that shaped and determined the ends and meanings of nature. "Nature" had become part of the human project.

Curran's fourth move in the construction of a new paradigm of natural law was to build on Bernard Lonergan's famous distinction between the classicist and historicist worldviews to argue for what he called a "process metaphysics." The classicist view of both human nature and the physical rested on an understanding of "essences" (itself a category that was now problematic) that remained unchangeable and could only undergo "accidental" changes in the flow of time. Intrinsic to that older model had been the belief that the "meanings" of human activity had been "spelled out" for all eternity: in that neo-scholastic model, human persons ostensibly came to know the truth and reality by abstracting from the "accidents" of time and arriving at immutable and unchangeable "essences" that defined the *real* meaning and identity at the heart of things. And because of the unchangeableness of this solid-state system, knowledge built on the "immutable essences" found in nature was both certain and unchangeable: human nature, the "meaning" of human acts, and the values toward which society aimed remained the same everywhere, all the time.[35]

But over against the classicist paradigm of neo-scholasticism, in which "human nature" was the same at all times in history and in all cultures, his own evolutionary, historicist paradigm was built on the proposition that modern human persons "differ quite a bit" (his words) from primitive *Homo sapiens* precisely because of the human traits that had evolved to ensure the survival of the species. With that proposition in mind, Curran's fourth move in paradigm construction asserted that everything—including the *metaphysical meanings* of flourishing—*was in process,* in flux. To borrow the older terminology, Curran thus argued that the very "essences" of things changed, as a result of the process of historical change. One could not assume, as the manualists did, that the essential identity of acts and decisions always remained the same. The very opposite was the case: metaphysics, no less than the physical universe, was "in process."

Curran believed that a more workable paradigm could not simply brush aide "accidental circumstances" in order to arrive at purportedly unchanging essences: the concrete, the particular, and the individual were *crucial* in understanding reality. And, of course, the *cause célèbre* of contraception offered a compelling example of just *this* proposition. The concrete experience of the Crowleys and other married couples regarding "bedroom issues" was *not* secondary or accidental in evaluating the moral meaning of contraception; indeed, just the opposite was the case. If moral theologians began with the concrete experience of the Crowleys and proceeded by an inductive method, they would (Curran confidently felt) arrive at very different conclusions about the morality of contraception. Thus, in Curran's approach, an inductive methodology—much closer to the presuppositions of the historicist worldview outlined by Bernard Lonergan—appeared to adumbrate a new day for Catholic ethicists. Curran allowed that "historical consciousness as methodology is an abstraction, but an abstraction or theory that tries to give more importance to *particular, concrete, historical reality.*" And he was the first to realize that "a classicist mentality is horrified at the thought that something could be right in one century and wrong in another"; but moral theologians had to explore the implications of that fact nonetheless.[36]

And Curran rested his argument for the dramatic need for moral theology to build on an historicist foundation on the highest author of all in Catholic theology: that of the pope in union with an ecumenical council:

> In the documents of Vatican II the bishops do not officially adopt any worldview or methodology. But Vatican II definitely portrays reality in terms of a more historicist worldview, and also employs a historically conscious methodology. . . . The bishops at the council also acknowledged that the Church has profited by the history and development of humanity. History reveals more about man, and opens new roads to truth. [Therefore] the Catholic Church must constantly engage in an exchange with the contemporary world.[37]

Curran's methodological turn undoubtedly reflected the heady experience of lay empowerment in the years immediately after the Second Vatican Council. Thus Curran's efforts in paradigm construction built on the experience of Vatican II to include the Church's new "dialogical reality" in ecumenical relations in the years immediately after the Council. Curran therefore emphasized the critical need for theologians to construct a newer paradigm in light of the energy and insight that had emerged in those dialogues: there was, he stated, a new dialogical reality to "doing theology" after the Council,

> The need for the Catholic Church to engage in dialogue—dialogue with other Christians, dialogue with Jews, dialogue with non-Christian religions, dialogue with the world. Dialogue is not monologue. Dialogue presupposes that Catholics can learn from all these

others. The call for dialogue presupposes the historical and pilgrim nature of the Church, which does not possess all the answers, but is open in the search for truth. The need for dialogue and ongoing search for truth contrast sharply with the classicist view of reality and truth.[38]

Finally, Curran's dialogical, inductive, process-oriented paradigm—in which humanity was not only a product of nature, but now also a "producer" and shaper of it—began its discussion of "nature" with the actual experience of human persons: to that extent it proceeded from an "experiential" starting point, rather than beginning with the propositional approach of neo-scholasticism. From Curran's point of view, *Humanae Vitae* stood 180 degrees away from where it should have begun its consideration of contraception. Whereas the 1968 encyclical had begun with *propositions* regarding the "ends" and purposes of human sexuality—which then declared certain sexual acts as "disordered" when measured against the propositions, which were always true—Curran now argued that Christian ethics had to begin *not* with propositions, but rather with an analysis of the actual "bedroom experience" of Christian couples. It was in light of that experience that moral theologians had to decide how to interpret the tradition of Christian teaching regarding human sexuality and marriage, especially in light of modern science and the new human ability to define what nature "meant."

Natural law, so understood, was best interpreted utilizing an inductive and historicist methodology that presupposed the truth of evolution and the human shaping of nature that resulted from the evolutionary process. Curran's proposed paradigm, then—based on a "process metaphysics" in which human beings had to be understood as *shaping nature*, no less than being shaped by it; offering a unified anthropology that rejected the idea that human persons were "part animal" and "part rational"; resting on a dialogical understanding of how natural law needed to be constructed, and not "found"; and proposing an experiential starting for the process, a starting point at which the particular, the concrete, and the contingent played starring roles—offered a totally different way of understanding the micro-tradition of natural law. Was it a "paradigm revolution" in Kuhn's sense, as opposed to an evolution from neo-scholasticism? As noted earlier, revolutions are in the eye of the beholder. But there is substantial evidence—at least for this student—that indeed it was.

5

Germain Grisez and the "New Natural Law"

A. A Natural Law of Basic Goods

One of the most prolific, and certainly one of the most brilliant, voices in the debates set off in the decades after the appearance of *Humanae Vitae* was that of Germain Grisez, who for thirty years taught Christian ethics at Mount Saint Mary's University in Emmitsburg, Maryland. Educated at the University of Chicago and a married father of four children, Grisez emerged early as a savvy and perceptive commentator in the theological battles that the 1968 encyclical set off, more than holding his own with the other figures involved, the overwhelming majority of whom were priests teaching in seminaries. Even before the appearance of his magisterial work, *The Way of the Lord Jesus,* Grisez had attracted the attention of others involved in the battle over the Church's teaching regarding contraception, not the least of whom was John Ford.[1]

In 1965, while Ford was busily engaged in the battles then roiling the Pontifical Commission charged with advising the pope on the issue of contraception, the American Jesuit asked Grisez to help in that work. Thus, during the final months of the Commission's work—from the spring of 1965 until early July 1966—Ford and Grisez worked closely together in Rome, while what would become the "Majority Report" was being crafted. At the explicit request of Cardinal Alfredo Ottaviani, then Prefect of the Doctrine of the Faith and chair of the Executive Committee overseeing the Pontifical Commission, Ford and Grisez prepared a highly critical commentary of that Report, a commentary that would become known, in time, as the "Minority Report." Ford's choice of Grisez for a theological collaborator during those months in Rome was not accidental: Grisez had been working on a major book studying precisely this question of the regulation of births, and had sought out Ford's advice. That work, *Contraception and the Natural Law,* was published in 1965 and became the basis of an entire school of moral discourse that would become known as the "new natural law."[2]

Grisez's broad knowledge of the Catholic theological tradition and his own native brilliance, evinced in his 1965 monograph as well as in his collaborative efforts in Rome, deeply impressed Ford, who sought Grisez's help several years later—in 1968—when Washington's Cardinal Patrick O'Boyle was dealing with something like a pastoral revolt in his diocese, not only among lay people but also from a significant number of his own priests who strongly dissented from the teaching of *Humanae Vitae.*[3]

Grisez is a complex and subtle thinker: he agreed with revisionist moralists like Fr. Charles Curran and Richard McCormick that the arguments advanced in the 1968 encyclical were intellectually thin, at best. Where he differed from Curran and McCormick was that Grisez believed that the Church *should* condemn birth control as a sinful act. That is, he completely agreed with the encyclical's strong condemnation of contraceptive acts as profoundly sinful and (as the encyclical had argued) "intrinsically disordered." But Grisez built on the earlier work of British philosopher Elizabeth Anscombe to construct, with Oxford philosopher John Finnis, a markedly different approach to natural law that he hoped would place the teaching of the 1968 encyclical on intellectually firmer ground.[4]

With Curran and McCormick, Grisez believed that the 1968 encyclical rested on a deeply flawed "physicalist" argument that was scientifically naive and intellectually dubious; that is, he—like his colleagues "on the left"—saw the profound intellectual incoherence of attempting to derive the "ought" from the "is." From Grisez's standpoint, the entire effort to derive important moral principles (the "ought") from the sheer physical facts of copulation (the "is") was doomed from the start. The "meanings" of human physical acts—viewed from the standpoint of a third-person observer—were, at best, opaque and multilayered. And without ever glossing the great British author Virginia Woolf, Grisez's critique of the 1968 encyclical's argument regarding the "meaning" of the physical act of coitus embodied her famous observation in *To the Lighthouse* as well: that "nothing is [ever] simply one thing."[5]

In the sometimes-arcane language of Catholic theology, Grisez's question focused on what theologians called the relationship of "practical" to "speculative reason." For the rest of us, that question might be translated thus: if God created human nature oriented to living a life of flourishing by choosing practical actions like helping the poor, caring for our neighbors, and telling the truth (ethical choices that result from concrete, *practical* decisions that we can immediately recognize as good and right), shouldn't those choices be apparent to us? Shouldn't those choices be "perspicacious" (i.e., immediately obvious to us)? And if that was the case, what need was there to resort to speculative arguments about what human beings should do and how they should behave? What need—in other words—was there for the immense and confusing superstructure of neo-scholastic philosophy to get us to "see" what we should do (what Catholic moral theology called "speculative reason")? Why would God, Grisez asked, create human nature without the ability to understand what our end or purpose was, thus necessitating the endless—and largely unconvincing—speculations of scholastic philosophy? To utilize Thomas Kuhn's terminology, Grisez was attempting to formulate a paradigm that would answer the many anomalies produced by neo-scholasticism—anomalies that had unleashed a "period of crisis" well before the publication of *Humanae Vitae* in 1968. That neo-scholastic tradition had—by the mid-twentieth century—offered a model of "reason" that seemed arbitrary, artificial, and—well—unbelievable. If the Catholic tradition of Thomistic theology had always asserted that one of the chief benefits of natural law discourse was its ability to bring persons of good will of different (or no) religious loyalties to an agreement about what the good person or society should be, shouldn't the "practical choices" that defined those decisions be obvious to all, whether they studied scholastic philosophy or not? Wasn't that part and parcel of what made "natural law" *natural*—that is, immediately available to everyone who shared the same human nature?

As Grisez saw it, the neo-scholastics (and to a large extent *Humanae Vitae*, which would borrow a number of their arguments) had made God into an arbitrary monarch by postulating a model of ethical behavior that asserted (on the one hand) that human beings were naturally oriented toward certain kinds of actions, while (on the other hand) asserting that they could only access the "ends" or purposes of those actions through a torturous appeal to speculative truths that seemed to transcend human nature—that seemed to be arbitrarily handed down by a monarchical God outside of time and space. And it was here that "nature" reared its pesky head: where was "nature" in such a model of natural law? If the clues about what kind of persons human beings should be—or what kind of societies human beings should construct—were not apparent in nature, how could one label such a model "natural law"? Nature seemed to be about theoretical constructs, rather than grounded in how human beings actually live. And the arguments proffered to "prove" the truth of the need for passing over that fragile bridge from practical reason to its speculative twin appeared both unconvincing and intellectually dubious (on a good day). Thus four years before the appearance of Paul VI's encyclical, even critics recognized the sheer brilliance of Grisez's critique, and the audacious paradigm he proposed to resolve the anomalies of the older model. Grisez believed (undoubtedly correctly) that St. Thomas Aquinas would repudiate such a model of "Thomistic" philosophy. Grisez believed (again, undoubtedly correctly) that Aquinas was far too smart to posit such a model of "nature."[6]

But at the same time—and yet again, this is a rather dramatic "at the same time"—Grisez knew that Catholic moral theology since Francisco Suarez in the seventeenth century had insisted on the *objectivity* of moral norms. That is, moral teaching was neither merely "emotive" (i.e., based on how human beings *feel* about certain issues or actions) nor socially constructed (i.e., based on what one's culture or society believed to be good or evil actions). Catholic moral theology had thus consistently emphasized that moral norms were *given*, and not constructed. And Grisez's brilliant rereading of this emphasis on objective moral norms outlined a paradigm that made crossing the bridge from theoretical to practical reason unnecessary, and even irrational. Grisez, in other words, made the entire sloppy business of "measuring" the goodness or badness of acts by comparing them to some purely theoretical pattern irrelevant. For as Grisez outlined the natural law basis for moral action, there was no need to cross *any* bridge to understand the moral "meanings" of human action, for

the moral norm simply *is* human nature as it is given—given of course, not to sense experience but to rational understanding. Moral goodness and badness can be discerned simply by *comparing* the essential *patterns of human actions* with the *intelligible structure of human nature* both in its inner complexity and in its essential relationships. The judgment whether an action conforms or not to human nature *is completely objective.*[7]

Grisez thus argued that moral norms—that is, guidelines for ethical living—had to be "objective" in the sense that they were immediately apparent as "goods in themselves," with no need for speculative or metaphysical arguments as to why or how they were desirable. This was the central component in Catholic theology's commitment to "realism." If natural law was truly universal and "graspable" by everyone, apart from religious faith or philosophical argument, then it had to be "objective" and real in the sense of being perspicacious—obviously true and desirable because it outlined actions that were in congruence with the "intelligible structure of human nature." And that intelligible structure had to be apparent to everyone, without philosophical or metaphysical argument.

Understood thus, one might reasonably argue that Grisez's entire academic project in elucidating a "new" natural law was about providing a much more believable and realistic explanation of how human beings attained "full flourishing" (Aquinas' own definition of the end of natural law) by constructing a paradigm of the real world in which the core moral truths could be apprehended directly and immediately. Hadn't Aquinas understood natural law in exactly this way, Grisez asked—that is, as being so basic and foundational to how the real world operated that it could be appropriated (or, as Immanuel Kant would say, intuited) *immediately, by everyone,* without appeal to theoretical arguments that only convinced the already convinced? Wasn't such an understanding of natural law "natural" in the same way that gravity was—that is, immediately grasped as "real" without proofs, and especially grasped without appeal to intellectually shabby "proofs," like those offered in neo-scholasticism, or cobbled together with phenomenological arguments like that offered in *Humanae Vitae*? Didn't such a foundation for natural law—analogous to Immanuel Kant's proposed "categorical imperative" as the ground for fulfilling moral duties—make it more believable and immediately relevant for understanding how the most fundamental moral truths were grounded in the real world? At the very least, such a paradigm for natural law would provide a far more secure basis for church teaching than what had been presented as "natural law" in recent ecclesial documents.[8]

One might therefore see the entire *"new* natural law" project undertaken by Grisez and Finnis as being about *saving* natural law by reestablishing it on distinctly different foundations that avoided any appeal to metaphysical claims—including appeals to the teleological meaning of historical action, among others—that modern science had long rejected as outdated and (well) unscientific. Understood such, Grisez's paradigm offered the possibility of grounding church teaching—including church teaching on contraception—on more solid intellectual foundations.[9]

Viewed from the standpoint of Kuhn, one could propose that Grisez had recognized, well before 1968, that the "normal science" of moral theology had encountered a series of anomalies from the application of nineteenth-century neo-scholastic propositions to the lived reality of believers. And those anomalies had become so widespread, and had caused such confusion, that the older paradigm had come to be widely recognized as untenable, particularly among the most respected "experts" in the field. Read thus, one could plausibly argue that Grisez had recognized that Catholic moral theology had entered a "period of crisis" well before the appearance of *Humanae Vitae* in 1968. And one could further plausibly argue that Grisez believed that a more disciplined retrieval of the actual thought of Aquinas would help to place the Church's teaching regarding contraception on much firmer intellectual ground. In undertaking precisely this kind of retrieval, Grisez clearly embodied one of Kuhn's canniest insights regarding paradigm change—that the period of crisis had freed up the willingness of one moral theology's most creative minds to "question even the most basic assumptions of the older science."

Grisez had argued that the neo-scholastics had, in the first place, misread Aquinas—a misreading that had led inexorably to the metaphysical muddle that was "Catholic natural law discourse" of the time. Grisez attacked the claim (basic to neo-scholastic thought) that Aquinas had identified moral norms—the guidelines for living an ethical life—by grounding them in "speculative reason." This sounds to nonacademics like an arcane and minor point, but this point is anything *but* that: the debate was over how human beings can know whether they're being good in their actions. This is thus a question of primal importance for people (including religious people) who seek to live a moral life. It is, then, the very opposite of what might be termed an "arcane" question.

Grisez argued that in his *Treatise on the Natural Law* (*ST* 1-2, q. 94), Aquinas had contrasted speculative over against practical reason, beginning with the first principle of natural law: *bonum est faciendum et prosequendum et malum vitandum*: "the good is to be done and fostered, and evil avoided." Such a principle was a classic example of "speculative reason" because it stated a principle that was universally true, but nonetheless remained an abstraction. This first principle was "speculative" in the sense that, while true, it offered no practical advice as to *how* it was supposed to be applied. While such a principle *speculatively*—that is, in the abstract—stated the foundational principle of the moral life, it offered no practical advice as to what "fostering the good" might mean in this or that particular situation. Should we give to this worthy charity, or that one? Should I support Mother Theresa's nuns in Calcutta or the Sisters of Charity working among Native Americans? Thus answering the practical question of which worthy charity should be supported was a function of practical reason, which had to be applied by making a prudential judgment: I'll give to this group, and not to that one. Such a practical judgment had to be—and, according to Grisez, *was*—made prudentially, "on the ground," so to speak, independently of any recourse to the ends of actions supplied by speculative reason. The prudential judgments as to which charity should receive my money were, to the moral actor, immediately grasped as the ones that should be made. And those judgments made by ethical actors (grasped as "good" by practical reason) defined the very heart of what natural law was about, and not the embarrassingly tenuous appeals to the metaphysical ends or meaning of human of action. For Grisez, this made much more sense in explaining why natural law was "natural": because it was obvious *on the ground* and graspable in itself, without any theoretical appeal to purported ends or purposes that one had to speculate about.[10]

Thus Grisez argued that Aquinas used the word "good" to refer to whatever human beings could immediately recognize as "worthwhile," without grounding the legitimacy of those goods in some speculative truth above history. The "good" for Aquinas, then, was *not* based in speculative reason, but rather in practical reason. Such goods could be grasped immediately, and without the need to appeal to some speculative principle to understand what helped people to flourish, and what hindered such flourishing. Grasping these basic goods, so understood, requires no knowledge of metaphysics or even authoritative teaching to undergird them. The most basic knowledge of such goods rests on practical insights. As Robert George cannily described Grisez's paradigm of the new natural law,

> the practical intellect itself grasps certain ends as reasons for action that require no further reasons. They are intelligible as ends-in-themselves. As such, their intrinsic choiceworthiness is self-evident.[11]

In a breathtakingly daring rereading of Aquinas, Grisez thus asserted that Aquinas never proposed to judge the goodness or badness of human acts by how well they applied speculative truths to concrete ethical situations. If there was, Grisez argued, such a thing as a transcendent "yardstick" against which one had to measure one's actions to see how good or bad they were, then it was hard to see how such a law could be called "natural." Didn't one have to believe in such a transcendent yardstick in the first place in order for that whole system to work? How could such paradigm be construed as found "in nature" if that were true? Rather, Grisez argued that the knowledge of the most basic goods that define human flourishing—"intelligible as ends-in-themselves"— did not depend on the human ability to discern a speculative anthropology that laid out how human beings should achieve their "rational ends," or indeed by any model of ethics that measured the goodness of individual acts by some kind of teleology. As Grisez read Aquinas, then, "nature" was indeed normative, but certainly *not* normative in the way in which neo-scholasticism had understood that term. Natural law, as presented by Grisez, was "normative" in the sense that it rested on precepts that were immediately obvious as "basic goods," desirable as "ends-in-themselves," and without need of "proof." Indeed, the very need to "prove" a model of natural law by appealing to metaphysical arguments (the purported "ends" of action) betrayed the dirty little secret that such a paradigm of natural law was nether normative nor natural: it was, rather, a jerry-rigged system that could not bear the weight of the ethical superstructure that had been constructed on its wobbly foundations.[12]

As Grisez read Aquinas, the motivation that drives the practical reason for doing certain things and for avoiding doing other things is the perception that there are "intrinsic human goods" that are self-evidently helpful to human flourishing. "Grisez's Aquinas" was therefore presented in a paradigm in which practical principles could never be deduced from purely theoretical truths about human nature: the necessarily prudential judgments of practical reason could never be deduced from speculative reason. The "goods" that form of objects of our moral concerns were intelligible as "ends-in-themselves," and were thus perspicacious—that is, so self-evidently true that offering "reasons" for them would be an insult to human intelligence. Grisez argued that, for Aquinas, the most fundamental precepts of natural law had nothing to do with lists of "good" actions (and concurrently lists of bad actions) that were evaluated by how well (or badly) they "fulfilled" theoretical models of human nature, as the neo-scholastic paradigm proposed. And Grisez asserted that Aquinas had never offered a systematic account of moral norms—adumbrating "rules" for defining virtuous and sinful behaviors—with an eye to measuring how well an act achieved its purported end. In the new natural law paradigm, human beings perceive actions they should perform because they are "opportunities for people to realize *for themselves (and often others) benefits whose rational value cannot be reduced to purely instrumental purposes.*" Grisez's brilliant articulation therefore offered a paradigm of natural law that was existentially immediate, grounded in actual human experience, and free of the embarrassing need for appealing to a purported teleological end that almost all non-Catholics (and most Catholic moralists, as well) found intellectually shabby and unbelievable.[13]

At the very outset, then, Grisez made four revolutionary moves that paved the way for a new paradigm for understanding the micro-tradition of natural law. *First,* Grisez postulated that Aquinas had been seriously misread by those very scholars who claimed the title of "Thomists." Aquinas had never intended to ground moral norms in speculative reason; indeed, such a reading of Aquinas laid the foundations of natural law on sand, and not on firm ground. *Second,* Grisez cut the all-important thread that neo-scholasticism had used to tie moral norms to an understanding of teleology (i.e., a speculative understanding of the ends or purposes of things and acts). In Grisez's paradigm, speculation about the "ends" of acts was irrelevant to the moral life. *Third,* Grisez radically redefined what "human flourishing" was, and how it was to be accomplished: human flourishing could not be proved or even argued about (certainly not rationally), precisely because, *fourth* (and in the long run most important), Grisez recentered natural law in such a way that radically redefined the role of human reason in living the moral life. More of this anon.

Further, Grisez had eschewed the paradigm outlined by his friend John Ford as well. Grisez recognized that Ford's resort to the "argument from authority" to ground the truth of natural law—that the precepts of natural law were "true" because they were authoritatively taught by a Church that Jesus had promised to always lead through the action of the Holy Spirit—undercut one of the most important strengths of natural law reasoning: the ability to talk about foundational ethical issues with those who espoused a different faith, or no faith at all. If Ford's paradigm was legitimate, then there was no discernable difference between arguments deriving from a faith commitment and those purportedly deriving from a natural law that was self-evidently true to anyone who cared to look at the real world. Quite unintentionally, Ford's attempt to "shore up" the authority of natural law thinking by resting it on the authority of the Church undermined the very independence and certitude that Aquinas had sought to invest natural law with in the first place.[14]

Therefore one might posit that the most brilliant single component defining Grisez's paradigm of natural law was his assertion that the "basic goods" that defined what it was to live as fully human could not be proved in any simplistic empirical manner, like one might execute a proof in geometry: it was (literally) impossible to "prove" the truths of natural law by reason, or indeed by any other way. It was therefore here, Grisez believed, that the neo-scholastics (among others) had misread Aquinas. The basic goods that grounded the norms for ethical living required no speculative knowledge of what "human flourishing" might mean: in place of just such metaphysical speculation, Grisez argued that Aquinas had posited self-evident "prescriptions" immediately graspable to human intelligence. It was in *that* sense that natural law was "natural"—that is, part of the very structure of the real world. Grisez argued that Aquinas had recognized that precisely because the prescriptions of natural law were *foundational* to human life, one risked making the prescriptions of that law into banal laundry lists of good and bad actions by measuring them against some theoretical construct. Further (and more to the point), all models of such rational "proof" might be (and usually were, at least eventually) disproved by critics. Something as foundational as natural law had to be well beyond the ability of human reason to disprove, at least as Grisez read Aquinas on this crucial point.[15]

Grisez and Finnis (who served as Grisez's primary conversation partner and even—to some extent—his "popularizer") thus elucidated an entirely new paradigm that they believed to be both sounder intellectually than the paradigms of the neo-scholastics and revisionists and much closer in outline to the paradigm offered by Aquinas. Grisez's paradigm has most commonly been referred to as the "new natural law," but it is also occasionally referred to in philosophy as "basic goods theory." The latter term is, in many ways, a useful one because Grisez's paradigm posits eight "basic goods" that, taken together, "tell us what human persons are capable of being, not only as individuals but in community." Four of the basic goods were what Grisez termed "reflexive"— that is, reflecting what kind of person one was: self-integration, authenticity, friendship, and justice. Three of the basic goods he labeled as "substantive"— defining the substance of human life: life and bodily well-being, knowledge of truth and the appreciation of beauty, and "skillful performance" and play. The eighth and last basic good he labeled "marriage and family." As the new natural law adumbrated the foundations of moral living, individuals could never morally act against any of these goods, which would be irrational precisely because to act against them would be to willfully undercut one's ability to achieve full human flourishing, and would also stymie efforts to achieve communal flourishing.[16]

As Philip Johnson has insightfully observed, missing from these lists of basic human goods are both "money" (which was merely "instrumental"— that is, merely a means for achieving more basic goods) and "pleasure" (which was not to be sought as an end in itself, but rather as a benefit resulting from the pursuit of a more basic good). And Grisez asserted that human actions could be evaluated as "rational" when they pursued one or more of these basic human goods, which were both "irreducible" and "incommensurable." By these two terms he simply meant that such basic goods could not be derived from any supposedly more fundamental good ("irreducible"), nor was there any standard by which one such good could be exchanged for another ("incommensurable").[17]

Further, as Grisez outlined what he took to be a paradigm much closer to what Aquinas had offered as a usable model of natural law, Grisez had offered self-integration ("integral fulfillment") as the first of his basic goods— fulfillment, which in this case meant striving to lead "coherent lives that give each of the basic goods its due." This first basic good enabled human actors to recognize and pursue what Grisez called self-evident "prescriptions" that defined ethical living. Among the self-evident prescriptions that furthered human flourishing derived from these basic goods were obvious truths like "life is a good which is to be sought" and "truth is a good which is to be sought." Precisely because such prescriptions defined the very meaning of what it was to be a rational human being,

> the goods they set for human action could not be directly attacked by man [sic] without his doing violence to his rational nature. To act against truth, to act against life . . . was to deny part of man's rational nature.[18]

Prominent among these self-evidently true prescriptions was one which declared that "procreation is a good which ought to be sought." In making this statement, however, Grisez was self-consciously distancing himself from the paradigm of moral theology that would be embodied in Paul VI's 1968 encyclical, which would argue that contraception was intrinsically disordered because it prevented the physical act from attaining its "natural end." As Grisez understood well before 1968, the confident assertion of Paul VI's encyclical that the "men of our day are particularly capable of seizing the deeply reasonable character" of such an argument was too sanguine by half. Grisez had already recognized that the very structure of that kind of argument regarding intrinsically evil acts was both ethically unconvincing and "naturalistic"—*not* because the meaning of such acts was discoverable in nature, but rather because it was naively and simplistically "physicalist." And by the latter term he meant the mistaken belief that one could discern moral meaning in the physical structure of human acts. The ethical meaning of human acts could not be so one-dimensionally evaluated—like one might evaluate the family dog by how well it followed the directives of its masters.

Rather, Grisez argued that natural law witnessed to the self-evident truth that human beings should never act against certain essential "human goods" because those goods furthered the human project as a whole and provided a framework for human flourishing, which was the purpose of living ethically in the first place. These goods, in other words, helped to shape the evolving personal journey of individuals toward greater openness to the world, toward greater awareness of the needs of others, and toward the kind of flourishing that defined a fully human life. His appeal, then, was not to human reason, but rather to human *experience*. And that experience—just as Aquinas had posited about natural law—was graspable and "choiceworthy" to all human beings, believers or not, pagans or Christians, Aristotelians or Hegelians. The sheer brilliance of Grisez's paradigm of natural law was here made manifest by the simple argument that the prescriptions of natural law were immediately intelligible as ends-in-themselves, without the need of theological or metaphysical superstructure of any kind. This was paradigm reconstruction on a world-class scale, and almost everyone in the guild of moral theology immediately recognized that Grisez's was a voice that had to be reckoned with.[19]

B. *Moral Precepts as "Choiceworthy"*

Grisez's brilliant insight was *not* that Paul VI's condemnation of contraception was wrong in itself; on the contrary, Grisez believed that Paul VI was quite correct in ratifying the consistent teaching of the Church regarding the immorality of contraceptive practice. Rather, it was the paradigm of natural law on which the encyclical rested its arguments that could be easily recognized as intellectually problematic. After 1968, Grisez read the critiques of the encyclical offered by his colleagues in the field—Curran, McCormick, and others—and recognized the intellectual weight of their critiques. The holes in the older neo-scholastic argument constituted anomalies that the defenders of the encyclical seemed unable to answer. And Grisez undoubtedly recognized that one could easily—too easily—multiply the examples of such anomalies. The very ease in multiplying such examples (which was precisely what many critics of the encyclical engaged in for several decades after 1968) revealed the desperate need to disengage orthodox Catholic teaching from the paradigm of natural law informing *Humanae Vitae*.

As Grisez saw it, a model of natural law organized around basic goods that contributed to "human flourishing" placed the condemnation of contraception on much firmer intellectual ground than that offered in the 1968 encyclical. Contraception's malice, understood within the context of Grisez's paradigm of natural law, was not to be explained by its supposed violation of the "ends" of sexual intercourse, or that it violated some speculative model of "rational creatures" who could reason their way to the purposes of things, but rather because it rejected one of the most basic goods that defined human flourishing: the good of procreation. And while that good could not be proved rationally, it did accord with the universal human experience of having children; it was *this* appeal to the universal and lived *experience* of parenthood that Grisez believed more correctly reflected the argument of Aquinas, and provided a firmer intellectual support for the Church's teaching regarding contraception.

But much of the brilliance of Grisez's articulation of a new paradigm of natural law resided in the care with which he argued the details of his model—for example, in critiquing the argument that each and every act of conjugal intercourse had to remain open to the "total giving" between spouses that the physical act embodied. Grisez sought to distance his own support of the 1968 encyclical's condemnation of the grave evil of contraception from the "phenomenological argument" that had been offered in paragraph 12 of *Humanae Vitae*, which had argued that coitus, simply as observable human behavior, evinced "two inseparable meanings"—the unitive and the procreative. The "phenomenon" of coitus, according to this line of reasoning, "while most closely uniting husband and wife, capacitates them for the generation of new lives." Paragraph 12 thus appealed not only to the rational "ends" of marriage (the classic neo-scholastic argument) but also to the phenomenological meaning of the "total giving" between spouses inscribed into the very structure of the act. But Grisez argued that no human act—precisely because it was a human act—could be "total" in the sense in which the encyclical argued. All human acts—to the extent that they were human—embodied a range of meanings, none of which could be taken as "total" in any final moral sense. And precisely because of that lack of totality, it was implausible (at best) to believe that each and every act of conjugal intercourse could embody the kind of "total giving" the encyclical seemed to make normative. Further, and more to the point, the basic precepts of natural law as elucidated by Aquinas prescinded from precisely *this* kind of unilateral linking of physical action with moral meaning. For Grisez, such an argument embodied the kind of "physicalism" that Aquinas was too smart to endorse. One could not so blithely deduce moral meaning from a human physical activity whose "end" could only be understood by an appeal to a speculative truth "above" nature.[20]

Grisez's strong denunciation of contraception thus witnessed to a widespread sense—even among *Humanae Vitae's* most fervent supporters—that although its *teaching* correctly passed on orthodox Catholic moral guidelines, the natural law arguments offered to support that teaching were both unconvincing and implausible. The paradigm on offer in the 1968 encyclical regarding the "total giving" implicit in the physical act of spousal intercourse represented a model of natural law that few—even fervent supporters of the encyclical's teaching like Grisez—could take seriously.

It boded ill for the reception of *Humanae Vitae* among the faithful if someone as critical of contraceptive practice as Grisez could recognize even before the promulgation of the encyclical in 1968 the pertinence of Richard McCormick's famous postpromulgation question regarding its authority: that if the natural law arguments adduced to support the teaching of Paul VI's encyclical *failed* to offer the kind of plausible proof that Catholic moral theology had come to expect in making ethical arguments, what—exactly—was the status of that teaching? Grisez had recognized well before 1968 the problematic nature of both the neo-scholastic paradigm of natural law and the weight given to (supposedly coherent) phenomenological arguments that failed to prove what they claimed. Grisez thus sought to offer a more plausible and understandable model of how a more correctly articulated paradigm of natural law could and did support the condemnation of contraception.

C. A Natural Law without Nature?

As creative (and, undoubtedly brilliant) as Grisez's paradigm of natural law was, however, it was criticized by both thorough-going critics of *Humanae Vitae's* condemnation of contraception like Richard McCormick "on the left" and other Catholic scholars—"on the right"—who shared Grisez's belief that its condemnation of contraception was correct. Thus Russell Hittinger (himself a complex thinker like Grisez, but probably closest ideologically to members of the latter camp) offered a resounding critique of Grisez's paradigm of what had come to be called the "new natural law." Taking aim at Grisez and at the constellation of Catholic scholars who had gathered around Grisez—Finnis, William May, and Joseph Boyle—Hittinger identified the work of both Grisez and Finnis as being part of what he called the "recoverist project"—a broad movement in contemporary philosophy to recover a credible premodern paradigm of ethics, in Grisez's case—in the thought of Aquinas from the thirteenth century.[21]

From Hittinger's point of view, both Grisez and Finnis had emerged as major voices within the "recoverist school" because they believed that they had correctly retrieved Aquinas' thought in a way that avoided the intellectual pitfalls of modern movements (like neo-scholasticism) that had been the easy targets of post-Enlightenment criticism: both Grisez and Finnis believed that they had successfully recovered the systematic core of natural law theory in a way that was congruent with the older tradition *and* in a way that could

be persuasive to contemporary ethicians wary of natural law discourse as it
had been practiced by the manualists. Further (and by no means least among
their concerns), Hittinger identified Grisez and Finnis as the chief figures in
the "recoverist school" because they believed that their recovery of a genuinely Thomistic basis for natural law discourse could be of immeasurable aid
in grounding Roman Catholic moral theology in a more intellectually robust
and defensible model than those previously on offer.[22]

But Hittinger believed that the "recovery" so successfully reported
represented something else again than a simple retrieval of Aquinas' famed
system, freed of misconceptions and misreadings for contemporary readers.
Without ever using Kuhn's nomenclature in his criticism of that recovery,
Hittinger nonetheless argued that Grisez's presentation of a genuinely
"Thomistic" understanding of natural law rested on a completely different
paradigm from that of the Angelic Doctor. Hittinger argued that the core of
natural law theory as it had been traditionally (and consistently) understood
posited that the "law" referred to could, in some way, be apprehended and
argued about by utilizing human *reason* (not human experience). Precisely
because it was part of the very structure of how the universe operated (like
the laws of physics), the human nature so explicated could be theoretically
recognized as *normative* because reason could recognize it as such. "Nature,"
then, as grasped by human reason, assigned moral values to certain kinds of
human activity, and condemned other activities as morally evil because such
activities violated the flourishing of human nature as uncovered by reason.
But it was exactly *this* connection between nature, normativity, and reason—
what philosophers and theologians called the relationship between "practical" and "speculative" reason—that Grisez seemed to dismiss. If the basic
goods that constituted the very foundation of natural law could not be rationally proved, what was the relation of human reason to human nature (if
any)? And if the basic goods that constituted the foundational components of
natural law could not be proved or argued about, what was the role of reason
in moral discourse—a role that had been consistently assigned a major part
in previous Catholic models of natural law discourse. And if reason played *no*
role in elucidating the meanings of those basic goods as they applied to specific human acts, in what sense could one refer to the "law" in natural law?[23]

Hittinger believed that Grisez's paradigm failed finally because it would
not (or could not) systematically interrelate moral norms, human reason, and
a philosophy of nature. That is, Hittinger argued that central to older mainstream traditions of Catholic natural law was the belief that "moral norms"
were not only present in "nature" but also could be discovered and postulated

by human reason. But Grisez seemed to take pride in the fact that his paradigm baldly rejected any sense that nature was normative in a way that enabled
human reason to derive moral norms from it. In Hittinger's estimation, then,
Grisez appeared to deny any rational basis for an identification of the "natural" with the "morally good"—indeed, the very core of Grisez's model seemingly rested on the firm belief that one could *not* derive the moral "ought"
from the "is" of human nature. In holding such a position, Grisez appeared
to reject the core presupposition of traditional natural law thinking: that the
most basic moral norm informing all natural law approaches to ethics had
been the imperative: "follow nature using human reason."[24]

As Robert George has noted, Hittinger's critique of Grisez's new natural
law paradigm brought together a spectrum of criticisms from various quarters
of the philosophical and theological forest, voicing the (sometimes trenchant)
critiques of scholars like Ralph McInerny and Henry Veatch. But the most
basic criticism that united all of them was the charge that Grisez appeared
to rest the entire superstructure of natural law on the older Kantian position
that the fundamental goods or prescriptions undergirding ethical living were
perspicacious and self-evident, and could not be rationally derived from *any*
understanding of human nature.

In the philosophical world, Grisez's paradigm had been most famously
elucidated by Immanuel Kant in the eighteenth century, and was usually
termed "intuitionism." Kant had believed that the most basic moral truths
had to rest on a firmer foundation than that of fallible human reason, which
was famously unreliable in discerning reality, moral and otherwise. Kant had
quite cannily pointed out how self-deluded moral actors often were—failing
to appreciate how morally tainted their self-professed "virtuous" behavior
often was. Any moral code resting on a foundation as thin and unreliable
as human reason was bound to miss the mark of the good and the right.
Kant had argued therefore that the core moral truths were "intuited" directly
and immediately by human beings, without the need for reasoning about
them. In his *Critique of Pure Reason* (published in 1781), Kant had argued
that only actions done out of duty have true moral virtue, and the "duty"
undergirding such moral action was founded on an immediately intuited
truth that he called the Categorical Imperative: "Act only according to that
maxim whereby you can, at the same time, will that it should become a universal law."[25]

Such a model of direct intuition as the foundation for moral action (labeled "Kantian ethics" by philosophers and theologians) appeared to rest the
foundations of moral action well beyond the shifting perceptions of human

actors, in the process providing a certain and secure basis for morality that was both universal and transcultural—precisely the benefits of natural law. And Hittinger argued that Grisez appeared to have constructed an analogous understanding of natural law: Grisez seemed to argue that if natural law was indeed what it claimed to be—a law that was accessible to everyone, regardless of culture or religious belief—then it had to be (by definition) universal in a way that indeed transcended culturally constructed patterns of understanding. The intuitionist model of ethics appeared to provide a secure model for precisely *these* aspects of moral reasoning.

But as many scholars had observed well before Hittinger elucidated his critique of Grisez, what Kant giveth, Kant can taketh away: if intuitionism of the Kantian variety was (by definition) unprovable because it was so obviously apparent to human intuition as true, how did one answer skeptics who *failed* to "intuit" these basic goods? How did one go about constructing an answer to those who could not—or refused to—see the perspicacious and obvious truth of the basic goods ostensibly supporting the entire edifice? As philosopher Henry Veatch had famously observed, in borrowing such a Kantian model, Grisez had borrowed all of its problems as well: "though the hands are those of Germain Grisez, the voice is that of Immanuel Kant."[26]

As Hittinger saw it, Grisez appeared to accept Kant's supposition that ethics could dispense with *any* philosophy of nature approached through reason, having made something like a "declaration of methodological independence" of ethics from metaphysics. But in thus presenting a "natural law without nature," Hittinger claimed that Grisez's paradigm sought to "recover natural law theory by way of shortcuts"—the chief shortcut being the invocation of Kantian intuitionism to obviate the need for human reason to discover what "following nature" might mean as a basis for ethics. But such a shortcut unfortunately created troubling anomalies that, in Hittinger's estimation anyway, opened up other problems in the "new" natural law.[27]

Further, Hittinger believed that there was a logical error in Grisez's belief that one could elucidate the "basic goods" of human flourishing *completely* independently of speculative or metaphysical knowledge. Hittinger argued that even in such an intuitionist paradigm as that presented by Grisez, there was a *certain* amount of speculative (nonintuited and rational) knowledge that was indispensable for the model to operate successfully. And Hittinger argued that Grisez had confessed as much—wittingly or not—in some of his early writing regarding the good of procreation and the evil of contraception. Hittinger thus claimed that in discussing the foundational prescription that "life is a good which ought to be sought" in *Contraception and the Natural Law* (1964), Grisez had argued that

> the good of human life must be judged as a whole rather than in rela-
> tion to the end of each faculty or physiological power. Accordingly,
> respiration and nutrition cannot be said to be basic human goods.
> However, from a biological point of view, the "work of reproduction is
> the fullest organic realization of the living substance." In other words,
> [reproduction] differs from respiration in the sense that it bestows the
> good of life as a whole, and therefore ought to be included within the
> basic good of life.[28]

Hittinger's claim here was simply this: that despite the new natural law
claim of superiority to older natural law paradigms by avoiding the need
for rationalizing about the applications of first principles to actual ethical
situations, Grisez had to rely on precisely *this* kind of theoretical argument
in laying out what was essential as opposed to accidental to human organic
health. As Grisez had argued the case, reproduction was a "basic good," in
the service of which nutrition and respiration served as secondary or "accidental" goods. As Hittinger saw it, such a distinction between "basic" and
"secondary" goods was not, and could not be, intuited—which was why
Grisez had to make and argue that distinction *rationally*. Hittinger argued
that Grisez's own analysis of at least one basic good was not consistent with
his foundational argument regarding the "inferential underivability of the
basic practical principles." From Hittinger's point of view, at least, the new
natural law paradigm betrayed the very same kind of marks of human construction as the older paradigms it sought to displace: the limits of the human
ability to construct models of reality—even in such a brilliant paradigm as
that of the new natural law—would always reveal themselves at some point.
While Hittinger never invoked Kuhn, his critique was based on an insight
that Kuhn had often repeated: that reality is more complex than any model
we can construct to explain it.[29]

Likewise, some neo-scholastic scholars added their own critiques of the
new natural law to critical voices like that of Russell Hittinger: from the point
of view of these scholars, Grisez's argument that practical reason operated
from its own first principles, independent of any knowledge drawn from theology, metaphysics, or anthropology, rendered those previously respected
disciplines all but redundant or irrelevant in Catholic discourse on ethics.
The argument that one could (or should) construct a model of natural law

without recourse to any understanding of metaphysics or theological speculation was indeed something new in Roman Catholic discourse, and *not* new
in a good way.

A number of scholars believed that Hittinger's critique of Grisez's paradigm scored some "hits." As Hittinger's criticism made apparent, Grisez did
indeed *appear* to accept Kant's supposition that ethics could dispense with
a philosophy of "nature" (at least as that term had traditionally been understood, anyway). Hittinger further voiced the concern shared by a number of
scholars regarding Grisez's apparent acceptance of the older (Kantian) belief that one could separate ethics from rationality, and from metaphysics.
Likewise, Hittinger had homed in on one of the most vulnerable aspects of
Grisez's paradigm: the very attempt to identify "basic human goods" without
any attempt to construct a clear connection between "nature" and "normativity" left moral discourse at a distinct disadvantage when debating with
those who failed to see the "basic moral goods" intuitively: what default position could one repair to in such a situation?

That said, however, a number of scholars came to the defense of the new
natural law paradigm, often quite brilliantly. Robert George was one of
these. George argued that Grisez had never denied that a certain amount of
speculative reason was necessary in elucidating the implications of the "basic
goods" that constituted the foundation of natural law: in George's estimation, new natural law theory simply posited that the basic goods of moral discourse were not (and could not be) *derived* from rational propositions in the
way that—say—neo-scholasticism had proposed. The precepts at the core
of natural law were not "rational" *in that sense.* But the application of those
precepts to actual circumstances (what George called "practical judgments")
could not be made in the complete absence of rational speculation. How
could it be other? In George's estimation, Hittinger seemed to assume that
Grisez's allowance of such rational, speculative activity in this way showed
that "he does in fact directly rely upon anthropological, if not metaphysical,
evidence for including procreation in the list of basic goods." But George
argued that Hittinger was mistaken in believing that Grisez's presentation of
at least one "basic good" (i.e., procreation) was "not consistent with his understanding of the inferential and deductive underivability of the basic practical principles." In George's estimation, Hittinger's critique was based on a
misunderstanding of Grisez's actual argument. In so arguing, George thus
expressed the opinion that the new natural law had indeed accomplished
what it claimed to have done: placing church teaching on firmer, less vulnerable foundations.[30]

Robert George's extended response to the critiques of the "new natural law"—published in the revered pages of the *University of Chicago Law Review*—was as lively and brilliant as Grisez' original elucidation of his paradigm and Hittinger's criticism of it. For those not familiar with the fierce intellectual combat waged by moral theologians and ethicists (often coming close to the hostility generated in contemporary political debates), these debates over Grisez's project will appear strangely vociferous and overheated. But they do witness to the intellectual high stakes involved in supposedly "dispassionate" and rational scholarly conversations.

What can't be disputed is that the "new natural law" produced widespread reinterest in theories of natural law within the Catholic community. In the first few decades after the closing of the Second Vatican Council in 1965, interest in natural law discourse had waned among both Catholic philosophers and theologians in favor of other (seemingly more contemporary and "relevant" paradigms) offered by theological systems utilizing existentialist and Marxian thought (e.g., liberation theology). Further, the Second Vatican Council had emphasized the need to put Catholic theology—especially Catholic moral theology—on firm biblical rather than speculative foundations. For many scholars in the years after the closing of the Second Vatican Council in 1965, it was far more important that moral theology be in conversation with the *biblical* witness of Jesus and the Hebrew prophets than with medieval scholastics, even scholastics as brilliant and creative as Aquinas.

But the work of both Grisez and Finnis became foundational to Catholic moral discourse with the accession of Pope John Paul II to the Throne of Peter in 1978. John Paul was easily the most prolific papal author of the past century, in large part because of the sheer length of his pontificate. The critiques offered by the new natural law of moral theories like "proportionalism" and "consequentialism" (both of which were adopted by a number of theological "dissenters" in the Church) provided the intellectual foundation for the formal Vatican condemnation of both of those theories, as well as providing the intellectual background for arguably John Paul's most famous encyclical, *Veritatis Splendor*.[31]

Likewise, "new natural law" as an intellectual movement came to attract the attention of avowedly secular scholars during the 1980s, especially among students of jurisprudence and political philosophy. As Samuel Gregg has observed, the publications of Grisez and Finnis elucidating the new natural law paradigm reawakened awareness among both analytical philosophers and legal scholars that "practical reason" (at least as interpreted by figures like Grisez) provided an extremely helpful resource for critiquing the arguments of intellectual heavy hitters like John Rawls, Ronald Dworkin, and Robert Nozick who had staked out avowedly "secular" positions on controversial issues like abortion, euthanasia, and homosexual unions. If anything, therefore, one could argue that Grisez's paradigm of the new natural law had an even more profound effect on pundits and public philosophers *outside* Catholic precincts who sought to answer intellectuals like Rawls and Dworkin, who were arguing in favor of the ethical permissibility of abortion and euthanasia, than it did on scholars in the mainstream of Catholic moral theology.[32]

As creative and protean as the paradigm outlined by Grisez was—and even his harshest critics admitted that it was both of those things—not everyone in the world of Catholic moral theology jumped onboard the bandwagon of the new natural law. Indeed, the vast majority of ethicists and moral theologians in the Catholic community preferred to stay on the sidelines of that parade, critiquing (often harshly) Grisez's "recovery" of Aquinas. From the standpoint of Kuhn's model of how scientific revolutions occur, this was neither surprising nor even a negative thing. For as Kuhn had predicted at almost the same time when Grisez was beginning to elucidate his own "alternate candidate" for the micro-tradition of natural law, there would always be "outliers" in any disciple who rejected the normativity—and even the very coherence—of new and improved models purportedly explaining how the real world operated. That, Kuhn noted, was not a bad thing, but rather a very good thing indeed, because it served as a lively reminder that no paradigm, however brilliant and comprehensive, could exhaust the complexities of the real world.

Kuhn had asserted that no science (and I would include theology in that group) could offer anything like a "blueprint for reality" that was totalistic: there would *always* be parts of the real world that eluded any paradigm's ability to explain totally. Thus Kuhn had asserted that it was more helpful (and truer) to understand scientific paradigms as humanly constructed, provisional models for predicting how the real world operated, than as blueprints for reality. And as he further argued, there would often be results in the day-to-day application of paradigms to reality (day-to-day applications that Kuhn had called "normal science") that implied that the operational paradigm not only was incomplete but also might be wrong. There would thus (he predicted) always be outliers in any discipline who nursed profound doubts as to the paradigm's worth and veracity, and who in fact would offer contrary models for explaining observed phenomena better, or more elegantly, or more completely. In a word, such outliers served the all-important function in any discipline of reminding its practitioners that "the paradigm informing normal science was confessedly arbitrary, provisional, and humanly constructed." That simply meant that the discipline producing such critics was alive, creative, and self-critical—very good things indeed. And paradigm production in the years after Grisez elucidated his own purchase on the theories of Aquinas proved that Kuhn knew what he was talking about.

6

Jean Porter and the Historical Project of Robust Realism

A. "Constructing Nature" in Moral Theology

Historians of Catholic theology in the United States would be on very safe ground to name Jean Porter as one of the most respected and sophisticated theologians writing in the twenty-first century. This perception has been recognized well beyond the Catholic tribe, evinced in "secular" honors like Porter's being named a Fellow of the prestigious American Academy of Arts and Science in 2012. The American Academy, founded by John Adams during the American Revolution, annually announces a highly select "class" of fellows that reads like a "who's who" of distinguished scientists and playwrights, diplomats and journalists, scholars and philanthropists. The stated brief of this high-powered company (in the language of John Adams) is to "cultivate every art and science which may tend to advance the interest, honour, dignity, and happiness of a free, independent, and virtuous people." To say, then, that Porter has been widely perceived both inside and outside the Catholic community as one of the most sophisticated and respected voices in contemporary natural law discourse is an observation well within the bounds of verifiable proof.[1]

On one level, Porter might be identified as part of the same "recoverist" movement into which Russell Hittinger placed Grisez. Porter's "recovery," like Grisez's, focuses on the thirteenth-century protean theology of St. Thomas Aquinas. But there Grisez and Porter part company, and their respective paradigms of natural law look very different. For Porter adumbrates a "Thomistic recovery" in marked contrast to that of Grisez's new natural law: her's is a far more "historical"—and "historicist"—recovery of the natural law tradition: "historical" in the sense of both appreciating and describing the context of the medieval world of the twelfth and thirteenth centuries that witnessed the emergence of the high scholastic tradition in institutions like the University of Paris; but also "historicist" in understanding how the intellectual presuppositions of our own postmodern culture differ dramatically from those of the medieval scholastics, precisely because of our embeddedness in the culture that has shaped our ideas. Part of this historicist recognition of the differences between our world and that of Aquinas is the presumption that all ideas—both ours and those of Aquinas—are imbedded in the stream of history, and thus need to be approached as historical artifacts shaped by intellectual and cultural presuppositions about which we are *sometimes* conscious, but often not. Porter therefore argued that—on one level, anyway— the conversation spanning many centuries is a worthwhile undertaking, because of some similarities of our era and that of the University of Paris in the thirteenth century:

> Like the scholastics, we are living through a period of rapid social change and corresponding institutional breakdown and reformation, including extensive and far-reaching changes in the practice of marriage. Like them, again, we are confronted with the two-fold need to understand these changes and to direct and regulate them through social and legal mechanisms. How might the scholastic's complex account of the purposes of sex and marriage serve to illuminate our own efforts to address these issues?[2]

But she also quickly balanced this recognition of the similarities between our era and that of the thirteenth-century scholastics with the warning that one of the most common mistakes made in retrieving medieval texts written about natural law has been a "widespread assumption that they understood such key concepts as reason and nature in the same way as we do." And that assumption had led scholars debating the tradition of natural law down a number of blind allies and simplistic conclusions regarding the supposed "continuity" of natural law discourse. That recognition on Porter's part—that the natural law "tradition" was one marked *at least as much* by ruptures and discontinuities as continuity, thus putting any emphasis on the "continuity" of that tradition in need of much qualification and nuance—makes her project important for the purposes of this book. Thus, as Porter argued it, the medieval scholastic concept of natural law could not be fully understood without first understanding two crucial contextual realities: the historical context of European social development and the intellectual context of scholasticism. And one of the biggest intellectual influences on *us* that makes a simple (or simplistic) application of medieval categories and definitions to the ethical questions of the twenty-first century difficult—or, actually, impossible—is the sheer fact of the advances made by the modern physical and social sciences in explaining the physical and social worlds we live in. Contemporary biology makes an attempt to "rehabilitate" the categories and definitions that Aristotle (himself the subtlest and most sophisticated scientific theorist available to scholastics like Aquinas) offered to explain the workings of the real world deeply problematic, or even risible. As Thomas Kuhn might have observed, we live in a different scientific world than that inhabited by the thirteenth-century scholastics: in Kuhnian terms, we now live in a physical universe many paradigms removed from that of Aquinas.[3]

For Porter, then, we must enter the project of retrieval with the understanding that the words "nature" and the "law" contained in Aquinas' paradigm of natural law stand worlds apart from how we understand both the words and what they define. The conceptual world that twenty-first-century scholars inhabit—built on the discoveries of both the physical and social sciences of the past few centuries—understands both physical and human "nature" in ways that would have been incomprehensible to Aquinas and his fellow scholastics. Thus, undertaking a rehabilitation of Aquinas' understanding of "nature" by simply updating his definition through the application of post-Kantian categories to his thirteenth-century paradigm was both problematic and profoundly ahistorical in the worst sense: yes, we have to begin by uncovering as clearly and concisely as possible what Aquinas understood the word "nature" to mean. But that was simply the *first* step in a many-staged process of critical engagement that was about the *replacement* of an older paradigm with a new one, fitted for our own time. "Rehabilitation" in this sense did *not* mean building on that paradigm: it meant replacing it in a way that was faithful to the *trajectory* of the Thomistic project. But replacing it was part of the task, nonetheless.

And that fact—of the multiple-paradigm distance separating Aquinas from ourselves—highlights another way in which Porter's recovery project might be considered "historicist": it rests on the profound Kuhnian insight that paradigm production in the micro-traditions of theology is ongoing, and applies to the Catholic tradition of natural law discourse no less than to molecular biology: "I speak of traditional *versions* or *accounts* of the natural law [in the plural]," Porter declared, "rather than speak of one traditional theory [in the singular] of the natural law, because there have been a *number* of such accounts." From the first, Porter recognized that the long history of Catholic discourse over many centuries had produced very different paradigms—often at significant variance with each other—reflecting the concerns and presuppositions of each of their historical contexts. For Porter, then, "manyness" was at least as important as "uniformity" in understanding Catholic discourse regarding natural law. And the pluralism she speaks of touches on the substance and *purposes* of those models, no less than their overall structure and form.[4]

Porter's project of "recovery" of the Thomistic foundations of Catholic natural law theory therefore sought a critical examination of the concept of natural law as it emerged in a *specific historical context,* with the aim of recovering it as one resource—not necessarily as the only resource, nor even necessarily the most important one—among a number of *other resources* for use in constructing a viable contemporary model of natural law. Thus Porter's exercise in recovery was motivated by her belief that the scholastic concept of natural law, as it was shaped by great thinkers like Aquinas, was both interesting and worthy of study in its own right, and by her belief that those medieval writings included a great deal that was relevant for consideration in contemporary discussions about ethics. But her project of recovery of natural law discourse was also grounded in a method that balanced her profound respect for Aquinas and his medieval scholastic peers with a critical approach that "problematized" any simple process of applying Thomistic answers to twenty-first-century concerns. Porter described that method as an

> *engaged reading* of selected texts. [In utilizing this method,] I hope to present the ideas and arguments of these texts accurately, but, at the same time, I hope to evaluate them precisely as ideas and arguments. This will involve both placing these texts in context of the assumptions and concerns that gave rise to them, and evaluating what we find there in light of our own best understanding of the issues at stake. *My aim in this project is thus constructive as well as historical.*[5]

And Porter's engaged, critical reading of medieval texts like Aquinas' *Summa*—resting on sophisticated historical and historicist principles—led to her to argue that many of the modern recovery projects had misread (or at least overread) Aquinas's understanding of the self-evident character of natural law, precisely because they were too eager to engage in *eisegesis*, rather than exegesis. It was one of the legacies of the Enlightenment of the seventeenth and eighteenth centuries, she noted, to think of "nature" and "reason" as opposing or contrasting realities, so that "nature" had come to be construed as "prerational" (i.e., as defining humans and other creatures as animals) over against "reason" (which distinguished humans from other animals). But Porter argued that while such a distinction was known to Aquinas and the scholastics, they nonetheless "generally emphasized the *continuities* between nature and reason."[6]

To nonspecialists, this sounds like quibbling over meaningless details that could only be of interest to ivory tower scholars with their head in the clouds. But this is to considerably underestimate the importance of the point being made: if Porter was correct in her reading of the thirteenth-century scholastics, then the process by which human beings arrived at their knowledge of moral goodness and badness was considerably messier and less "rational" in the strict sense than either the neo-scholastics or the new natural law theorists allowed. An entirely new—and very broad—area of "moral discernment" opens up with Porter's recovery of scholastic philosophy: Aquinas and his colleagues seemed to have accepted the view that even the "precepts of the Decalogue express fundamental tenets of the natural law, and that other scriptural precepts, or *even human laws and customs, can also be said to be part of the natural law in some sense.*" It was that simple phrase—"or even human laws and customs"—that opened up creative new possibilities for elucidating what a robust, contemporary understanding of natural law might mean. And this richer understanding of the "sources" for understanding the meaning of natural law (enveloping "human laws and customs") constituted the *first* feature of her distinctive paradigm.[7]

Building on this first distinctive insight of her paradigm, Porter thus argued that some modern readers of Aquinas' emphasis on the singularly *rational* character of natural law (and here she had Grisez and other proponents of the new natural law clearly in mind) had correctly recognized *some similarities* between the medieval scholastics' argument about the *rationally* self-evident character of natural law and the modern paradigm of the new natural law. But she cautioned that this similarity of argument should not be pressed too far, or too strongly: yes, she noted, Grisez was quite correct in arguing that Aquinas had posited that natural law was, *in some sense,* rational and self-evident. But, Porter, noted,

> there is a fundamental difference between the "new natural law" of Grisez and Finnis and the scholastic concept of the natural law that cannot be brought out simply by a comparison of relevant texts on the natural law and reason. Grisez and Finnis share in the modern view that nature, understood in terms of whatever is pre- or non-rational, stands

in contrast to reason. . . . [But] no scholastic would interpret reason
in such a way as to drive a wedge between the pre-rational aspects of
our nature [on the one hand,] and reason [on the other.] They always
presuppose an essential continuity between what is natural and what
is rational, since on their view nature is itself an intelligible expression
of divine reason.[8]

And unpacking that first insight, Porter elucidated what we might take to
be the *second* feature that distinguishes her "recoverist project" from that
of Grisez and the new natural law theorists: far from creating a wedge between nature and reason, Porter's engaged reading of Aquinas and the medieval scholastics led her to assert that the "discovery" of the lineaments of
natural law might be uncovered in any number of ways "natural" to human
beings: certainly through rational analysis, but also from reflection on social
and cultural norms imbedded in cultural institutions; from the study of the
insights of physical and social science as to how the real world operated; from
consideration of the best traditions of human society. All of these sources
represented how natural law had embodied reason in the world.

And as an example, Porter argued that Aquinas and the scholastics had defined the "proper ends" or purposes of marriage and sexuality after reflecting
on how society and the Church understood the institution of marriage, not
after rationally analyzing physical processes: it is on the basis of *that* reflection that they judged particular kinds of acts to be "unnatural"—because they
were not in accord with purposes revealed to theological and social reflection.
With that second insight alone, Porter significantly recrafted the Thomistic
recovery project.[9]

"Reading nature"—in Porter's engaged reading of Aquinas—was not a rationally neutral exercise, coolly dependent on human reason and free from
other (more messy, more *affective*) human loyalties—like faith. "Reading
nature" was—in Porter's take on Aquinas—an engaged, invested enterprise that emerged in theological reflection. It was *not* "neutral," but rather
committed to a specific model of right and wrong; it was "somewhat" based
on reason—but not reason completely devoid of other commitments. And
while this made St. Thomas, and Jean Porter herself, sound like the project
of constructing of a natural law paradigm either *nscientific* and irrational, just
the opposite was the case.

Porter's "engaged reading" of medieval texts, then, was *scientific* in a way
that was startlingly analogous to Kuhn's understanding of how modern
science operated, and in a way that most physical scientists would recognize as

reflecting their own presuppositions. Just as Kuhn had reminded his readers that no respectable scientist believed that one could dispense with humanly constructed paradigms in order to study nature "directly," so Porter reminded her colleagues that the very same truth applied to the study of natural law. And to make her point, she quoted approvingly, and at some length, from Alister McGrath's famous work, *A Scientific Theology* (the very title of which brings to mind Kuhn's project):

> "Nature" is thus not a neutral entity, having the status of an "observation statement": it involves seeing the world in a *particular way—and the way in which it is seen shapes the resulting concept of "nature."* Far from being a "given," the idea of "nature" is shaped by the prior assumptions of the observer. One does not "observe" nature; *one constructs it.* And once the importance of socially mediated ideas, theories, and values is conceded, it is impossible to avoid the conclusion that the *concept of nature is, at least in part, a social construction.* (And) if the concept of nature is socially mediated, it cannot serve as an allegedly neutral, objective, or uninterpreted foundation of a theory or theology. *Nature is already an interpreted category.*[10]

Reading Porter is often like reading Kuhn: "one does not observe nature; one constructs it." "The concept of nature is, at least in part, itself a social construction." But Porter, like Kuhn, reminds her readers that simply because we can't have anything like an "objective access" to nature—that is, seeing nature "as it is" apart from human constructs—does *not* mean that we cannot gain a certain amount of reliable information about the nature of things. Porter refers to this reliable information we can gather about the nature of things as *"robust realism,"* and that phrase comes very close to defining the core of her brilliant project. The robust realism she posits as the firm basis for constructing a reliable paradigm of natural law rejects *both* the kind of relativism that asserts that, because we cannot have purely objective knowledge of nature, we lack any accurate knowledge at all (on the one hand), and the intellectually naive argument posed by some advocates of natural law that *their* paradigm of nature represented an exact, one-to-one model of some purported nature "out there" (on the other). Porter's label for her approach—robust realism—in fact reflects the sophistication of her own unique project of recovery.[11]

But Porter's recognition of the need to "construct" nature in any paradigm of natural law—resting on an intellectual model of "nature" that almost exactly parallels Kuhn's understanding of how both science and "nature" operate, and supported by the arguments of theologians like Alister McGrath—represents the *third* distinguishing feature of her paradigm: by studying human nature and reflecting on it theologically, we "construct" a model of nature and natural law to both interpret and order the sheer randomness of lived reality.

Kuhn had pressed home precisely this point in stressing the arbitrary and humanly constructed nature of paradigms in his discussion of the incommensurability of *all* scientific models: he argued that one cannot determine which paradigm is truer by "comparing them with each other over against nature." As theologian McGrath had observed along the same lines, precisely because the concept of nature is *already* socially constructed, it could never serve as an "allegedly neutral, objective or uninterpreted foundation of a theory or theology: nature is already an interpreted category." Can such an approach be labeled "realist?" Again, both yes and no. Certainly "no" by neo-scholastic standards; but by postmodern standards, there is enough "yes" implied here to fall under a broad Catholic umbrella of epistemology. More of this in time.

But building on these three insights, Porter further argued that part and parcel of the project of constructing such a natural law paradigm involved serious dialogue with the modern disciplines of the natural and social sciences, no less than critical historical study of the histories of theology and philosophy. Just as Aquinas and the great thinkers of the High Middle Ages had mined the thought of Aristotle—the most perceptive and most respected scientific voice of their day—in constructing their models of natural law, so it was incumbent on contemporary scholars of Christian ethics to mine the best insights of evolutionary biologists and physical and cultural anthropologists to arrive at a clearer understanding of the real world in a robust way.

What this meant concretely was that the advocates of any robust paradigm of natural law *had* to come to terms with the widely accepted insights of disciplines like evolutionary biology, especially the insights of Charles Darwin, in postulating any kind of design or order in the universe. In Porter's estimation, even Darwin's hypothesis regarding the randomness of natural selection—a hypothesis seemingly so hostile to the kind of "ordered design" posited by traditional natural law theory—*is* compatible with a more sophisticated and capacious understanding of how "teleology" operates in the universe. And coming to grips with so fundamental a building block of the modern consciousness as the evolutionary theories of Darwin, Porter believed, was incumbent on any theory of natural law that purported to offer anything like a model of the real world:

> If biological teleology is interpreted in a way that implies that the process of evolution is itself intrinsically directed toward some ultimate goal (such as ourselves), or else that specific features of living creatures are the direct products of conscious design, then this idea is indeed ruled out by Darwinian biology. However, if an appeal to teleology is meant to indicate that individual living beings characteristically act in certain ways that can best be interpreted as goal-directed behavior, then in *that sense* the idea of teleology is fundamental to biological science. Indeed, [in that sense,] the distinctive mark of living as opposed to inanimate creatures, is precisely that they engage in goal-directed behavior.[12]

Porter's project therefore was defined by a sophisticated balancing of careful historical research with a deeply critical awareness of the *differences* as well as the similarities in the use of words like "nature" and "law" in the tradition. Porter therefore balanced a genuine appreciation for the "Thomistic synthesis" achieved during the high scholastic period with a keen awareness of how modern physical and social science has "moved the marker" in our understanding of human flourishing and social relations.

B. Applications I: Marriage and a Natural Law of Robust Realism

The single most creative component of Porter's paradigm—a component that echoes the scientific insights of Kuhn, and that finds an important theological ally in Alister McGrath's important work *Scientific Theology*—is her dedication to the fact that "nature" is not (properly understood) discovered, but rather "constructed." In Porter's breathtakingly inventive paradigm of natural law, nature is not "observed," nor is it a "given" that one uncovers and then utilizes to build upon. Nature—and more particularly *human* nature, which is the object of her scholarly project regarding natural law—is the result of social construction. In asserting this Porter is *not* implying that the concept of nature is totally arbitrary, nor that it is completely relativistic or nonfoundational, in the cavalier sense of "nature is whatever works for me." But it is certainly not "realist" in the absolute sense that the nineteenth-century neo-scholastics took it.

Porter argues that she does offer a *realist* paradigm of natural law, in the same sense that Aquinas offered a "realist ethics." But realist in this sense does not mean "objective" in the sense of something outside of, or over against, human experience. It is rather constructed *out of human experience.* Nature is a social construction in the same sense in which Kuhn talks about the "laws" of nature—not laws extracted *from* nature, but rather laws constructed to talk *about* nature. Such laws are human strategies for describing and predicting what will *most probably* happen in a given situation. It is in that sense that Porter quotes approvingly from Alister McGrath—that "nature" does not have the status of an "observation statement": nature is not what we find from impartial observation; it is, actually, just the opposite. Nature refers to the socially constructed paradigm that results from the human effort to explain what makes human beings and communities flourish, and why they do. And no single example of the application of Porter's insights illustrates the rich possibilities inherent in her paradigm of robust realism more clearly than her discussion of what natural law reveals about the "ends" of marriage.

Porter argued that while Aquinas and his fellow scholastics certainly understood both human sexuality and marriage to be ordered toward pro-creation, she also noted that, in retrieving the emphasis of precisely those scholastics, we had to construe "procreation" more broadly than simply the physical continuance of the species given the insights of modern thought, es-pecially the insights provided by developmental psychology and cultural an-thropology. Porter therefore proposed that "procreation" had to include both the education and socialization of children, in addition to their physical re-production. And she so argued because it was otherwise "difficult to see how a plausible analysis of sexuality and marriage could fail to take account of the role that these play in the human reproductive process."[13]

The flourishing of human persons, as Porter read the arguments of the high scholastic thinkers of the thirteenth century, certainly began with sexual reproduction. But in her critical engagement with the medieval texts, she fur-ther argued that interpreting their arguments today involved educational and formational valences as well, in addition to explicitly sexual ones. And she argued—persuasively—that such a "thicker" reading of the Thomistic tradi-tion actually stood much closer to what the scholastics meant in proposing "human flourishing" than what the nineteenth-century neo-scholastics had proposed. What Aquinas meant by the phrase "human flourishing" *certainly* began with the facticity of birth: but human babies were not puppies, born in litters and ready to grow into adult versions of themselves. Babies needed to be socialized and educated in order to achieve a fully human adult identity, thus making socialization and educational processes part and parcel of the procreative process that took place in the context of marriage. As Porter read the tradition of natural law, then, "reproducing the race" had a far thicker and more complex meaning than simply human physical generation: it ineluctably involved patterns of socialization and education as intrinsic components of the procreative process—patterns that were intrinsic to the process, and not add-ons. The "procreative end of marriage," so understood, had broader and deeper resonances than simply physical coitus between a man and a woman, with the resulting fertilization of eggs.[14]

What Porter proposed, then, in *her* version of the "recoverist" project, was a critical engagement with historical natural law texts like that of Aquinas' *Summa Theologiae*. But the word "critical" played just as important a role as the word "engagement" in that phrase. And this was because she repeatedly stressed the fact that we can only approach classic historical texts like the *Summa* (the engagement part of the process) from within the framework of *our own* presuppositions and our best understanding of the essential components of that process (the critical part of the process). Of necessity, as actors embedded within the stream of history, we have to engage the classic texts *on our* terms, while recognizing and respecting *their* purposes and questions. Each pole of this conversation—both our own and that of thirteenth-century scholastic thinkers—needs to be given its proper weight. They can't answer our questions simply because our own undertaking of the recovery has been profoundly shaped by ideas and insights that have emerged in the centuries after the thirteenth century: how could it be otherwise?

Through this process of critical engagement with ancient texts, the *differences* (as well as the similarities) between their conceptual framework and ours will progressively emerge—"if we are open to seeing these differences." But the process of critical appropriation that Porter proposes would help contemporary scholars avoid two of the intellectual pitfalls which many have fallen into: one was the danger of "anachronism"—reading thirteenth-century authors as though they were using terms in the same way we do, or utilizing them toward the same purposes as we do. And the other was the danger of "hasty appropriation": using medieval thinkers as intellectual forebears without remainder, or as proof texts for our own intellectual project many centuries after them.[15]

Porter believed that utilizing this process of critical engagement with seminal thinkers like Aquinas would—necessarily—help contemporary scholars studying natural law craft an even richer and more capacious understanding of the "flourishing" of human organisms that represented the purpose and goal of natural law as defined by Aquinas. Further, Porter expended considerable time (and considerable brilliance as well) in exploring precisely the question that defined one of the "hot spots" of interest that united the concerns of both medieval natural law thinkers and contemporary scholars: that of human sexuality and its relation to the institution of marriage. To place the question of the "ends" of marriage within a more robust understanding of "human flourishing" would, Porter believed, provide a richer context for approaching an issue that many contemporary Catholic scholars have framed in far too narrow a way. Positing physical procreation as the *sole* purpose for the valuation that society, and more specifically Christian society, places on the institution of marriage hardly exhausted what the moral theology meant by the human flourishing of spouses as the *telos* or "end" of marriage. "Flourishing" needed to be considered within the much broader context of contemporary insights into what makes human beings fulfilled and happy: we are, Porter reminds us, more than simply mammals with reason. We are also social, creative, and meaning-seeking animals:

The critical point here is that sex and marriage need to be seen within the context of an overall pattern of life, one which we share with the other primates to some extent, even though it both informs and is transformed by our capacities for rationality. Certainly, on any plausible account of the place of sexuality in a mammalian species such as our own, sex will serve a reproductive purpose; but the fact that we are social primates as well as mammals points to a more complex account of the overall purposes of sex. That is to say, we are not only animals, which reproduce sexually, but social animals, for whom sexual exchange and interaction serve to express and cement social and personal bonds—and hence to some extent and with many qualifications, to shape and form personal identity.[16]

If such an understanding of the "natural" purposes of marriage and its relation to human sexuality were taken as the *real* model that did justice to both the insights of the scholastics and the important sociological and scientific insights of our own time, then the possibility opens up that the institution of marriage—considered even from a distinctly *Catholic* standpoint—might also serve *other purposes,*

legitimate and worthy of promotion, so long as they do not undermine the orientation of the institution [of marriage] towards procreation, comprehensively considered to include the extended processes of education and socialization. Indeed, it would be surprising if such a centrally important institution, shaped by a complex history and responsive to diverse social exigencies, did not serve a wide range of purposes both for individual participants and for the community as a whole.[17]

And Porter observed that one of the chief purposes for the institution of marriage in our own day was exactly analogous to how thirteenth-century scholastics understood it: providing for the "decent regulation and expression of sexual desire." But given the insights of social and physical science of the past few centuries, there were other reasons that the institution of marriage was "natural" to the human species—beyond the mere regulation of sexual desire within socially approved bounds and the procreation of children. One of the most important social functions of marriage as part of any robust reading of what was "natural" to the species was the sustaining of networks of social relations within communities, providing a framework for establishing claims for mutual support (both personal and financial) and for securing society's recognition of those legitimate claims through a variety of social mechanisms. And not least among those social mechanisms was the institution of marriage's role in enforcing demands for care and sustenance between spouses. Finally—and by no means least—the institution of marriage served the centrally important function of "providing a framework for the public expression and support of interpersonal love."[18]

From Porter's vantage point, then, *all* of these values—educational and formational, no less than sexual—had to be reflected in a robust understanding of the "procreative ends of marriage." To focus just on the sexual reproduction of the species was to both misunderstand and impoverish what contemporary society intends by the phrase "human flourishing." Indeed, her approach asserts that such a richer definition of that phrase provided a much better understanding of the evolution of the Catholic tradition, epitomized in formulations like that of Cardinal Joseph Bernardin's famous "consistent ethic of life" argument articulated in 1984: Cardinal Bernardin's argument, since espoused by Catholics around the world, was that Catholic Christianity was committed to human flourishing from cradle to grave, and not just focused on procreation and the birth of children. Bernardin's point, of course, was that issues like affordable health care were also intrinsically part of the Catholicism's commitment to "life issues."[19]

Further, and arguably just as brilliant in adumbrating her stunningly creative paradigm, Porter had emphasized (with a clear eye on a number of contemporary contested issues like gay marriage) that marriage in our cultural context had to serve "other purposes, legitimate and worthy of promotion so long as they *do not undermine the orientation of the institution toward procreation, comprehensively considered to include the extended processes of education and socialization.*"

For Porter, then, a robust, contemporary understanding of natural law had to include these *other* purposes—"purposes both legitimate and worthy of promotion." The paradigm of Porter's version of the recoverist project regarding "procreation" thus looked considerably different from the paradigms offered by *Humanae Vitae*, John Ford's model in the "Minority Report," and the new natural law adumbrated by Grisez. She therefore quite unapologetically set about *constructing* "nature" in her paradigm, using the best insights at hand.

Porter's explication of the "other purposes" of the institution of marriage can be glimpsed in her position regarding possible Catholic recognition of same-sex marriage. If it were suggested, she argued, that same-sex unions should constitute either the only, or the paradigmatic, form of marriage, "*this would be ruled out by a natural law analysis of marriage*" in which procreation played an important and privileged role. But, she quickly observed, no one is in fact proposing such an understanding of marriage: what rather is envisioned, she argues, is simply the

> extension of institutional claims and restrictions of marriage to a class of unions which cannot fulfill the reproductive purpose of marriage, but which may well embody other aims served by the institution. This, it seems to me, is a very persuasive claim. We already extend the institution of marriage to include heterosexual couples who are incapable of reproduction, as is the case when both partners are elderly. These extensions are justified because for us marriage represents more than just a framework for sustaining reproduction; it also provides a framework for expressing and supporting the mutual love of two people. By the same token, refusing to extend this framework to same-sex couples appears to be arbitrary, and therefore unjust, given the *purposes* [in the plural] of marriage as we understand and practice it today.[20]

In Porter's engaged reading of the Catholic natural law tradition, then—in the service of a paradigm of robust, contemporary realism—extending the right of entering into the institution of marriage to same-sex couples would seem to be required by simple justice. And, precisely on the basis of a more robust understanding of Catholic natural law principles, refusing to extend that recognition can be said to be both "arbitrary, and therefore unjust."

C. Applications II: Contraception and a Robust Understanding of Natural Law—"This Prohibition Raises Complex Questions"

Just as in her recovery of the Thomistic bases for a richer, more contemporary understanding of marriage, so Porter began her exposition of what a modern natural law approach to contraception might look like by a careful "engaged reading" of what Aquinas and the other medieval scholastics had stated regarding this issue. And Porter began by freely asserting that

> neither Aquinas nor any other scholastic (to my knowledge) affirms that the pursuit of sexual pleasure for its own sake is [ever] morally legitimate, even within marriage. For the scholastics, there is only one unambiguously good purpose for sexual intercourse within marriage: procreation. . . . By the same token, the scholastics condemn any use of contraceptives, even within marriage. *This prohibition raises complex questions, however.* The scholastics inherited a tradition on contraception that included two quite different rationales for the prohibition of the practice.[21]

And those two rationales were rooted in a tangled historical record that needed careful recovery, critical examination, and a "robust" elucidation before they could be applied to contemporary ethical situations undreamed of by the medieval scholastics. The first tradition that needed retrieval and critical consideration was a position that Aquinas and his thirteenth-century colleagues inherited from St. Jerome in the fourth century, which argued that contraception was a form of homicide—a singular position that (Porter drily noted) is difficult to evaluate in terms of "how far [it] is meant to be taken literally, by [either] Jerome or by his followers." The second question was rooted in the 1968 encyclical *Humanae Vitae*, and is based on that document's famous appeal to the structure of the sexual act and its purported "inherent orientation toward procreation."[22]

Porter's engaged reading of the tradition regarding the first question begins by observing that, based on her own careful reading of early medieval texts, it was impossible to believe that the scholastics took Jerome's equation of contraception with murder at face value. Well before the thirteenth century, the ecclesiastical penalties prescribed for the use of contraceptives differed in both type and gravity from those prescribed for homicide. But considerably more to the point, Porter observed that the scholastics had largely rejected Jerome's argument by the thirteenth century in favor of St. Augustine's view that contraception was more properly understood as sinful because it sought sexual pleasure as an end in itself. Albert the Great (himself the teacher of Aquinas) had gone so far as to explicitly repudiate Jerome's equation of contraception with homicide, observing that such an argument appeared specious because there was no guarantee in any case that a given act of sexual intercourse could produce offspring. "More tellingly," Porter noted, a number of scholastic theologians did not even mention contraceptive practice at all, either when discussing grave sexual sins or homicide.[23]

As Porter read the trajectory of opinion on this issue, then, it was difficult to find anything like a consistent theological justification for the Church's condemnation of contraceptive practice. That being said, Porter was nonetheless sympathetic to the trajectory of the arguments against contraception in the history of the tradition: given the values of respect for life, care for the vulnerable, and commitment to the common good of society which defined her rich understanding of the natural law tradition,

> the scholastic defense of procreation helps us to see that this sentiment reflects a deep and sound doctrinal instinct. [But] *this does not imply that other possible values are unimportant, or much less legitimate; but it does reflect a sense that a commitment to procreation should have a central place in the witness of the church.*[24]

Along with that confession, however, Porter also observed that "it does not follow that the use of contraceptives is never morally justified. Nor does it imply that the Christian community should not attempt to formulate the circumstances in which contraceptives may or may not be used." And her justification for this reimagining of what the tradition had taught regarding contraception began with her honest assessment of the distance—both in terms of our understanding of science and in terms of understanding of how we understand the purposes of marriage—between ourselves and our medieval forebears. It was a simple fact that

> there is probably no point at which we feel the distance between the scholastics and ourselves more sharply than in their evaluation of sexuality. Their almost unanimous conviction that sexual pleasure is morally problematic seems perverse to us, and their view of marriage seems chilly at best. As for the claim that procreation is the only legitimate purpose for sexual intercourse—even the most sympathetic observers regard this as critically insupportable.[25]

Precisely *because* the theological justifications proffered by the scholastics seemed problematic—or even "perverse" and "insupportable"—to us, theologians had a profound duty to both their craft and to the Church to revisit the question in light of contemporary understandings of sexuality, and to consciously *construct* a better model of what the "natural" purposes of sexuality meant for our time. As John Noonan had famously remarked in his own magisterial study of contraception in 1965, "it is a perennial mistake to confuse the repetition of old formulas with the living law of the Church."[26]

Porter observed that *Humanae Vitae's* appeal (in paragraph 16) to the *structure* of the sexual act and its "inherent orientation" toward procreation represented a dramatic departure from how the Church had structured its justification in the past. And it represented a dramatic departure from how Aquinas and the scholastics had understood natural law. At least since the High Middle Ages, the Church had begun its justification for the condemnation of contraception *not* by an appeal to science or physiological processes (which were based on what we would now consider very dated Aristotelian presuppositions about the physical universe in any case), but from a theological understanding of what marriage meant. The Church's argument thus rested *not* on what physiological processes revealed, but rather on theological reflection. Aquinas and the centuries-long Thomistic tradition he founded

> focus[ed] on the proper purposes of sexuality and marriage as these are *revealed through theological reflection*, and *then* they judge particular kinds of acts to be unnatural because they are not in accordance with those overall [theologically derived] purposes. They do sometimes speak in terms that suggest that unnatural sexual practices violate the purposes of sexual organs, but it is important to realize that this way of speaking *itself presupposes a particular understanding of the purpose of sexuality.*[27]

Porter's point here is both quite simple and quite important: that there was little—if any—evidence in the medieval sources to warrant the belief that Aquinas or his fellow scholastic conversation partners believed that their theological understanding of the moral gravity of contraception derived from the rational analysis of the physical act of sexual intercourse, as though "nature" (in some disembodied sense "out there," apart from human meaning-making) outlined the physiological purposes of sexual intercourse, which then provided the "natural" basis for theologians to build on. Porter argued that the history of the Catholic tradition on this revealed that the Church's teaching rested on a structure of reasoning that was *exactly opposite* to this: Aquinas' understanding of the evil of contraception derived *not* from a dispassionate physical analysis of the "purposes of sexual organs" and their inherent orientation; rather, Aquinas' understanding of the "inherent orientation" of human coitus derived from his *theological* understanding of the ends of marriage.

Further, the 1968 encyclical's appeal to the "moral rationality" of its argument—that is, its confident assertion that the men and women of the time would understand and assent to its condemnation of contraception, quite independently of a faith commitment—had no foundation at all in the scholastic understanding of natural law:

> Modern commentators have come to the conclusion [that the scholastics believed] that a natural law argument must necessarily be couched in universally accessible terms of moral rationality. But this is not the scholastics' view. On the contrary, they see no incongruity in developing their understanding of the natural law through theological arguments. . . . We will misunderstand the claim that the proper purpose of sexual activity is procreation unless we realize that this is a *theological judgment,* grounded in the theologically-informed philosophy of nature current at the time, taken together with a particular reading of scripture. It is not an unsupported intuition, *nor is it intended as an observational report, or a scientific theory in the modern sense.*[28]

And just as Aquinas and the medieval scholastics sought to construct a consciously theological understanding of the ends and purposes of marriage and sexuality according to the very best scientific and scriptural data available *to them,* so were we obliged to construct the most informed and responsible model of natural law in light of the data available *to us.* Given her own robust understanding of the "ends" of marriage and the place of sexuality within it, it should come as no surprise that Porter constructs an analogously complex and sophisticated understanding of contraception in light of a contemporary understanding of natural law. She begins by simply dismissing *Humanae Vitae's* problematic appeal to a universally accessible moral rationality as historically anomalous in terms of the ancient tradition of Catholic natural law discourse; it was, in any case, unpersuasive "and—to some, anyway—offensive." Certainly, she argued, the scholastics' defense of both procreation and marriage based on a profound theological argument about the goodness of creation *had* to be taken seriously; and an important component of that stance had been the recognition that "children are among the greatest blessings of the marriage relationship . . . and are a gift that should not be refused lightly."[29]

But as Porter had argued so lucidly (and even elegantly) regarding the "other purposes, legitimate and worthy of promotion" in considering the institution of marriage from a natural law perspective, so here she "complexified" the question of contraception in an analogous way, Yes, the emphasis on the goodness of both creation and procreation remained central to the Christian message. Nonetheless, she also observed that at least for the past two or three decades, responsible people (and deeply committed Christians) have come to something like a *theological* awareness

> that a deliberate policy of family limitation may be necessary if we are as species not to outstrip the earth's capacity to sustain human life. At the same time, there has been considerable debate over whether birth control is either necessary to keep the human population in check, or the best means for achieving this goal. Without attempting to resolve this debate, we can at least say that a collective policy of family limitation is expedient, and may be necessary, in light of the risk of global overpopulation.[30]

The Christian community had an important stake in that conversation in terms of how that policy would be carried out. And as a very much "public" tradition, Porter believed that the Catholic community had to participate as an engaged conversation partner in that debate. But while asserting all of this, Porter also observed that it was critically important—in terms of its own witness to the goodness of God's creation and the human procreative participation in it—that the Christian community "not fall into the trap of regarding procreation as undesirable in view of our planet's limited resources." It might well be, she allowed, that the community's witness to the goodness of creation might have to "place more emphasis on the social and communal dimensions of this process, but that should not take the form of denying the fundamental goodness, the natural joy and hopefulness, of pregnancy and birth."[31]

As Porter elucidated her quite creative and unique "natural law position" on contraception, then, a deliberate refusal of a married couple to have children was "problematic" (her word) from a Christian standpoint because the procreation of children constituted one of the primary goods of a fully Christian understanding of sexuality within the context of marriage. But "problematic" in this context did *not* mean intrinsically disordered: such a choice might be practically necessary and morally justified, or even morally required—if the woman's health would be endangered by a pregnancy, or if the economic or social condition of the couple challenged their ability to raise children decently and appropriately. A choice for contraception under these kinds of circumstances, Porter believed, was *in accord* with a natural law understanding of the good of procreation because the word "procreation" had intrinsic educational and formational meanings that had to be considered if a proper understanding of natural law was to be achieved. But under these circumstances, Porter advised that the Christian community should "encourage couples to express the *value of procreation in other ways*," for example through adoption, or the care of foster children, or even through committing themselves "as a couple to fostering the life of the wider society."[32]

It is important to recognize how Porter's paradigm of "robust realism"—while utilizing terms and insights from the neo-scholastic tradition deriving from Aquinas, and while undertaking a unique version of the "recoverist" project parallel to, if quite different from, that of Grisez,—can't be said to actually build on or *extend* the project of either of those paradigms, in that sense representing a classic instance of Kuhn's argument regarding the structure of paradigm *revolutions,* and not evolutions.

From Aquinas and the scholastics of the High Middle Ages, Porter (like the neo-scholastics) had borrowed a commitment to the study of "nature" (specifically human nature) as the most fruitful way of discovering the kinds of virtuous living that supported "human flourishing." But one of Porter's most seminal insights was her argument that Aquinas' understanding of natural law—whatever else it might teach—did not (and could not) offer the kind of objective, essentially rationalist and propositional approach to the moral life that the neo-scholastics had canonized in the nineteenth century. Natural law (in Porter's reading of Aquinas) was quite unapologetically chock full of theological presuppositions, and not the "universal ethic" free of faith commitments that the neo-scholastics had posited. Likewise, Porter's replacement of Aristotle's scientific and philosophical presuppositions with the insights of modern physical and social science led to a vastly different understanding of what the word "nature" referred to (and, as a result, what might be considered "natural"). Indeed, the neo-scholastics would have been extremely hard-pressed to see in Porter's paradigm anything like an "updating" of their understanding of natural law, or an "evolved" version of their own project. This was *not* an evolution in any meaningful sense of that word. Yes, many of the words and phrases were the very same ones utilized by the neo-scholastics; but their meanings had undergone something of a sea change: same-sex genital relations and gay marriage as positions supported by a "natural law" reading of the meanings of sexuality and matrimony? Couples working for the "common good" in lieu of having and raising children as a legitimate embodiment of a serious commitment to "procreation"? To that extent, anyway, Porter was a "Thomist" in a vastly difference sense than either the neo-scholastics or Grisez, and with a very different understanding of terms like "nature" and "law" than Fr. Charles Curran. Indeed, Porter might be said to have refashioned what "human flourishing" was, and how it was to be achieved.

But Porter was likewise a participant in the "recoverist project" in a way singularly different from Grisez and other advocates of the new natural law. Central to Porter's entire project of recovery was her belief that Grisez and the advocates of the new natural law had seriously misread Aquinas and the mainstream scholastic tradition in positing a series of "basic goods" immediately apparent to human beings as obviously true, but unprovable by human (speculative) reason. Porter argued that Grisez and his conversation partners had misread and misconstrued the "Thomistic argument" at the most basic level of their paradigm, in the process seeding anomalies into their model that made the resulting paradigm seem easily refutable and, well, unreasonable. Aquinas had never posited such "self-evident truths" immediately apparent to the practical reason as the basis for his own understanding of natural law. Further, and more to the point, any list of "basic goods" that human beings could arrive at were by their nature historically determined to specific cultures and faith traditions, and were—as such—nonapplicable in any "global" sense to people of other (non-Christian or non-theistic) cultures. The Aquinas that Porter "recovered," then, seemed to be from another planet than the Aquinas interpreted by Grisez. And therefore, just as Kuhn had predicted, the paradigms of the neo-scholastics, Grisez and Porter were "incommensurable"—that is, unable to be compared with each other to measure which one(s) had gotten Aquinas "right." And that was because each one "built" on a very different Aquinas.

D. *The End of Global Ethics?*

As brilliant as Porter's version of the "recoverist project" undoubtedly was (and no one questioned the sheer brilliance of her scholarship), there were critical voices raised about its implications for moral theology and Christian ethics. Among the most important of those critics was Lisa Sowle Cahill, a distinguished feminist Christian ethicist. One of Cahill's most important long-term projects was the elucidation of a contemporary "global ethics" that was able to bridge cultural and religious particularities in setting out ethical guidelines that touched issues like marriage and procreation. But Cahill's project began with the intention of exploring one of the most important purposes of natural law discourse: the effort to craft ethical guidelines and understandings that engage people of good will who do not share the same philosophical, theological, or cultural presuppositions.

For Cahill, the imperative for such a global approach to ethical issues became even more critical and challenging after September 11, 2001, when the "clash of civilizations" raised fundamental questions about how cultures evincing very different religious and social values might engage in meaningful conversations about the moral meaning of violence.[33]

But even granted the challenges involved, it was precisely *this* project— that is, engaging in cross-cultural conversations in order to arrive at a set of global, as opposed to culturally specific, values—that was needed. And it was precisely *that* aspect of natural law as globally applicable that Porter's paradigm seemed to make more difficult. Cahill believed that the Catholic tradition of ethical reasoning had always proceeded on the assumption that some social visions were more reasonable and beneficial to human flourishing than others, and that a genuine argument engaging people of good will but of varying beliefs could and would elucidate the difference between "better" and "worse" social visions. Central to that task was a resolute focus on the "common good"—an understanding of the arrangement of human societies that posited the material and social welfare of its citizens as of preeminent importance.[34]

But Cahill noted that Porter's work seemed to imply that anything like a "global ethics" was impossible, and that—moreover—such an ethic was un-necessary because diverse cultures could overcome moral disagreements by considering individual ethical issues on an ad hoc and pragmatic basis. One of the most important facets of Porter's historical recovery of the thought of Aquinas and the scholastics was, of course, her penetrating insight that Aquinas and his conversation partners never understood their own natural law arguments to be couched in "universally accessible terms of moral rationality"; that is, Porter had argued that Aquinas and his peers understood the natural law arguments they offered to be based in an explicitly Catholic *theological* understanding of sexuality and marriage, and not in some "universal" set of values that transcended theological and philosophical approaches to reality.[35]

Porter had rejected the idea of a "common morality" that transcended specific cultural locations partly because such a model of natural law seemed to lack any foundation in the history of the Catholic tradition (a position derived from Porter's brilliant recovery of the thought of Aquinas and the scholastics). But Porter also rejected the idea of a common morality because of her suspicion—shared by a number of other scholars—that it actually rested on cultural imperialist foundations. Making Western models of rationality and morality "normative" for everyone, especially for those in former colonies of Western Europe and the United States, was (she feared) one more example of cultural imperialism. Talk of a "global ethic" in which every moral tradition might find a "fundamental core, which amounts to a universal valid morality," seemed both suspicious and impossible to find. But equally relevant was Porter's further argument that any resulting "common core" presented was so nonspecific and platitudinous as to be almost useless for resolving specific ethical questions.[36]

Just part of the brilliance of Porter's impressive project of Robust Realism was her historically driven insight that we—like the medieval scholastics—had to bring *our* best theological, scientific, and sociological insights to the project of constructing a relevant paradigm of natural law. The upside of this approach was that we were free to construct a contemporary model of natural law that took older (scholastic) models into account, but moved beyond them in elucidating what a contemporary paradigm might look like, in the process "constructing" a new paradigm. A classic instance of this was Porter's famed argument that the "procreation of children" involved dedication to educational and formational values, no less than spousal intentions in the act of sexual intercourse. But as Cahill recognized, the downside of this very same argument was that Porter sought to remind her readers of the explicitly theological basis of their approach to natural law, as opposed to its purported basis in some "universally graspable" exercise of reason that transcended theological loyalties. It was in light of precisely *this* argument that Cahill observed that Porter's project seemed to deny anything like an "objective, universal, or common ethic in fact or in principle."[37]

Porter's paradigm, as Cahill limned it, argued that it was simply better and more honest to seek practical, ad hoc consensus among conversation partners from different moral, cultural, and religious traditions on specific ethical issues than to participate in the "misleading and impossible quest for a moral Reason which stands outside the flow of time and contingency." Recourse to such practical, ad hoc agreements across cultural and religious differences might not completely replace the kind of "universal common core" that some ethicists sought; but such a stance was both more intellectually responsible (as the moral values advanced by Catholic natural law advocates were themselves the products of a specific historical and theological tradition that defied generalization into "universal values") and less likely to be coopted by imperialist strategies of Western dominance.[38]

As Cahill admitted, Porter understood the "fragmenting" implications of her approach to Robust Realism. But Cahill, like some other feminist ethicists, feared that lacking "universal standards," there would seem to be no basis on which to critique cultural practices that were harmful and oppressive to women, regardless of theological or religious practice. Over against that fear, Porter had argued that there was in fact an alternative, third strategy,

> a strategy of pragmatic negotiation that builds on areas of overlapping consensus to develop human rights claims that can be defended from within the perspectives of a wide range of [religious and cultural] traditions.[39]

As smart as Porter's argument was regarding the real possibility of such a "third way" of pragmatic negotiation, Cahill nonetheless harbored concerns about its implications for the feminist commitment to the full flourishing of women, flourishing that included issues like contraception and the purposes of marriage. Thus it was that Cahill's paradigm of natural law looked very different from that of Porter.

7

Lisa Sowle Cahill and the Search for a "Functionalist" Paradigm of Feminist Global Ethics

A. "No Labels Please"

It was hardly a coincidence that Jean Porter's brilliant project of elucidating a robustly realistic paradigm of natural law represented an important conversation partner for Lisa Sowle Cahill. Like Porter, a member of what might very well be the most selective "club" in the United States (the American Academy of Arts and Sciences), Cahill's career at Boston College has been marked by receiving both the John Courtney Murray Award (granted by the Catholic Theological Society of America, and considered by many to be the highest accolade that Catholic scholars can bestow on one of their own), and the Yves Congar Award for outstanding contributions to her field. Like Porter, a widely respected scholar deeply conversant with the Catholic Thomistic tradition, Cahill's theological project has been referred to by some as the Middle Way, and represents yet another attempt to construct a paradigm that negotiates the anomalies discovered in previous models of natural law—even models as sophisticated as those of the "new natural law" and "robust realism."[1]

Like Germain Grisez, Cahill studied at the University of Chicago under the famed Protestant theologian James Gustafson, and developed the reputation of being a very smart and savvy bridge-builder, making connections between different theological traditions, but always with an eye toward shaping the broader conversation about faith and ethics. It is, thus, challenging to categorize her more than 200 articles and fifteen books as fitting neatly into any one ideological or theological school. She has, therefore, been labeled as a champion of everything from "feminist ethics" to "Thomistic recovery." But

Cahill resolutely refuses to be constrained within any of those labels. As one of her most perceptive and canny observers put it, in an article entitled, "No Labels, Please,"

> Cahill has found herself increasingly drawn into highly inflamed debates over the practical applications of Christian theology to social issues. One of them concerns the politics of the U.S. bishops and what Cahill has described . . . as their almost singular preoccupation with abortion and other culture-war issues. With her challenging but usually diplomatic forays into such issues, Cahill may be serving as a test case of whether any high-profile theologian can transcend the polarization that now comes with the fiercely contested territory of Catholic moral discourse.[2]

A case in point of this "no labels, please" approach was her stated belief that the Catholic tradition is "internally diverse and constituted by plural traditions." Further, as she argued in her article entitled, "Catholic Feminists and Tradition," it is *precisely* the role of diverse local churches and of the laity to challenge distortions in past teachings." And she identified closely with a new *global* model of theological feminism, which comprised

> [m]any different locations and styles of theology. . . . Some of these theologies have arisen in the same western cultures that have been the primary sites of thinking. Others are the expressions of global Catholicism, and respond to the limits of North Atlantic theology. . . . [Thus] Catholic feminists differ on what they regard as *usable* "*tradition*."[3]

But Cahill is unapologetic about her debt to past Catholic theologians (like St. Thomas Aquinas) and to her work under the magisterial Protestant ethician James Gustafson at the University of Chicago. As Cahill surveyed the landscape of public conversation in the twenty-first century, she sensed that much that was both valuable and revered in the natural law tradition seemed to be under attack—or at least seemed to be challenged. And that challenge could be summarized by a simple question: can the concept of the "common good" survive globalization?[4]

With Porter, Cahill recognized that working toward a politically and economically useful understanding of the common good was difficult enough, even within a reasonably unified national or ethnic community; but if that project was extended to "planetary lengths"—that is, undertaken to find anything like a global ethic—it seemed well-nigh impossible to secure (a position strongly implied by Porter). Further, Cahill understood the distrust of many feminist scholars that previous models of morality based on *supposedly* universal laws of nature usually turned out to be the "mothers of all oppression": what was offered as a "liberating" ethic based on a purportedly transcendent (and/or ahistorical) set of values that was always true almost inevitably turned out to offer decidedly male, Western, and profoundly oppressive directives that took no account at all of cultural difference, political loyalties, or gender concerns. The "liberation" promised by paradigms like that of the neo-scholastics turned out to be chock-full of misogynist and distinctively Western presuppositions that failed to deliver on precisely its most important promise: a model of ethics that *was* genuinely universal, freeing, and believable.[5]

Cahill recognized the intellectual coherence of Porter's argument that, even if one believed that an objective and universal "common ethic" applicable globally was either intellectually naive or politically suspect as yet another form of cultural imperialism (as both Porter and Cahill believed it often was), it *was* nonetheless possible to work toward structures that sponsored intercultural conversation, and even possibly arrive at "paths toward [the] resolution of difficult social problems"—especially difficult social problems in which women tended to be the victims. Further, Cahill was committed to elucidating a "revised natural law" to ground the feminist moral claim that women worldwide, regardless of cultural location, were owed certain "substantive material goods and protections"—goods that included family, labor, and health protections—that were essential to their well-being. And those goods and rights transcended mere formal or procedural guarantees like the right to equal protection under the law.[6]

Porter had observed that the surprising success of a number of structures of intercultural conversation *do* "at least suggest that there *are* significant commonalities in human existence that make cross-cultural moral consensus a real possibility." But Cahill also noted that Porter's allowance for such a possibility could *not* be construed in any way as some kind of "given, bestowed on us by a universal morality. . . . Such a development will have to do without hope for a 'global ethic.'"[7]

Thus, while sharing Porter's very smart suspicion of the real motives informing many models offered as projecting a purportedly global ethic, Cahill recognized that one of the most useful and attractive elements of the Catholic tradition of natural law discourse was its abiding commitment to spelling out a concept of a "common good" to which people of diverse cultural, philosophical, and legal loyalties—and of both genders—might assent. Such a concept had provided Catholic natural law practitioners with an approach to ethical issues that helped to bridge cultural, religious, ethnic, and gender differences. And it was *that* dimension of natural law discourse— of sponsoring intercultural and interreligious dialogue about specific issues affecting the flourishing of human beings as both individuals and as members of society—that Porter's paradigm had now made problematic. And the problem seemed compounded by emergence of one of the most distinctive challenges defining the last quarter of the twentieth century, and the first few decades of the twenty-first: globalization.

Globalization is, of course, almost as old as human civilization, discernable millennia before the Common Era in the Silk Road across Central Asia, and by Phoenician traders sailing around the Mediterranean, exchanging goods for barter or cash payment centuries before the birth of Christ. The exchanging of ideas and of goods could thus be dated to the earliest emergence of civilization. But the *processes and extent* of globalization had reached exponential speed by the twenty-first century, abetted by information technology, international investment, and massive migration cycles. Both international trade policies and technological developments since the end of World War II had spurred remarkable increases in cross-border trade, migration, and the exchange of ideas, so that many observers argued that the "world [has] entered a qualitatively new phase" in its development in the past half century. Since 1950, observers had noted that the sheer volume of world trade (and the intercultural interaction that accompanies it) had increased by twenty times. And while fans of the globalization process have argued that it has allowed poor countries and their citizens to raise their standard of living, critics of globalization have argued that the creation of an unfettered international free trade market has primarily benefited multinational corporations in the West, largely at the expense of local cultures and peoples in the developing world.[8]

Cahill argued that precisely *that* process of exponential economic growth and intercultural exchange posed considerable challenges for traditional Catholic understandings of the "common good," especially after 9/11. Indeed, the question of the survival of a robust understanding of the common good

became acutely urgent in September 2001, when the terrorist organization al Queda heightened its visibility among the ranks of transnational actors. The continuing value of the "common good" concept will depend on its ability to encourage intelligent communal discourse about the possibility and shape of a "good society," avoiding both gross injustice and the violent, anarchic solutions it can provoke.[9]

Cahill thus believed that such an effort toward constructing a truly global understanding of the common good seemed warranted for several reasons, not least by the surprising success that several scholars, including Porter, had recognized in *functional* and *pragmatic* agreements reached by conversation partners from very different cultural traditions on a variety of important ethical and political issues: "The very success of these processes does at least suggest that there are *significant commonalities in human existence* that make cross-cultural moral consensus a real possibility." But Cahill wanted to build on that recognition of "real possibilities" to be found in the "significant commonalities in human existence" to construct a more robust understanding of the possibilities for a "common morality" than Porter seemed to allow. And that goal was especially urgent given the fact that women were consistently denied an equal part of the "common good."

A concrete instance of the discovery of such "significant commonalities in human experience" was the statement issued by the International Criminal Court (established in 1998 by an agreement among 120 nations) that declared sexual assault to be a "crime against humanity." That declaration—built on the global rise in consciousness regarding women's human dignity—bore witness that nations manifesting diverse cultural and religious backgrounds *could* nonetheless agree on certain moral boundaries that all could accept as "normative" in a pragmatically applicable sense. Likewise, the 2001 conviction of eight Rwandans and a Bosnian Serb general in separate war crimes tribunals in Arusha and The Hague clearly testified to a growing sense shared in two very different cultural loci that certain acts violated common understandings of human rights. Further, the widespread international support accorded the Kyoto Protocol on the issue of global warming testified that there was a common international sense that humans everywhere required certain natural conditions of life, and that something *like* a moral obligation to protect nature could be agreed upon by very diverse societies. Cahill believed that all three of these instances illustrated the fact that there are some issues on which it was possible to mobilize action around something like *global* ideals of social responsibility, even if those ideals could not be uniformly applied, or necessarily understood in the same way. Therefore she was quick to observe in offering these examples of the successful marshalling of global action that global ethics does not stand or fall with a universal set of specific moral prescriptions, which few today would defend, but with the idea that there are after all some moral non-negotiables and some clearly identifiable injustices to which all cultures and religions should be responsive for humanistic reasons.[10]

Cahill believed that a critical retrieval of the thought of Aquinas would offer an important basis for constructing a paradigm of genuinely global ideals of social responsibility; but Cahill's retrieval began at a very different place than that of Porter, and its articulation resulted in a distinctively different paradigm. And Cahill's own paradigm construction was marked by a number of (typically) smart methodological moves: the first of these smart methodological moves was her argument that even a modestly realistic model of a common or global ethics needed to follow the "pragmatist turn" in contemporary philosophy. By this Cahill simply meant that any paradigm of intercultural or interreligious ethics that purported to be describing moral duties in the real world must begin by exploring how ethical questions are intimately tied to the concrete experiences in *specific* (often *religiously diverse*) communities. In other words, Cahill called for a reversal of starting point in constructing a "universal" or common ethics—starting *not at the level of the universal or global, but rather on the local level* of specific, concrete issues, examining how and in what ways ethical agreements were reached by communities:

the issue is not so much whether moral truth exists at all, but how it emerges from the relation between agents or knowers and their contexts, and how radically it varies with history, communities, and traditions. Do individual subjects or groups create disparate realities and truths ... or is there such a thing as reasonable evidence on which different communities can agree? ... *Over against the stark alternatives of objectivist foundationalism and relativist nonfoundationalism, one possibility is a refigured model of rationality that encompasses radical contextuality as well as cross-contextual, interdisciplinary conversation.*[11]

And Cahill's first methodological move proceeded from profoundly *Thomistic* principles, albert in a very different way from Porter's use of Aquinas. Cahill believed that Aquinas' insights into natural law elided in important ways with the concerns of feminist ethicists. As Cahill read him, Aquinas' generalizations about human inclinations were, in essence, appeals to *human experience*, and not to human reason. *Unlike* Kantian approaches to natural law (like that of the new natural law), Aquinas did not begin with abstract principles or values, but rather began "from the ground up," generalizing from what he *observed* regarding human desires, behavior, and social institutions. To that extent anyway, Thomistic and feminist concerns overlapped in their commitment to undertake an ethics grounded in the "pragmatist turn," taking careful account of cultural differences and the ways those differences could not fit into any single neat model of homogenized cultural "sameness."[12]

And in this first methodological move, Cahill turned to Aquinas. She observed that Aquinas had noted in the *Summa Theologiae* that in living the moral life it was not enough to simply *know* general principles of action, as though morality were some kind of "score card" that one used to judge how well one was behaving according to some speculative system. Rather, Aquinas had argued that the virtue of prudence was central to the moral life precisely because prudence was a "habit of choosing." Cahill therefore argued that there was a *pragmatic* basis to the foundation of Aquinas' understanding of the moral life, and in presenting this argument she turned—approvingly— to the argument made by Daniel Westberg in his monograph *Right Practical Reason.* According to Westberg, it was a misconception to think that Aquinas believed that reason knew the course of action that should be taken in a specific situation that the will—subsequently—would then choose or not choose, as though morality were somehow a "speculative" enterprise that the will would then act upon (or not). Rather, it was to totally misunderstand Aquinas' argument to believe that

> the reason first knows goods that the will subsequently does or does not choose ... [For Aquinas,] moral "truth" is found *not* in apprehension as such, but in judgement leading to action. *Acting* is the chief end of practical reason as well as the central aspect of moral virtue; reason, will, and action are *simultaneous in moral relationships, and in the attainment of moral truth.*[13]

The "pragmatist turn" that feminist ethics utilized for grounding its own concerns would thus seem to have a profound Thomistic basis as well. But Cahill believed that Thomistic and feminist concerns elided on a number of other issues also: similar to feminist arguments, Aquinas construed "human goods" as substantive, and not merely formal. That is, Aquinas offered *content* in his discussions of "human flourishing." The flourishing of persons and communities in politics, economics, and marriage involved a range of quite *specific* emotional, intellectual, and material supports that fostered the flourishing that he posited as the "end" of the good life. In this, the Angelic Doctor mirrored precisely the concerns of feminist ethicists, who tended to begin their analysis of women's flourishing on the concretely personal level, listing *specific* goods that women required—and specific harms that had to be avoided or corrected—if women were to successfully navigate the messiness of the human condition toward the full flourishing that constituted the *telos* of human life.[14]

Thus, even in the global context of intercultural conversation, Catholic feminists retained certain concerns that united them in their open-ended conversations with representatives of other cultures and religious traditions: concerns regarding gender-based economic disadvantage that fell disproportionately on women: slavery, trafficking, and environmental exploitation. Indeed, some of their most serious concerns were aimed at the Catholic tradition: while identifiably Catholic by their sacramental and liturgical participation in local Catholic communities, their concern was that "cultural practices that subordinate women are too often reflected in, rather than challenged by, Catholic ecclesial structures and practice, including the all-male priesthood."[15] Where feminists and Aquinas—or at least Aquinas' epigone—parted company, of course, was in the "homogenized" understanding of human embodiment that defined Thomistic models of natural law. Indeed, one could argue that feminism emerged as a distinct philosophical and theological movement precisely at the moment when it offered an incredulous, justly angry *reaction* against ideas (offered by some of Aquinas' followers) regarding what was "natural" or "good" for both male and female persons—especially the part that the human body should play in defining sexual roles. It was exactly that question—of *which* bodily capacities, *which* human desires, and *which* social relations constituted authentic goods for women (as opposed to the presumed "man" at the heart of neo-scholastic theories)—that gave feminists serious pause, and inclined them to reject Thomism as a totalistic system for understanding women's flourishing. Cahill *was*, therefore, a Thomistic thinker—but in a very different sense than the neo-scholastics who also claimed Aquinas as their patron saint. "No labels, please."[16]

Cahill's first methodological move—which mirrored the "pragmatist turn" among contemporary philosophers—turned on their heads many of the natural law paradigms explored thus far in this book. Instead of starting the discussion of natural law by studying the purported structures of universal reason shared by all human beings, or by studying the "intrinsic meaning" of human acts inscribed into the structure of the acts, or by elucidating certain

"basic goods" that all human beings (to the extent they were human) could recognize as basic to the flourishing of human persons, Cahill proposed starting
the project of defining a truly global ethics by examining *how*, and in what
ways, it emerged in very specific agreements reached between communities.
That is, Cahill proposed starting a "cross-contextual, interdisciplinary" conversation about global ethics on the *local level*, focused on the very specific,
actual *contexts* in which conversation partners reached agreement regarding
specific ethical issues. One therefore began the construction of such a model
not on the level of the universal principles or theoretical understandings
of "universal reason" (whatever that might be). Rather, one began the construction of a paradigm about global ethics by focusing on what she termed
"radical contextuality": the concrete, hard-edged reality of specific issues in a
specific time, a specific place, and specific debates. This was what Cahill was
presenting as her "refigured model of rationality."

In Cahill's supple recasting of the natural law project, any exposition
of a truly global understanding of social ethics *began* by presupposing that
agreements on important ethical issues emerged out of the concrete and
pluralistic, conversational give-and-take reality of radical contextuality. The
"truth" did not need to be imposed on the messy business of human debate
and conversation: it was present *in* the messy give-and-take. To that extent,
one might argue that Cahill presented a "messy truth," at the opposite end of
the spectrum from the clear, simple ideas beloved by male ethical thinkers.
Cahill presupposed (like all of her Catholic colleagues dedicated to a "realist" ethics) that there certainly *was* "reasonable evidence on which different
communities could agree." But it did not need to be imposed, stretched, or
applied: it *emerged* in the complex relation of moral subjects (in all their diver-
sity) and their contexts. But Cahill's understanding of what "moral realism" in
the Catholic tradition involved was rather more capacious than many of her
predecessors'. Thus, while certainly allowing that the normative requirement
for any genuinely Catholic theological ethics was moral realism, she defined
that normative requirement as a shared conviction

> that there are shared and "objective" moral and political values that
> are visible cross-culturally, if [understood] rather differently. Examples
> are freedom from violence, adequate food and shelter, and political
> participation. There are also objective violations of the human good,
> evil, sins. The ideas of "moral realism, objective goods, and objective
> evils" *will require qualification, and may be open to dispute. . . . Today,*
> *the Catholic commitment to moral realism is qualified in the direction*

of a more inductive method, more sensitivity to concrete experience, more tentative and revisable conclusions, and more awareness of genuine differences among cultures.[17]

Cahill's second (equally brilliant) methodological move in constructing her paradigm was a rejection out of hand of the need to choose either pole of what she considered a false bipolarity. In constructing a workable paradigm for intercultural conversation, the choice was *not* between an "objectivist foundationalism" (positing that any ethical issue could be "solved" by simply applying a universally true set of standards for a predetermined answer), on the one hand, or a "relativist nonfoundationalism" (which posited that there were no universal values that people from different cultures could agree to), on the other. Such a choice, from Cahill's perspective, presupposed a false "either-or" approach to issues far too complex and varied to be settled by such a ham-fisted choice. Both poles of that dilemma, Cahill now implied, had outlived their usefulness in contributing to a *truly* realistic understanding of anything like a natural law.

"Nonfoundationalism" had opted to retreat from any effort to arrive at a cross-cultural or global understanding of guidelines for human action. In thus opting for a "relativist" understanding of the ethical life ("this ethical guideline may work for me, but I can't apply it to you, as you live in a very different cultural context," or "these values work for me, but since you aren't a Christian, they don't apply to you"), nonfoundationalism appeared to betray one of the core commitments of the tradition: the commitment to arrive at an understanding of the ethical life that persons of very different backgrounds could agree to. And "foundationalism"—which presupposed an "objective" set of laws or guidelines independent of, and prior to, the human attempt to arrive at agreement about complex social and moral issues—swam against the "pragmatic turn" that defined most of modern philosophy. The tendency of foundationalists to begin their discussion of natural law on the "universal level"—positing speculative prescriptions or guidelines that were offered as "universally true," regardless of context—tended to be so abstract and removed from the messy reality of human life as to be useless in navigating ethical situations, each one of which was different and unique. And it was precisely Cahill's interest in constructing a model in accord with that pragmatic turn that led to her second methodological move.[18]

Cahill's third methodological move built on the first two, but moved beyond them: she argued that it would serve the purposes of both feminist and Thomistic natural law scholarship to revisit—and to redefine—the older idea of "practical reason." That revisiting and redefining could lead to a *"refigured* model of rationality that encompasses radical contextuality as well as cross-contextual, interdisciplinary conversation." Cahill argued that such a refigured model had to be *"pragmatic, interactive, and provisional."* It would be these three characteristics of her refigured model of rationality that would characterize the unique brilliance of her paradigm: a paradigm of natural law that presupposed that the search for "rationality" began *not* on the level of the universal, but rather on the level of practical agreements reached on specific issues of ethical concern. The result would be a paradigm of rationality that "decentered" Western presuppositions about "reason," so that genuine intercultural and intercontextual conversations could take place between participants. And the result would also be a paradigm that was self-consciously "provisional"—a model of rationality that was perhaps not true for everyone all the time, but true enough for now to reach accord on important issues. It would be very safe to say that nothing like such a project had been undertaken before by a Catholic social ethicist. [19]

For the purposes of this study, it is important to recognize how seamlessly Cahill's paradigm construction fit into Thomas Kuhn's own understanding of how and why paradigms (including the paradigms of micro-traditions like natural law) *worked* for understanding the real world. Like Kuhn, Cahill called for *pragmatically constructed* models of reality: the worth of those pragmatic models was not to be found in how they *proved* the reality of universal principles: their worth was rather to be found in the fact that they actually *worked* in reaching agreements about ethical issues across ethnic, racial, and gender lines. Likewise, Cahill was at pains to argue that her model was *provisional*: it did not (and probably could not) claim to be true for all time, everywhere, to the same degree in every culture. But it was valuable now, in these cultural contexts, applied to these specific issues. As Kuhn had argued, successful paradigms worked "for the time being," in allowing the day-to-day business of normal science to proceed, valuable until too many anomalies arose demanding another paradigm to replace it. And last but by no means least, Cahill's project was interactive: it allowed, indeed it demanded, that all participants in the experiment take part and contribute to the final product: it was democratic and nonhierarchical; indeed, it was antihierarchical. This was paradigm construction on a magisterial scale.

B. A Refigured Model of Rationality: A "Less Pernicious Form of Moral Realism"

Cahill freely rehearsed the often-penetrating critiques of previous models of "universal rationality" and Western-inflected paradigms of natural law, not least the thorough-going critique of Porter. Quoting from Porter's famous article, "The Search for a Global Ethic," Cahill allowed that much of Porter's critique was both well placed and intellectually valid: Porter's wariness of moral traditions that posited a fundamental core which purportedly constituted a "universally valid morality" more often than not promised considerably more than they could deliver. The concrete, practical applications of such purportedly "universally valid" morality were almost invariably controversial and/or intellectually thin, and were also invariably found to contain Western and Christian (actually, usually explicitly *Catholic*) and male presuppositions that were often experienced as thinly veiled imperialist constructs. Thus Porter had famously argued that it was simply better (and more intellectually honest) to seek practical consensus on specific issues, free of the cant of some "universal morality" that never worked "in the weeds." Cahill likewise recognized the validity of the thorough-going critique of the static, ahistorical models of natural law that were often founded on the "misleading and impossible quest for a moral Reason which stands outside the flow of time and contingency." All such static, "classicist" models of natural law and/or "universal reason" had to be jettisoned if anything like a truly *global* model of ethics was to be constructed.[20]

Cahill argued that, even granting the validity and power of the criticism leveled at the baggage carried by previous "universal" models of natural law (baggage usually involving Western, northern hemisphere, and heteronormative presuppositions of what was presented as "universal reason")—there nonetheless remained "other, less pernicious forms of moral realism available" to serve the project of constructing a more promising model. Cahill's concern expressed here—for "other, less pernicious forms of moral realism"—may sound purely arcane or rarified to nonacademics. But it was anything but rarified or arcane, at least for those concerned with elucidating a pragmatically workable working model of global ethics.

"Moral realism" is the useful, short-hand phrase that refers to the belief that debates over ethical duties or moral responsibilities involve actual moral *facts* that matter, and not just human speculative positions ("wouldn't it be nice if both the rich and the poor were judged equally fairly?"), or idealized fantasies ("one shouldn't steal, even if no one is looking"). "Realists" in moral theology and social ethics therefore believe that, in debates over guidelines and duties, conversation partners are debating actual ("real") obligations and duties, based in reality, to which there are right and wrong answers. For moral realists, "morality" refers to something just as real (even if just as ineffable) as gravity.

But the "stakes" in the debate over moral realism are especially high for Catholic participants because the Catholic tradition of moral theology has been consistently "realistic." That is, Catholic moral theology, following in the footsteps of Aquinas, has fairly consistently argued for a "moral realist" understanding of personal and social duties, in which the responsibilities of the moral law outline actual, *real* duties oriented to a specific end ("telos"): full human flourishing. And that flourishing is not achieved by accident, or by "sort of" doing or avoiding certain kinds of behavior or attitudes. To attempt a genuinely Catholic model of social ethics is—almost by definition, then— to build on a moral realist foundation.

But Cahill recognized that holding to moral realism while also rejecting most previous models of objective foundationalism was a tall order: the force of the criticisms leveled at many (all?) previous models of natural law themselves made holding onto moral realism as the foundation for any project aimed at constructing a universal ethics extremely difficult. As Cahill was aware, the coherence, strength, and liberating force of feminist, postcolonialist, and nonheteronormative criticisms of previous models of "universal rationality" (even models as brilliant as that of Aquinas) made contemporary applications of that once-revered tradition problematic, or at least extremely challenging. And it was precisely here—at what appeared to many as an intellectual dead-end—that Cahill posed her famous question: "can historically-located moral reasoning still lead to generalizable knowledge of human goods and relationships, and [to] at least *some* concrete specifications, even if not [to] a universal 'code' of behavior?" More specifically, Cahill sought to pursue the question of whether "moral reasonableness" might be *reconstructed* to allow for *both* the historical nature of moral knowledge (the recognition—following the pragmatist turn—that all moral and ethical questions arise in specific historical contexts, and are framed by those contexts) *and* for a common, even global, morality. Might one be able to *begin* with admittedly historically embedded and historically crafted moral insights, but then *ascend* to ever-larger patterns of moral agreements across cultural and religious contexts that would eventually take on the appearance of a global—even if provisional and purely pragmatic—ethics? This was an entirely new question, breathtaking in its intellectual daring. This was a project endeavoring to construct an entirely different kind of paradigm than ever attempted before.[21]

Cahill thus sought to construct a paradigm of natural law to address the anomalies produced by *both* the classicist, foundationalist paradigms, like that of the neo-scholastics (which did indeed claim to offer a "global" ethic, but one so static and infused with Western notions of rationality as to be unusable in intercultural contexts), *and* the anomalies produced by nonfoundationalist paradigms, like that offered by Porter (which *was* historically aware of the "tribal" nature of Thomistic discourse, but as a result posited moral knowledge as a "language game" available to Catholic Christians, but few others). Cahill's "hunch" was that a creative rereading of "practical reason" might contribute in important ways toward such a refigured model of a contextually aware but global ethics. And a further hunch was that revisiting the theology of Aquinas—more specifically, Aquinas' understanding of the "practical reason"—might provide an extremely useful path out of the impasse between an understanding of the "historicity of reason" (on the one hand) and the universality that a truly global ethics demanded (on the other).

Cahill therefore undertook a very different kind of "recoverist project" than Porter had so brilliantly undertaken. And she took on that daunting task because she believed that Aquinas' understanding of moral realism as *fundamentally practical* illuminated a pathway between the problems posed by both the classicist, static model of moral realism of the neo-scholastics and the relativist stance of the nonfoundationalists. Cahill recognized that Aquinas might "provide insights that resonate with other cultural views of the practical and 'narrative' character of morality and its bearing on moral relations among communities." And that was because, "for Aquinas, *moral reason is practical reason,* perfected by the virtue of prudence."[22]

Cahill began her own, singularly unique form of the recoverist project by emphasizing the fact that, for Aquinas, the key virtue of prudence sought *not* speculative truth, but rather "truthful action." That is, at the heart of Aquinas' understanding of moral theology was his belief that practical reason sought to discover the truth "in contingent matters, for human action is always *particular and historical.*" Far from challenging the starting point of the nonfoundationalists that all moral action was embedded in specific cultural and historical contexts, Aquinas presupposed the same thing: "moral reasoning *always takes place within ongoing patterns of action.*" Aquinas simply presupposed that ethical questions began not on the level of universally applicable guidelines, but rather in the messy reality of peoples' lives, wherein one had to discern meaning "within ongoing patterns of action."

The deductive method of neo-scholasticism, and its claim to timeless certitude in the specific conclusions proposed on the basis of its principles, is clearly untenable, [for Aquinas]. Aquinas himself says that in defining prudence that "the intellect cannot be infallibly in conformity with things in contingent matters" (ST 1–2, q. 57, a. 5).[23]

And based on that insight, a number of scholars had already observed that, for Aquinas, the practical reason's purchase on natural law was "narrative" in character. What that meant specifically was that moral knowledge was "discovered progressively over time, and through a process of reasoning engaged with experience." Referencing the important work of Pamela Hall on just this point, Cahill argued that a *true* Thomistic reading of moral reasoning asserted that all such moral reasoning took place within the ongoing life of specific, concrete communities, and therefore itself *had a history*. In such a reading of the case, "we learn the natural law, not by deduction, but by reflection upon our own and our predecessors' desires, choices, mistakes and successes." What this meant concretely was that human nature was *not* something "discovered" as a completed construct, a "thing" already existent—like some unchanging entity that floated above the vagaries of history and its "choices, mistakes, and successes"—but was something *contingent*: something deeply shaped and influenced by its specific cultural locus and time.[24]

Cahill's point here is both brilliant and extremely important for understanding her paradigm of a contingent and provisional natural law: Cahill argued that moral reason—historically shaped and tradition dependent, and not eternally "fixed" as both the neo-scholastics and the new natural law advocates posited—nonetheless gave access to genuine *truth* in moral matter, but truth with a specific meaning:

> A point to be stressed perhaps more strongly is that human nature, its ends, its flourishing, and its moral standards are not "discovered" as already existent and unchanging entities. *They too* are "contingent" and perhaps in some degree mutable; the extent to which this is the case is a matter of debate. . . . A somewhat different implication of Aquinas' view is important for the present discussion: moral reason, though historical and tradition-dependent, nonetheless accesses truth. . . . But truth and reason in moral contexts have to be understood as integrally bound to action, indeed as emerging within action, not only as "leading to" it as their effect.[25]

Among the several levels of work being accomplished here, Cahill was taking the truth of Porter's important (and demonstrably true) insight regarding the historically shaped and contingent nature of Aquinas' understanding of natural law, but building on it to arrive at a very different conclusion regarding both its global nature and its reliability. Yes, Cahill argued, Thomistic natural law discourse was both historically shaped and tradition dependent (just as Porter had shown). But the model of moral reason it offered nonetheless accesses a "working truth" that is usable for the present in arriving at agreement on ethical issues.

It is important for the overall argument of this book to elucidate the exact relationship of Porter and Cahill's paradigms at this point. Some might argue that Cahill "built" onto Porter's insight of the historically contextualized thought of Aquinas in making her own arguments regarding the contingent, narrative character of moral truth. And there are clear and important parallels between Porter's recovery of the historically inflected nature of Aquinas' understanding of practical reason and the arguments of Cahill. Yes, Cahill took as "givens" important parts of Porter's paradigm: for instance, that moral truth was always "practical," emerging in concrete situations as the result of the application of the Christian virtue of prudence (the "cardinal virtue" for Aquinas). But the overall structure and "meaning" of Cahill's paradigm was something radically new, and quite different from the meaning and structure of Porter's paradigm. Cahill *began* with the seeming anomalies produced by Porter's model—that the radical historicity uncovered in Aquinas' moral reasoning seemed to *challenge* the possibility of a truly global ethics—and turned those anomalies on their head to make them the foundation of her understanding of moral truth.

For Cahill, the contingency and practical nature of the moral knowledge and agreement reached in concrete ethical situations *guaranteed* that the resulting ethical knowledge was (to use an extremely indelicate formulation) "provisionally *true.*" It was, in other words, *both* contingent *and* a solid foundation on which to build ethical agreements across cultures. Far from challenging the possibility of a truly global ethics, such moral knowledge derived from the application of practical reason to the thorny questions posed by practical dilemmas offered the only form of moral certainty possible—a contingent, pragmatic certainty "for the present." And it *was* certain and— more to the point—it was globally *true*—or at least as globally true as any other kind of human knowledge available to human beings. This last point is critical for understanding how Cahill's paradigm represented a totally different paradigm from that of Porter: for Cahill, a "universally graspable exercise of reason" *was possible* (a possibility rejected by Porter as the foundation of the "false universalism" she found in previous models of Catholic natural law) if one truly understood what Aquinas had meant by the phrase "practical reason."

But in terms of the purposes of this book, it is important to underline how plastic and provisional were Cahill's definitions of central categories of the natural law tradition—even seemingly nonnegotiable categories like "human flourishing" that some would posit as close to the core of Catholic natural law. Thus Cahill can refer to "revisable universals" that define human flourishing in outlining her feminist, inductive approach:

> Catholic feminists go beyond sex and gender to reinvent Aquinas' basic natural law approach as an ally for gender justice. . . . The importance of inductive practical reasoning allows for variety in specific depictions and realizations of the good, and anchors them in an ongoing tradition of critical social analysis while still permitting "revisable universals."[26]

Thus Cahill took for granted that a true understanding of moral reason—and thus of natural law—was to be found not in eternal, ahistorical principles, nor in fixed and always-true "basic goods" that set the ends and meanings of human flourishing quite apart from, and anterior to, human action. Rather, both truth and moral reason emerged within human action. Practical reason *was* "practical" in the root sense of the Greek word on which that word was based: *praxis*. The truth was found in the doing—in action—of human interaction with both the real world and with other human beings. Practical reason (just as Aquinas had argued centuries earlier) was the key to understanding how Christian ethics worked. But in this, Cahill offered a completely new understanding of what Aquinas had meant by the phrase "universally accessible terms of moral rationality." With Porter, Cahill allowed that the only possible "global" understanding of moral guidelines had to be found in contingent, practical agreements: where Cahill parted company with Porter was in her belief that the resulting accords were considerably *more* than simply ad hoc working agreements that lacked any basis in a genuinely real universal moral foundation. That foundation, for Cahill, *was natural law*, but a natural law that allowed for "reversible universals" nonetheless.[27]

In her own recovery of the thought of Aquinas, Cahill argued that for the Angelic Doctor the "practical reason" arose "*only within contingent states of affairs.*" That is, the context of decision making in which the practical reason operated was one in which the moral actor or actors had to choose between competing options, *not* knowing ahead of time which option, or set of options, would be chosen as embodying the "true" moral position. For Cahill, then, moral truth was a truth of action: it did not depend on some comparison between a specific human act with some universal yardstick that was (somehow) always true, even before human action commenced. But unlike Porter, Cahill believed that the ethical decisions reached by conversation partners in contingent situations, always utilizing the cardinal virtue of prudence, was *not* contingent: it was both ethically true and (with a nod to the Catholic tradition of moral realism) *real* ethical knowledge. Thus, while the situation in which ethical accord was reached was contingent, historically defined, and approached in different culturally determined ways by the various participants, the ethical accord hammered out was genuinely reliable as a basis for ethical action. And part of that ethical certitude was based in the central role that Cahill accorded the idea of pluralism.

A second component distinguishing Cahill's paradigm from that of Porter is her focus on cultural and religious pluralism as central to her understanding of why ethical reasoning was *true*. And in this she turned—quite counterintuitively—to Aquinas. Aquinas had famously drawn a crucial distinction between the first (basic) principles of natural law and the pragmatic application of those principles to specific cases. Aquinas had therefore distinguished the basic principles of natural law from the pragmatic patterns of behavior that contribute to human flourishing, which all human societies legislate about and categorize, although they do so in very different ways. This last point—at first glance, anyway—might seem like a "throw-away" line that Aquinas offered to acknowledge the sheer "manyness" of human reality: yes, of course various human societies had legislated differing kinds of behavior as morally good or bad. But for Cahill that insight was the opposite of a throw-away line. Cahill argued that it was important to remember that this latter category (the welter of human cultures that approached everything—including ethical decisions—in various ways) constituted the "real world" in which all ethical decisions had to be made. That pluralism constituted not a challenge to the possibility of global ethics but also the foundation on which global ethics was both possible and crucially important: a truly global ethics did not depend on a uniform set of moral guidelines completely understood and categorized before intercultural conversations began. The exact opposite was the case: for global ethical discussions to be genuinely *global*, "manyness" was the required context, as opposed to a uniform speculative understanding of moral truth.[28]

What all of this implied, Cahill was quick to point out, was that "moral truths" were not so much discovered as "realized" inductively, experientially, interactively, and "in the midst of *concrete human problems and projects.*" Further, and considerably more to the point, all of this implied that the real possibility of elucidating a truly global ethics need not (indeed, should not) begin in the realm of abstract (or deductive) reason or speculation; on the contrary, a truly global ethics—establishing agreement and accord on common concerns—had to begin with considerations of *practical* political and cultural issues and affairs. If the construction of a viable *global* ethics were to begin on the concrete, local level of quite specific issues, then

> the question is whether there are some human relationships, undertakings, or crises that are, or are becoming, "global" in scope, and some equally wide moral truths that *are known by engaging them.* The fact that certain transnational or even global institutions have de facto emerged due to communication, information, and transportation technologies, and are *already shaping patterns of relationship among human persons and communities, means that there is a transnational and even global moral sphere,* not just a "political" or "economic" one.[29]

Cahill's paradigm for a truly global ethics thus began "in the midst of concrete human problems and projects," and *not* on the universal, speculative level that everyone agreed on before conversation began: it was in the process of tackling specific practical issues that certain patterns and webs of meaning began to emerge. Those patterns were not imposed on the specific issues and questions, but rather emerged from *within* the thorny questions being addressed. What Cahill predicted was that this inductive process of analysis would yield the discovery that there *were* some human relationships or undertakings that evinced deep commonalities and shared concerns—commonalities about which one might appropriately use the term "global." And those global commonalities would come to be known *only* by engaging them. It was in the process of engagement, then, that certain values and beliefs would come to be understood as part of a truly global moral sphere—a sphere as real and as relevant as the global political and economic spheres that preoccupied transnational corporations. Indeed, this process of working toward a global ethics from the most local level would reveal that "moral concern, moral obligation, and the possibility of moral action exist today in expanding circles of relationship, and *it is here that reasonableness and truth find their practical meaning and are tested.*"[30]

C. A Truly Global Ethics: "Expanded Circles of Relationship"

The third feature of Cahill's paradigm that distinguished it in important ways from that of Porter was her argument that awareness of moral obligations—and the possibility for considered moral action across the divides of cultural, religious, and political differences—existed in "expanded circles of relationship." Those expanded circles progressively drew in more (and more diverse) groups of stakeholders who had come to see the moral "truth" of the stance taken on the ethical issues considered. It was *there*—in the expanding circles of relationship—that reasonableness and even truth found their meaning and (equally to the point) were tested. And the "test" that would be applied in those expanding circles, across cultures and national loyalties, would involve hard questions: are international relationships and agreements advancing or demeaning the *global* common good? Are there, in fact, common moral values to guide the long-term and increasingly complex relations among cultures? Is there really anything like "common values" that might command a reasonable consensus because they are recognized as embodying a "human truth" that transcends specific cultures and religious settings? And these questions had special pertinence for understanding the ethical rights of women, and the duties of societies to protect those rights—rights which included reproductive and family issues. What Cahill therefore proposed was a test for discerning in some detail the possibility of genuinely *shared* moral perceptions on a global scale; and it would be a hard test.[31]

Part and parcel of testing the possibilities inherent in these "expanding circles" was her assertion (resting on insights elucidated by the famed Vietnamese Catholic theologian Peter Phan) that "praxis is the criterion of truth." That is, the truth of a statement can only be measured or tested by how well it worked *in practice*—by how well (or badly) a proposed moral value or insight actually fostered and abetted global consensus and accord. In such a methodological approach to global ethics, theory and practice were always dialectically related—they were always "in perpetual motion, so that the pendulum of cognition never comes to a dead stop."

And it is precisely here that the fourth component of Cahill's paradigm emerges to mark it as both unique and distinctive in terms of Porter's model. In Cahill's deft handling of the possibilities for a truly global ethics, the only reliable test for understanding moral truth was the experience of how well any given value, commitment, or set of guidelines *actually fared* in eliciting assent and concerted action on a concrete ethical question. It was this very inductive system that turned the reductive systems of both neo-scholasticism and the new natural law on its head. Further, such an inductive approach to the question of "moral truthfulness" opened up the possibility of a genuinely "global" understanding of ethics that distinguished Cahill's paradigm from Porter's. As Cahill would have it, one began the consideration of a workable paradigm of a global "natural law" by examining where the conversations between diverse partners, studying issues that crossed international borders, *actually went*. Like Phan, Cahill understood her project to be about "fellow travelers on a common journey to a new destination." The end of that journey was not predetermined or already understood by any or all of the conversation partners. And the end or "telos" of that common journey would be to "construct a new harmony" (which is not the same as a *false universalism*"). In terms of the concerns of this book, that "new harmony" resulting from the common journey of diverse pilgrims described by Cahill *functioned* remarkably like what Catholic theologians had termed "natural law." But it was a model of natural law that could only emerge contingently from conversations "on the way," conversations in which no set of participants already possessed the "right answers."[32]

Cahill's project thus had the feel of a high-wire act of considerable energy and brilliance; it also felt like a high-wire act without the net of a "preset" natural law that already had the answers. In Cahill's paradigm there was no cosmic "crib sheet" that one could check to see how close to the "right answer" one was. And Cahill was the person most aware of the stakes involved: the core question here was whether there was anything remotely like that "new harmony" outside of Christian theology. The question was a searching one— "searching" in several senses because no such journey had ever been proposed by an advocate of natural law committed to the Catholic idea of a common good that transcended specific cultures. It was thus a "searching question" in that the search itself would reveal an answer that was not predetermined or historically limited. The answer would avoid *both* the "false universalism" that Porter had identified as one of the problematic inheritances of both neo-scholasticism and the new natural law *and* the kind of "tribal," historically determined understanding of natural law discourse that Porter had recognized as necessarily culturally specific and *nonglobal*—nonglobal precisely because it emerged in, and was specific to, the language games of specific religious and cultural "tribes."

Not only was the common journey toward some "new harmony" proposed *without* giving precedence or pride of place to Christian or Catholic principles, but the test for the success of that journey also had to be *practical*. The resulting moral truth emerging from this approach had to be not only intellectually coherent and understandable but also, just as important (and arguably more important), it had to *work* in actually bringing fellow travelers from various backgrounds and beliefs to a common understanding of moral issues. Cahill thus offered a paradigm that eschewed Porter's understanding of natural law as the discreet product of a historical and theological tradition whose values *could not* be generalized to other religious and cultural traditions, while also eschewing the "false universalism" of the kind that Porter had identified in most previous models of natural law (epitomized perhaps most famously in neo-scholasticism): it would have nothing to do with the easy—if false—confidence that all religions were equal, but (as it usually turned out) that Christianity was the most equal of all.[33]

Because it was based on the "hard" data of genuine intercultural accords *already* reached, Cahill believed that such expanded circles of (ethical) relationship were not only possible but also highly likely as the basis for a new understanding of natural law. Thus, to the question of whether any kind of global ethics of the common good might exist outside of Christian ethics, Cahill offered a resounding "yes"! But the test for such an ethics had to be resolutely *practical* (following the lead of Aquinas regarding the practical reason), and the case for its truth could not be advanced primarily as an intellectual enterprise, "but on the basis of *facts*."[34] In Cahill's estimation, the possibility of expanded circles of relationship "*can* support the kind of truth claims about reasonableness in contingent matters that is proper to the moral realm." Ever the realist, Cahill predicted that critics of this understanding of global ethics would object that the kinds of United Nations consensus statements she pointed to as evidence for the practicability of her model actually reflected selfish national interests more than shared moral values—that they proceeded from self-interested and not altruistic motives. She also (correctly) predicted that critics would argue that such international accords often voiced general aims in language so vague that they were unhelpful in addressing thorny concrete situations; or they would object that the disingenuousness of some of the signatories to the agreements resulted in very uneven implementation. Cahill acknowledged that

> there is truth in all these criticisms. *Nevertheless, pragmatic moral statements give moral leadership a global face, encourage grassroots activism, support local and regional structural change, and stimulate concerted resistance to non-cooperative nations.* They aid the "mobilization

of shame" that pressures outliers to international agreements to reconsider their policies. This whole process both relies on and reveals the
appeal of widely shared values rooted in perceptions of justice and injustice, funding a *global ethical process that is most successful in eliciting
transformative outrage when concrete abuses are on the table.*[35]

From Cahill's perspective, then, even allowing for the admittedly self-
interested, overly generalized nature of many United Nations "consensus
documents," such accords demonstrated that there *were* certain basic needs
and goods that are *not* all that difficult to recognize globally, basic needs
and goods that could provide a sturdy (if admittedly contingent) basis for
truly global norms and values. For Cahill, *this* was how the practical reason
operated "on the ground," offering reliable intercultural moral knowledge
while eschewing the false universalism of older reductive models of "speculative reason."

While neo-scholastics and the advocates of new natural law discourse
might argue that the resulting "moral truths" that Cahill proffered looked
substantially different—and even foreign—to their own conceptions of how
"universal reason" was discovered, and how it operated in determining the
moral meaning of human action, Cahill's model nonetheless *functioned* as
something remarkably similar to what Catholic theologians had always understood the "natural law" to be and do. Cahill's paradigm thus represented an
inductive, contingent, nonpredetermined, and culturally interactive model of
conversation and cross-cultural exchange that provided the context in which
moral truths *emerged*—as opposed to being discovered or applied—and in
the process providing convergent points for a genuinely *global* understanding
of human flourishing, while also allowing for "revisable universals."

In other words, Cahill's paradigm quite consciously addressed the
anomalies of neo-scholasticism (the anomalies of a "false universalism" and
a Western, imperialist, misogynist model of moral reasoning), as well as the
anomalies found in both the "new natural law" and Porter's brilliant (if finally "tribal") recoverist project. And what seemed to be the most vulnerable
aspect of all in Cahill's paradigm—that she offered a resolutely *functionalist*
understanding of natural law—might also be seen as its strongest virtue: functionalism, after all, presented the most resolutely "modern" and "American"
option for understanding how reality worked.

As first elucidated by the patron saint of American philosophy, William
James, functionalism had scared the bejesus out of continental philosophers
because it simply declared that the "idealist" basis for their systems was neither

true nor false, but was rather unprovable, and to that extent irrelevant, in understanding how things *really worked* on the ground. Just one of the many virtues of Cahill's paradigm of a functionalist natural law understanding of global ethics was that it elided perfectly with the "pragmatist turn" that contemporary philosophy had taken while also taking Aquinas seriously as a resource for practicing Catholic social ethics. Her paradigm addressed "full on" the concerns of feminist and postimperialist scholars in moving beyond the "false universalism" offered by paradigms like that of neo-scholasticism, while nonetheless offering a "realist" understanding of social ethics that remained true (if in a new and singular war) to the realist impulses in Catholic moral theology. Cahill's paradigm—like that of Porter—remains one of the most creative and protean constructs in the world of natural law discourse today.

PART IV

So Now What?

8

"In the Beginning Was the Grab Bag"

A. John Meier and Biblical Paradigms

The meta-narrative linking the previous chapters was the conscious attempt to apply Thomas Kuhn's theory of "paradigm revolutions" (utilized by Kuhn to understand the history of the physical sciences) to the history of Catholic theology—more specifically to understand the micro-tradition of "natural law discourse" within Catholic theology. And the application of Kuhn's theories to that discourse—a discourse that might be broadly construed as "Thomistic" if one allows for a *very* capacious understanding of the word— was undertaken to problematize what I have always taken to be an overly serene understanding of the development of Catholic theology, no less than of Catholic doctrine. As was mentioned at the very outset of this study, my own (experimental) project was undertaken in full recognition of the magisterial studies of the development of Catholic theology and doctrine already done by John Henry Newman (*An Essay on the Development of Christian Doctrine*) and John Noonan (*A Church that Can and Cannot Change*); those two works have been "received" in an almost technical theological sense by most Catholic theologians as foundational for understanding how Catholic theology "develops."[1]

Notwithstanding that broad reception among contemporary scholars of Catholic thought and practice, I was always made uncomfortable by the easy way in which some students of the tradition referred to the "development" of Catholic thought, as though development was synonymous with "linear growth" or "organic extrapolation." My discomfort with such an understanding was my hunch that hidden behind the word "linear" lay a great deal of rupture and discontinuity—indeed, at least as much rupture and discontinuity as continuity. Thus I would tend to avoid using that word in talking about how theology "develops." My devoted ("devotional"?) reading of the works of Stephen Jay Gould and other evolutionary biologists during the past few years has led to my sense that no biologist would use the word "organic" to mean "a process of linear development in which 'z' built on 'y' which had built on 'x.'" Such a sanguine view of how biology (say) develops its theories about the physical universe bears no relationship to how that science actually goes about its business.

Cardinal Newman, of course, baptized the word "development"—or at least made it safe for Catholic theologians to utilize it when writing about the history of church doctrine. Newman allowed that what he meant by "development" was capacious enough to include rupture and discontinuity, perhaps even serious rupture and discontinuity. But evolutionary theory was still in its infancy when Newman penned his magisterial work; a century and a half later we find that science in a very different place, a place where rupture—not continuity—plays the starring role in the explanations of evolution offered by historians of science. I bring this up not to critique Newman, but rather to point out that when scientists like Gould and Kuhn use the words "development" and "organic," they mean something very different than Newman's generation took those words to mean.

Some might protest that Newman, after all, was writing about doctrine, not evolution, which is certainly true enough, the implication being that he was borrowing a scientific term to utilize as a metaphor for discussing how the nineteenth-century Roman Catholic Church was related to the church of St. Augustine's day. That was most certainly the case, but the strength of Newman's use of the metaphor about evolution was that it reflected the best *scientific* thought of his time regarding evolution. And thus, while one might *still* claim Newman as the most lucid voice for understanding how Catholic doctrine "develops," one would now have to anchor that metaphor (no: Use "claim" instead of metaphor) in something other than contemporary understandings of evolution. No contemporary historian or philosopher of science whom I know of would argue that evolution unfolds in a linear fashion, or takes the "organic" nature of physical processes to mean the slow but steady unfolding of processes already in place; they would rather privilege radical discontinuity, competition, and the wholesale displacement of species by other species as intrinsic to the process. No Catholic historian of dogma whom I know of would feel comfortable positing *that* model of evolution for limning the history of doctrine.[2]

My sense is that the radical discontinuities that the contemporary physical sciences posit as a simple "given" for understanding the physical universe have made their way into both contemporary postmodernist and postcolonialist philosophical discourse, and even into theology and biblical theory. I pursued that "hunch" by a systematic reading of John P. Meier's magisterial (and immense) four-volume work, *A Marginal Jew*. In tracking Meier's study, I found his application of "tradition criticism"— that is, the critical study of how the traditions behind the writing of the current form of the New Testament developed—to be especially pertinent to the argument presented in this book.

For instance, in a very dense (and highly illuminative) examination of the gospel story of Jesus walking on the water and stilling the storm on the Sea of Galilee (Mark 6: 45–52), Meier argues that Mark's account of this "nature miracle" actually represents taking the Old Testament metaphor of Yahweh, the God of Israel, striding the chaos of the seas at creation, and applying that metaphor to Jesus. As Meier notes, such an application "is nothing less than astounding" when one considers that it is found in Mark's narrative; St. Mark's has been generally held to be the earliest written gospel, and as such was marked by a "low Christology," as opposed to, say, the "high Christology" to be found in St. John's Gospel, which was written a generation or two after St. Mark's. Thus the reason for Meier's use of the word "astounding" to talk about the discovery of such a high Christology in St. Mark's narrative (i.e., Jesus represented in the same way that the Hebrew scripture talked about God) is because the "evolution" of Christian ways of talking about Jesus was presumed to have proceeded from a "low" understanding of who Jesus was (prophet, worker of wonders, and rabbi) to a "high" one (Jesus as Son of God and "of the same stuff" of Yahweh) over the course of several generations of Christians in the early church, eventually recorded in St. John's Gospel. Meier therefore observes that a previous generation of biblical critics simply presupposed a "neat progression" of Christological language developing in a linear way from Mark through Luke to John (Jesus as "God striding the earth" in Rudolf Bultmann's famous phrase). But as Meier drily notes,

> such tidy evolutionary schemas should always be suspect, and in reality they simply do not mirror the complexity of New Testament christology. . . . Instead of engaging in rectilinear patterns of development, we should recognize that, once the early Christians believed that Jesus had been raised from the dead, a theological explosion was set off that assured *both creativity and disorder for the rest of the first century A.D. When it comes to New Testament, it is best to recite this mantra: "in*

the beginning was the grab bag." The next couple of centuries would be taken sorting out the grab bag.[3]

By this time it should be obvious that I think that Meier's *rejection* of the idea that the traditions behind the writing of what we now consider the New Testament developed or evolved in a "rectilinear pattern" (Meier's phrase) exactly mirrors my own understanding of how the micro-tradition of natural law discourse developed. Just as Meier argues that there never was anything like a neat progression from the prewritten, oral traditions of the sayings of Jesus ("Q," "M," "L," etc.) to Mark's written account, and then on to Matthew and Luke, and finally to St. John's Gospel, which privileged a "high Christology," so I take it to be obvious that an analogous explosion took place in the micro-tradition of natural law within Catholic theology. In the beginning was the big bang, or as Meier would have it, "in the beginning was the grab bag."

The authors of the four canonical gospels in the Christian New Testament certainly *did* draw on common sources in crafting their various narratives— common sources that include the "sayings of Jesus" found in an unknown document that Bible scholars call "Q" (from the German word "Quelle," meaning "source"); a now-lost "Book of Miracles" or "Signs" that reported Jesus' "mighty deeds"; a primitive "Passion Narrative" that formed the core of the final section of all four gospel narratives, and so forth. But the differences between the four gospels are almost as dramatic as the similarities, making any "harmonization" of the four narratives difficult, if not impossible. One searches in vain in Luke's Gospel for the "Messianic Secret" that provides the glue for St. Mark's narrative, and Matthew's portrayal of Jesus' self-understanding as the promised Jewish Messiah presents a very different portrait from St. John's "preexistent word," calmly ordering events from a magisterial height, including his own arrest and death. If Meier is correct (and I obviously think he is), then the "explosion" set off by Jesus' death and resurrection went in various directions during the first two or three generations of the early church, sparking *both* creativity and disorder.

This book was written with the selfsame understanding of the micro-tradition of natural law: after Catholic Christians came to an understanding of the utility and cleanness of line of St. Thomas Aquinas' use of the Aristotelian construct of natural law for framing moral discourse, a theological explosion took place exactly analogous to the one proposed by Meier for understanding the writing of the canonical gospels. There was no rectilinear "development" or evolution of the micro-tradition of natural law discourse in a set direction, or toward a commonly agreed-upon end, for the next seven centuries.

Although members *within* the discreet schools of the micro-tradition certainly *did* build on the insights of their predecessors (e.g., nineteenth-century
neo-scholastics developing earlier work within that same school of thought),
natural law discourse *didn't* progress or "evolve" in a unified direction whose
end or *telos* was agreed upon or set. Rather, later schools of natural law discourse *displaced* earlier paradigms by proposing totally new ones, in the salutary effort to address the anomalies that earlier paradigms couldn't answer, or
even allow for. While usually deploying the very same phrases and technical
terms (e.g., "common good," "human flourishing," "practical and speculative
reason"), they nonetheless put together those phrases and technical terms
in such substantially *different* ways that the resulting structure and its parts
looked and operated in new ways. And that perception of difference was more
than just a perception: the resulting structure and its attendant parts were a
new paradigm, displacing older ones.

Emphasizing that the micro-tradition of natural law was so marked by disjunction and rupture that the phrase "paradigm revolution" seems warranted
is, I understand, a question of calibration and perception. But I do believe that
the very question of calibration warrants the use of "paradigm revolutions"
when considering the centripetal forces that eventuated in very different
models of what "natural law" actually was, the kinds of human behavior that
resulted from living in accord with that law, and what the ends or purposes
of living such a life in accord with that law brought to a person. Germain
Grisez's argument that the very strength of his "basic goods" understanding
of human flourishing lay in its *inability* to be proved "rationally" (or even reasonably) finally represents a different model of human reason and its purposes
than, say, the model offered by Jean Porter. Likewise, the latter's sense that—
when all is said and done—Thomistic natural law language is finally *tribal*
and historically and culturally bounded offers a very different understanding
of its utility than that of the models offered by Fr. Charles Curran and Lisa
Sowle Cahill, for both of whom it was essential to its very purpose that natural law discourse be ecumenical, interreligious, and indeed "global" in a way
close to that posited by Aristotle. To argue, as Porter so brilliantly does, that
natural law offers warrant for both same-sex marriage and the regulation of
births presents a model of natural law that is worlds removed from the model
of John Ford and the "credible manualists." To simply dismiss those deep
differences as "matters of a secondary order" is to belittle the genius of their
authors, as well as to belittle the larger purposes of their respective projects.

Precisely because of those dramatic differences, it seemed better to conceive of the various models offered by natural law thinkers as being much

closer to the "explosion" set off by Aquinas (analogous to the explosion posited by Meier by the resurrection of Jesus), which resulted in not only creativity but also a certain degree of disorder (if not chaos). As Meier so correctly observes, "tidy evolutionary schemas should always be suspect" precisely because as he (and Kuhn) have argued, reality is never rectilinear, but rather is messy, chaotic, and finally nonlinear.

Thus talking about natural law is messy and chaotic, and the development of human models of it are, by definition, nonlinear because reality is always more complex than any model we can construct to explain it.

Acknowledgments

MANY FINE INTELLIGENCES helped in the writing of this book, only some of whom are named here. I am very grateful to colleagues at Boston College (BC) and further afield who read parts or all of the manuscript-in-progress and made helpful (and often trenchant, but infallibly correct) suggestions to fine-tune its arguments: my very smart colleagues Cathleen Kaveny (of BC's Law School and Theology Department) and James Bretzke, S.J. (of BC's School of Theology and Ministry) read the entire manuscript in an earlier incarnation and offered a significant number of helpful suggestions and editorial points. Further afield, Meghan Clarke (a rising star in the Theology Department at St. John's University in New York) offered smart comments that helped me hone the last three chapters. I am also grateful to the very smart members of the Faculty Colloquium on American Religion at Boston University (under the able convening of Professor Jon Roberts) who read the first two chapters when freshly written, and offered important insights that helped me rewrite them. Professor Andrew Jewett in the latter group was especially helpful to me for understanding Kuhn's place in the larger context of the history of science. Peter Fay, a gifted doctoral student in BC's Theology Department, answered my late-night emails for same-day library research with an amazing alacrity and cheerfulness, given that he was simultaneously engaged in writing seminar papers for his own courses. My editor at Oxford, Theo Calderara, read the entire manuscript with his famous editorial acumen, sending me questions about style and substance that always turned out to be apposite and unnervingly correct in clarifying the arguments of the book. To all of these talented colleagues I gratefully acknowledge a debt that can be confessed but not fully repaid.

David Quigley, BC's able and supportive Provost and Dean of Faculties, provided a welcome sabbatical and generous research support at the end of my term as Dean that enabled me to write a significant part of this book. The rector of the Jesuit community at BC, Robert Keane, S.J., supported this project from the first, and offered me generous financial support during the 2016–17 academic year.

Finally, this book is dedicated to three individuals who, in very different ways, helped me on my scholarly journey, and made that journey both lively and memorable. Ruby Hugh (whom I first met while a graduate student at Harvard, and now happily a Chestnut Hill neighbor) and Jim Breztke (a fellow Jesuit and himself a much-respected moral theologian) have been, as the inscription at the beginning of this book confesses, "the best of friends" to me, and filled my year of writing with much laughter and good food. And at long last I can make good on a debt incurred in 1981, when I walked into C. Conrad Wright's office in the Andover Harvard Library and asked him to serve as my mentor in the study of American religion. Conrad was a wry and witty but intellectually demanding classroom presence, and as Bartlett Lecturer in New England Church History at Harvard a magisterial scholar of one of the most revered religious traditions in our country. He was a superb mentor to me, and I acknowledge my debt to him with gratitude and affection.

Notes

EPIGRAPH

1. "Se voggliamo che tutto rimanga come e, bisogna che tutto cambi." Giuseppe Tomasi di Lampedusa, *Il Gattopardo*, 1.

INTRODUCTION

1. Edwin El-Mahassni, "Kuhn's Structural Revolutions and the Development of Christian Doctrine: A Systematic Discussion," *Heythrop Journal* (2017):. El-Mahassni was referencing Peter Toon, *The Development of Doctrine in the Church* (Grand Rapids: Eerdmans Publishing Company, 1979). "Nearly thirty years [after the publication of Kuhn's book], Hans Kung provided an exposition of Kuhn's ideas with applications to theology by dividing the history of Christianity into epochs. Toon agreed with Kuhn when he noted 'doctrine is seen as a historically conditioned response by the Church to questions put to her at a particular time and place by the world or by her members.' If theology is the framework by which questions about God are asked, then doctrines are the answers given to those questions. Further, if theology underwent several paradigm changes through history, then it is imperative that the sorts of answers which a particular worldview also be expounded upon." 2.

2. My very smart colleague Dr. Cathleen Kaveny (with joint appointments in the Law School and the Theology Department at Boston College) suggested that I use the categories of "macro-traditions" and "micro-traditions" to get at these issues, and I gratefully acknowledge her help on this.

3. Among the best studies of the history of Catholic moral theology are: John Mahoney, *The Making of Moral Theology: A Study of the Roman Catholic Tradition* (New York: Oxford University Press, 1987); Charles Curran, *The Origins of Moral Theology in the United States* (Washington, DC: Georgetown University Press, 1997); Albert Jonsen and Stephen Toulmin, *The Abuse of Casuistry* (Berkeley: University of California Press, 1988); James F. Keenan, *A History of Catholic Moral Theology in the Twentieth Century*

(New York: Continuum, 2010). Keenan's work has been especially important in shaping my own understanding of the development of Catholic moral theology.

4. Margaret Farley, "Ethics, Ecclesiology, and the Grace of Self-Doubt," in *A Call to Fidelity: On the Moral Theology of Charles Curran*, eds. Timothy O'Connell, Thomas Shannon, and James Walter (Washington, DC: Georgetown University Press, 2002), 55–75.

CHAPTER I

1. John Henry Newman, *An Essay on the Development of Christian Doctrine* (London: J. Toovey, 1846), chapter 1, section 1, part 7.

2. Oliver Wendell Holmes, "The Deacon's Masterpiece, or The Wonderful 'One-Hoss Shay': A Logical Story." The first stanza reads:

> *Have you heard of the wonderful one-hoss shay,*
> *That was built in such a local way*
> *It ran a hundred years to the day,*
> *And then, of a sudden, it—ah, but stay.*
> *I'll tell you what happened without delay,*
> *Scaring the parson into fits,*
> *Frightening people out of their wits—*
> *Have you ever heard of that, I say?*

Exactly one hundred years to the day after its construction,

> *The parson was working his Sunday's text,*
> *Had got to fifthly, and stopped perplexed*
> *At what the—Moses—was coming next,*
> *All at once the horse stood still,*
> *Close by the meet'n-house on the hill*
> *First a shiver, then a thrill,*
> *Then something decidedly like a spill—*
> ....
> *And what do you think the parson found*
> *When he got up and stared around?*
> *The poor old chaise in a heap or mound*
> *As if it had been to the mill and ground!*
> *You see, of course, if you're not a dunce,*
> *How it went to pieces all at once—*
> *All at once, and nothing first*
> *Just as bubbles do when they burst.*
> *Logic is logic. That's all I say."*

3. On Puritanism's—or Reformed Protestantism's—much-vaunted intellectual system building, the classic work is the first volume of Perry Miller's *The New England*

Mind: The Seventeenth Century (Cambridge: Harvard University Press, 1939). See especially chapters 1 ("The Augustinian Strain of Piety"), 3 ("The Intellectual Character"), and 4 ("The Intellectual Heritage"). The *Westminster Confession of Faith*, hammered out by Calvinist theologians meeting in London in the seventeenth century, represented the official confession of faith for the "Non-separating Congregationalists" (Puritans) who settled in New England after 1620. It embodied the British "take" on John Calvin's classic work, *The Institutes of the Christian Religion*, and was considered the best creedal interpretation of Christianity by Congregationalists, Presbyterians, and (certain) Baptists from the seventeenth century to the emergence of the Unitarian movement in Massachusetts in the first few decades of the nineteenth century. See J. H. Leith, "The Westminster Confession of Faith in American Presbyterianism," in *The Westminster Confession in the Church Today*, ed. A. I. C. Heron (St. Andres [Scotland]: St. Andrews Press, 1982). The best account—by far—of the emergence of Unitarianism in North America is C. Conrad Wright's *The Beginnings of Unitarianism in America* (Boston: Beacon Press, 1955). I refer to the Puritans as Calvin's "stepchildren" because, while Calvin was one of the main sources for British Puritanism, it was not the only source. And by the time of the migration to New England, British thinkers like William Ames and William Perkins had constructed significant additions to the pure Calvinist system, most notably the "Federal" (covenantal) understanding of God's foreknowledge. They were, then, less children than stepchildren—once removed—from Calvin's *Institutes*.

4. Aristotle, *Rhetoric*, Book 1, chapter 13 (http://rhetoric.eserver.org/aristotle/rhe1-13.html). Max Shellens, "Aristotle on Natural Law," *Natural Law Forum* 4V (1959): 72ff. Ross Corbett, "The Question of Natural Law in Aristotle," *History of Political Thought* 30 (2012): 229ff.

5. J. Ackrill, "Aristotle on Eudaimonia," in *Essays in Aristotle's Ethics*, ed. Amalie Oksenberg Rorty (Berkeley: University of California Press, 1980), 15–34.

6. St. Thomas was identified as "Aquinas" after the name of the Italian town where he was born (Aquino). His teaching was respected and was considered so authoritative by Catholic thinkers that he was named a "Doctor of the Church" (i.e., a teacher who helped define the authoritative teaching of the Church itself). Ralph McInerny, "Ethics," in *The Cambridge Companion to Aquinas*, eds. Norman Kretzmann and Eleonore Stump (Cambridge: Cambridge University Press, 1993), 196–216. Vernon Bourke, "Is Aquinas a Natural Law Theorists?" *The Monist* 58 (1974): 52–66. Anthony Liska, *Aquinas' Theory of Natural Law: An Analytic Reconstruction* (New York: Oxford University Press, 1997).

7. Quote from Charles Curran, *Tensions in Moral Theology* (Notre Dame: University of Notre Dame Press, 1988), 97. See also Stephen Pope, "Overview of the Ethics of Thomas Aquinas," in *The Ethics of Aquinas* (Washington: Georgetown University Press, 2002), 49ff.

8. Eleonor Stump, "Aquinas on Faith and Goodness," in *The Concept of the Good in Metaphysics and Philosophical Theology*, ed. Scott MacDonald (Ithaca: Cornell University Press, 1991), 188. John Jenkins, *Knowledge and Faith in Thomas Aquinas*

(Cambridge: Cambridge University Press, 1997), 190. Alasdair MacIntyre, *Three Rival Versions of Moral Inquiry: Encyclopedia, Genealogy, and Tradition* (Notre Dame: University of Notre Dame Press, 1991), 133–135.

9. Scott McDonald, "Introduction: The Relation between Being and Goodness," in *The Concept of the Good in Metaphysics and Philosophical Theology* (Ithaca: Cornell University Press, 1991), 5. Norman Kretzmann and Eleonore Stump, "Being and Goodness," in *Divine and Human Action: Essays in the Metaphysics of Theism*, ed. Thomas Morris (Ithaca: Cornell University Press, 1988), 287.

10. St. Thomas was known as the "Angelic Doctor" because of the beauty and clarity of his teaching, as well as because of his own ascetic life ("angelic"). In referring to the scholastics' teaching as "positivistic," I mean that the scholastics of the late Middle Ages and early modern period came to emphasize an understanding of the Christian life that could be encapsulated in objective propositions (that is, positive statements) that presupposed an unchanging universe and human nature. See David Kelley's very smart use of the term "ecclesiastical positivism" in *The Emergence of Roman Catholic Medical Ethics in North America* (New York: Edwin Mellen Press, 1979), 230. Thomas F. O'Meara, *Thomas Aquinas, Theologian* (Notre Dame: University of Notre Dame Press, 1997), 172ff.

11. See Richard McCormick, "Moral Theology from 1940 to 1989: An Overview," in *Corrective Vision: Explorations in Moral Theology* (Milwaukee: Sheed and Ward, 1994), 1–7. Gerald McCool, SJ, *Nineteenth Century Scholasticism: The Search for a Unitary Method* (New York: Fordham University Press, 1989). The neo-scholastics' understanding of such an unchanging universe was based on their belief in an unchanging law governing the universe, whose author was God, that could be discovered and described by human reason ("natural" law). By the nineteenth century, this neo-scholastic tradition had found its dominant form in the "manualist tradition"—that is, it was explicated in manuals written for priests who were hearing confessions. See Keenan, *A History of Catholic Moral Theology in the Twentieth Century* (New York: Continuum, 2010), 118.

12. Charles Curran described neo-scholasticism as a "legalistic, voluntaristic interpretation which sees natural law as a source of obligation and restraint, rather than as a rational guide for the free development of man's existence." Charles Curran, *New Perspectives in Moral Theology* (Notre Dame: University of Notre Dame Press, 1976), 7. Likewise, John Courtney Murray, SJ, portrayed neo-scholasticism as a "detailed code of particularized do's and don'ts, nicely drawn up with the aid of deductive logic alone, absolutely normative in all possible circumstances, ready for automatic application, whatever the factual situation may be." John Courtney Murray, SJ, *We Hold These Truths: Catholic Reflections on the American Proposition* (New York: Sheed and Ward, 1960), 295.

13. PaulVI, *Humanae Vitae* (Washington, DC: US Catholic Conference, 1968). Hereafter *"Humanae Vitae."* See also "Statement Accompanying the Encyclical *Humanae Vitae*," *Catholic Mind* (1968): 49–57.

14. Paul VI, *Humanae Vitae*. The quote is taken from paragraph 4 ("Interpreting the Moral Law") of the first section of the encyclical ("Problem and Competency of the Magisterium"). Italics added.

15. Part II of *Humanae Vitae* ("Doctrinal Principles") offered this in the section under "God's Loving Design": "Married love particularly reveals its true nature and nobility when we realize that it takes its origin from God, 'Who is love,' the father 'from whom every family in heaven and on earth is named' . . . . As a consequence, husband and wife, through the mutual gift of themselves, which is specific and exclusive to them alone, develop that union of two persons in which they perfect one another, cooperating with God in the generation and rearing of new lives."

16. Quote from paragraph 10 of *Humanae Vitae* ("Responsible Parenthood").

17. Paragraph 10, *Humanae Vitae*. Italics added.

18. Second part of paragraph 14. Italics added. For the spectrum of responses to paragraph 14, see Richard McCormick, *Corrective Vision: Explorations in Moral Theology* (Milwaukee: Sheed and Ward, 1994), 10; John Ford and Germain Grisez, "Ordinary Magisterium," *Theological Studies* 39 (1978): 258–312; William H. Shannon, *The Lively Debate: The Response to "Humanae Vitae"* (New York: Sheed and Ward, 1970), chapter 5: "The Second Phase of the Debate Over the Pill." My thanks to James Bretzke, SJ, who pointed out that the original Latin of the encyclical refers to contraceptive practice as *"inhonestum malum,"* perhaps better translated as "dishonestly evil" or disordered. Such a translation, of course, opens up even more questions about how the "dishonesty" of contraception violates the sexual intercourse.

19. *Humanae Vitae*, paragraph 12. Italics added. I follow William Shannon's argument here and in the next two paragraphs.

20. Paragraph 12, *Humanae Vitae*. Italics added. See William H. Shannon, *The Lively Debate: The Response to "Humanae Vitae"* (New York: Sheed and Ward, 1970), 108–109. On the "reasonableness" of Catholic natural law teaching, Cathleen Kaveny has observed: "In the Roman Catholic community, the arguments for or against the morality of a particular practice are in principle accessible not only to members of that community but also to all people of good will, as a matter of 'natural law.' To illustrate, Catholic teaching on matters of abortion, euthanasia, and contraception presents itself as based in reason, not merely in the tenets of the Catholic faith." *Prophecy Without Contempt: Religious Discourse in the Public Square* (Cambridge: Harvard University Press, 2016), 35.

21. "Theologian Discusses Encyclical," *The Tablet* 222 (September 1968): 924; "Statement Accompanying the Encyclical *Humanae Vitae*," *Catholic Mind* (1968): 49–57. The final vote of the episcopal governing board appointed to oversee the committee appointed by John XXIII to consider the question of whether contraception was "intrinsically evil" was: nine "no"; three "yes"; three "abstain." James F. Keenan, *A History of Catholic Moral Theology in the Twentieth*

Century (New York: Continuum, 2010), 122. Robert McClory, *Turning Point* (New York: Crossroad, 1995), 127.

22. John Lynch, SJ, "Notes on Moral Theology," *Theological Studies* (1964): 235.

23. Ibid.

24. The title for Section C comes from Garry Wills, *Bare Ruined Choirs: Doubt, Prophecy, and Radical Religion* (Garden City, NY: Doubleday, 1970). Wills argued that the Second Vatican Council "let out the dirty little secret, in the most startling symbolic way, the fact that the *church changes*. No more neat a-historical belief that what one did on Sunday morning looked (with minor adjustments) like what the church had always done, from the time of the catacombs. All that lying eternity and arranged air of timelessness (as in Mae West's vestmented and massive pose) was shattered. The house of arrested clocks, like Miss Havisham's Satis House, collapsed, by reverse dilapidation, out of death's security into uncertain life." 21. Italics in original.

25. In the first published study of Catholic marriage practice, produced by the National Opinion Research Center at the University of Chicago in 1963, 50% of self-described Catholic women admitted to using some form of birth control to limit the size of their families. This and other demographic data led sociologist and Catholic priest Andrew Greeley to argue that the 1968 encyclical had actually occasioned "an experience of emancipation for the most devout of Catholic women—exactly the opposite of Paul VI's intention," in part because the encyclical seemed so out of touch with actual Catholic marriage behavior, and in part because its arguments were so difficult to understand. Andrew Greeley, *The Catholic Myth: The Behavior and Beliefs of Catholics* (New York: Charles Scribners Sons, 1990), 91, 92. See also "Contraception Utilization," *National Survey* (Hyattsville, MD: Office of Health Research: Statistics and Technology, 1979), series 23, no. 2, Table 18, 32.

26. The best description of this older Catholic world and worldview was offered by Garry Wills in *Bare Ruined Choirs: Doubt, Prophecy, and Radical Religion* (Garden City, NY: Doubleday, 1971), 65ff. This paragraph and the four subsequent paragraphs follow very closely the argument I made in the *American Catholic Revolution: How the '60s Changed the Church Forever* (New York: Oxford University Press, 2010), 8–12.

27. Bernard Lonergan, "The Transition from a Classical Worldview to Historical Mindedness," in *Law for Liberty: The Role of Law in the Church Today,* ed. James E. Biechler (Baltimore: Helicon Press, 1967), 127.

28. Ibid., 127, 128.

29. Ibid., 129.

30. Ibid., 130. Italics added to "changing meaning" in Lonergan quote.

31. Ibid.

32. Keenan, *History of Catholic Moral Theology,* chapter 5, "Bernhard Haring," 83–110.

33. Richard McCormick, SJ, "Moral Theology 1940–1989," *Theological Studies* 50 (1989): 22.

34. The English translation of Haring's magisterial work is *The Law of Christ: Moral Theology for Priests and Laity* (Westminster, MD: Newman Press, 1961). Wills, *Bare Ruined Choirs*, 21.

35. Ibid., 44. McCormick quote from McCormick, "Moral Theology 1940–1989," *Theological Studies* (1989): 22. As Cathleen Kaveny pointed out: "As John T. Noonan has demonstrated, Catholic teaching on issues such as usury, marriage, slavery, and religious liberty has developed by dialogue with those who have different views in the broader world, and by adopting their insights into its own analysis and judgments. It is beyond dispute, for example, that *Dignitatis Humanae*, Vatican II's Declaration on Religious Freedom, was inspired by the manner in which Roman Catholics had flourished in the United States, which constitutionally protects the free exercise of all religions while prohibiting the establishment of any of them." *Prophecy Without Contempt: Religious Discourse in the Public Square* (Cambridge: Harvard University Press, 2016), 35–36. Keveny was referring to John T. Noonan, *A Church that Can and Cannot Change: The Development of Catholic Moral Teaching* (Notre Dame: University of Notre Dame Press, 2005), as well as to his *The Scholastic Analysis of Usury* (Cambridge: Harvard University Press, 1957); *Contraception: A History of Its Treatment by Catholic Theologians and Canonists* (Cambridge: Harvard University Press, 1986).

36. "The Church, nevertheless, in urging men to the observance of the precepts of the natural law, which it interprets by its constant doctrine, teaches that each and every marital act must of necessity retain its intrinsic relationship to the procreation of human life." Article 11 ("Observing the Natural Law") in *Humanae Vitae*.

37. Richard McCormick, SJ, "The Encyclical *Humanae Vitae*," *Theological Studies* 29 (1968): 728, 729.

38. Ibid., 728, 729.

39. Ibid., 729, 730.

40. Ibid., 731.

CHAPTER 2

1. Thomas Kuhn, *The Structure of Scientific Revolutions* (Chicago: University of Chicago Press, 2012), 4th edition, 1962, 1. For scholars pursuing the "Kuhn thesis" more recently, see I. G. Simmons, *Interpreting Nature: Cultural Constructions of the Environment* (London: Routledge, 1993), 6–17; Ian Hacking, *The Social Construction of What?* (Cambridge: Harvard University Press, 1999), 4–6, 35–62. In the middle of writing this monograph, Edwin El-Mahassni of Flinders University published an article entitled "Kuhn's Structural Revolutions and the Development of Christian Doctrine: A Systematic Discussion," *Heythrop Journal* 58 (2017): 1–14. I found Dr. El-Mahassni's article to be stimulating and insightful, although focused on a somewhat different project (the systematic development of doctrine).

2. "Newton wrote that Galileo had discovered that the constant force of gravity produces a motion proportional to the square of the time. In fact, Galileo's kinematic theorem does take that form when embedded in the matrix of Newton's own concepts. But Galileo said nothing of the sort. His discussion of falling bodies rarely alludes to forces, much less to a uniform gravitational force that causes bodies to fall. By crediting to Galileo the answers to a question that Galileo's paradigms did not permit to be asked, Newton's account hides the effect of a small but revolutionary reformulation in the questions that scientists asked about motion, as well as in the answers they felt able to accept." Kuhn, *The Structure of Scientific Revolutions*, 138–139.

3. Ibid., 3–5.

4. Florian Cajori, ed. *Sir Isaac Newton's Mathematical Principles of Natural Philosophy and His System of the World* (Berkeley: University of California Press, 1946), 21. Kuhn compares Newton's claim with Galileo's own speculations in the latter's *Dialogues Concerning the Two New Sciences*, trans., H. Crew (Evanston, 1946), 154–176. The block quote is from Kuhn, *The Structure of Scientific Revolutions*, 139.

5. On "normal science" and "paradigms" as Kuhn utilizes those terms, see Kuhn, *The Structure of Scientific Revolutions*, 24–25, 27–30.

6. Ibid., 103–110.

7. Ibid., 5.

8. Ibid., 5. Italics added.

9. On normal science, see ibid., 27–34, 100–101.

10. Ibid., xxvi.

11. Ibid., 64–65.

12. Quotes (respectively) from ibid., 38 and 78. "The very fact that a significant scientific novelty so often emerges simultaneously from several laboratories is an index both to the strongly traditional nature of normal science, and to the completeness with which the traditional pursuit prepares the way for its own change."

13. Ibid., 82.

14. Ibid., 68. Italics added. Kuhn notes that Albert Einstein, reflecting on the period of crisis he encountered preceding his articulation of the relativity theory, wrote: "It was as if the ground had been pulled out from under one, with no firm foundation to be seen anywhere upon which one could have built." And Wolfgang Pauli, before the articulation of the Heisenberg Principle, wrote: "At the moment physics is again terribly confused. In any case, it is too difficult for me, and I wish I had been a movie comedian or something of the sort, and had never heard of physics." Both quotes in Kuhn, *The Structure of Scientific Revolutions*, 84.

15. "Such explicit recognition of the breakdown [of a paradigm] are extremely rare, but the effects of crisis do not entirely depend upon its conscious recognition. What can we say those effects are? Only two of them seem to be universal. All crises begin with the blurring of a paradigm and the consequent loosening of the rules for normal research. And all crises close in one of three ways. Sometimes normal

science proves able to handle the crises-provoking problem. . . . [Or] scientists may conclude that no solution will be forthcoming in the present state of the field. The problem is labeled and set aside for a future generation. . . . Or, finally, a crisis may end with the emergence of a new candidate for paradigm." Ibid., 84.

16. Ian Hacking, "Introductory Essay," in Kuhn, *The Structure of Scientific Revolutions* (2012), xxvi.

17. Ibid., 6. The italics are added, and the phrase in italics is Kuhn's best definition for "paradigm": "a new basis for the practice of science."

18. Ibid., 77.

19. Ibid., 77–78.

20. "As for a pure observation-language, perhaps one will yet be devised. But three centuries after Descartes our hope for such an eventuality still depends exclusively upon a theory of perception and of the mind. And modern psychological research is rapidly proliferating phenomena with which that theory can scarcely deal. . . . Psychology supplies a great deal of other evidence to the same effect, and the doubts that derive from it are readily reinforced by the history of attempts to exhibit an actual language of observation. No current attempt to achieve that end [i.e., an 'objective' observation of nature] has yet come close to a generally applicable language of pure percepts. And those attempts that come closest share one characteristic that strongly reinforces several of this essay's main theses: from the start, they presuppose a paradigm. . . . Their result is a language that—like those employed in the sciences—embodies a host of expectations about nature, and fails to function the moment these expectations are violated." Ibid., 126, 127.

21. "These hint at what our later examination of paradigm rejection will disclose more fully: once it has achieved the status of paradigm, a scientific theory is declared invalid only if an alternate candidate is available to take its place. No process yet disclosed by the historical study of scientific development at all resembles the methodological stereotype of falsification by direct comparison with nature. That remark does not mean that scientists do not reject scientific theories, or that experience and experiment are not essential to the process in which they do so. But it does mean that the act of judgment that leads scientists to reject a previously accepted theory is always based upon more than a comparison of the theory with the world." Ibid., 77–78.

22. Ibid., 7.

23. Ibid., 148. Italics added.

24. Ibid. Italics added.

25. Ibid., 149.

26. Ibid., 84–85.

27. Ibid., 85. Kuhn quotes the great philosopher of science, N. R. Hanson, who said that the change to a newer model of science is like "picking up the other end of the stick," so that the scientist continues to handle "the same bundle of data as before, but places them in a new system of relations with one another by giving

them a different framework." Norwood Russell Hanson, *Patterns of Discovery* (Cambridge: Cambridge University Press, 1958), 1.

28. St. Augustine "responded forcefully to pagans' allegations that Christian beliefs were not only superstitious but also barbaric. . . . He felt that intellectual inquiry into the faith was to be understood as faith seeking understanding (*fides quaerens intellectum*). It is an act of the intellect determined not by reason, but by the will. In *On Christian Doctrine* Augustine makes it clear that Christian teachers not only may, but ought, to use pagan thinking when interpreting Scripture. He points out that if a pagan science studies what is eternal and unchanging, it can be used to clarify and illuminate the Christian faith. Thus, logic, history, and the natural sciences are extremely helpful in matters of interpreting ambiguous or unknown symbols in the Scriptures. Augustine believed the Platonists were the best of philosophers, since they concentrated not merely on the causes of things and the method of acquiring knowledge, but also on the cause of the organized universe as such." James Swindal, "Faith and Reason," "St. Augustine," *Internet Encyclopedia of Philosophy* (www.iep.utm.edu/faith-rel/).

29. Geoffrey Wainwright, *Doxology: The Praise of God in Worship, Doctrine, and Life* (London: Epworth Press, 1980), 224–227. Catherine LaCugna, *God for Us: The Trinity and the Christian Life* (San Francisco: HarperCollins, 1973), 112.

CHAPTER 3

1. John Noonan, *Contraception: A History of Its Treatment by Catholic Theologians and Canonists* (Cambridge: Belknap Press of Harvard University Press, 1965), 532. See also Robert Blair Kaiser, *The Encyclical that Never Was: The Story of the Pontifical Commission on Population, Family, and Birth, 1964* (London: Sheed and Ward, 1985). See especially chapters 2 ("1963: Birth Regulation Goes on the Agenda") and 11 ("Spring 1967: The Report is Published").

2. "Text of the Statement by Theologians," *New York Times*, July 31, 1968, 16.

3. Charles Curran, *Loyal Dissent: Memoirs of a Catholic Theologian* (Washington, DC: Georgetown University Press, 2006). My narrative of the Caldwell Hall meeting follows the account offered by William H. Shannon, *The Lively Debate: The Response to "Humanae Vitae"* (New York: Sheed and Ward, 1970), 147–148, and as reported in *The New York Times*, July 31, 1968, 1. The Caldwell Hall document was printed in "Text of the Statement by Theologians," *New York Times*, July 31, 1968, 16. "Ordinary magisterium" (from the Latin, *magister*, teacher) refers to the official teaching of the Church, which was usually voiced by either a pope or an ecumenical council.

4. Shannon, *The Lively Debate*, 147ff.; "Text of Statement by Theologians," *New York Times*, July 31, 1968, 1.

5. *New York Times*, July 31, 1968, 1, 16.

6. Ibid., paragraphs 6 and 7.

7. Ibid., paragraph 4.

8. Ibid., paragraph 4.

9. That is, "an inadequate concept of natural law": "Text of Statement by Theologians," *New York Times,* July 31,1968, paragraph 4.

10. Thomas F. O'Meara, *Thomas Aquinas: Theologian* (Notre Dame: University of Notre Dame Press, 1977), 172–173; Charles Curran, *Tensions in Moral Theology* (Notre Dame: University of Notre Dame Press, 1988), 97; Josef Fuchs, "The Absoluteness of Moral Norms," in *Readings in Moral Theology, Number 1: Moral Norms and Catholic Tradition,* eds. Charles Curran and Richard McCormick (New York: Paulist Press, 1979), 106. "Text of the Statement of Theologians," *New York Times,* July 31, 1968, 16.

11. Ibid., paragraphs 6, 7. Further (excellent) contemporary commentary was offered by Mary McCrory, "Dilemmas of Pope and President," *America,* August 17, 1968, 91. See also the comments of John Noonan in the cover story, "On the Pope's New Encyclical," *National Catholic Reporter,* August 7, 1968, 1.

12. Malcom Gladwell, "John Rock's Error," in *The New Yorker's Archive,* "The Annals of Medicine," at *Gladwell.com/category/the new-yorker-archive/annals-of-medicine.* Posted on March 10, 2000. First page. John Rock, *The Time Has Come: A Catholic Doctor's Proposals to End the Battle over Birth Control* (New York: Knopf, 1963).

13. Gladwell, "John Rock's Error," 2. B. Asbell, *The Pill: A Biography of the Drug that Changed the World* (New York: Random House, 1995), chapter 1. For a very different reading of these events, see William May, "A Profoundly Different Understanding of the Moral Life Undergirding Contraception and Respect for the Rhythm of Cycles," in *The Catholic Faith* (San Francisco: Ignatius Press, 1997), 25–29.

14. Ibid.

15. Ibid.

16. This entire paragraph follows the narrative of Malcom Gladwell in "John Rock's Error," 2–3.

17. William Shannon, "The Papal Commission on Birth Control," in *The Lively Debate: Response to Humanae Vitae* (New York: Sheed and Ward, 1970), 76–79. Robert McClory, *Turning Point: The Inside Story of the Papal Birth Control Commission, and How Humanae Vitae Changed the Life of Patty Crowley and the Future of the Church* (New York: Crossroad, 1995), chapter 1.

18. Shannon, 78ff.; McClory, chapter 1. Thomas Fox, "New Birth Control Commission Papers Reveal Vatican's Hand," *National Catholic Reporter* 25 (March 2011): 1.

19. "Responsible Parenthood: Majority Report of the Birth Control Commission," Appendix 1, in *Turning Point,* ed. Robert McClory (New York: Crossroad, 1995).

20. Robert Hoyt, ed. "Documents from the Papal Commission, Part I," in *The Birth Control Debate* (Kansas City: National Catholic Reporter, 1968), 15–23. Fox, 1ff.

21. "Majority Report of the Papal Commission for the Study of Problems of the Family, Population, and Birth Rate" (http://www.bostonleadershipbuilders.com/ochurch/birth-control-majority.htm). Quotes are from the first, fifth, and sixth

paragraphs of the Introduction. Italics added. Kaiser, *The Encyclical that Never Was*, chapter 5 (pages 112–137); chapter 9 (pages 199–226); and chapter 12 (pages 240–264).

22. Ibid., fourth paragraph of chapter 1. I am indebted to James Bretzke for pointing out how "The Majority Report" incorporated a new paradigm for "conscience" itself, replacing the older neo-scholastic understanding of conscience as the "faculty of right reason" with an understanding of conscience as rather a modality of the human person, sacrosanct in itself and responsible for making moral judgments in light of God's invitation. Conversation on January 15, 2017.

23. Ibid., chapter 2: "Responsible Parenthood and the Regulation of Conception," paragraph 1. Italics added.

24. Ibid., chapter 2, paragraph 10.

25. Ibid., paragraph 5 in chapter 3. Italics added.

26. Ibid., paragraph 7 in chapter 3. Italics added.

27. Ibid., paragraph 3 in chapter 3. Italics added.

28. A *peritus* (Latin for "expert") was the term applied to the scores of theologians present at the Second Vatican Council to help the bishops understand the finer points of Catholic theology and the development of the larger Catholic tradition. Baum himself would go on to a quite distinguished career as a progressive theologian during the 1960s and 1970s. My own reading of the "Minority Report" has been strongly influenced by John Galvin, "Was *Humanae Vitae* Based upon the Majority or the Minority Report of the Papal Commission?" at https://www.traditioninaction.org/Questions/WebSources/B_313_Humanae_Vitae-Report.pdf.

29. John Ford, "The Morality of Obliteration Bombing," *Theological Studies* 5 (1944): 261–309. See also McCormick, "Moral Theology 1940–1989: An Overview," *Theological Studies* 50 (1989): 5ff. James F. Keenan, *A History of Catholic Moral Theology in the Twentieth Century* (New York: Continuum, 2010), 115–116. See also the very fine biography of Ford by Eric Marcelo Genilo: *John Cuthbert Ford, S.J.: Moral Theologian at the End of the Manualist Era* (Washington, DC: Georgetown University Press, 2007). I found the first two chapters to be especially helpful in understanding Ford's intellectual world and manualist training.

30. "Authoritatively sound" from James Bretzke, SJ, *Handbook of Roman Catholic Moral Terms* (Washington, DC: Georgetown University Press, 2013), 90–91. On "tutiorism," see note 31.

31. This classicist tradition of moral theology has also been termed "tutiorism" (from the Latin word meaning "safer." It is, as a tradition in moral theology, closely related to rigorism because it holds that in cases of *dubium* (doubtful issues) or in a debate among experts, one should always follow the safest or strictest opinion. See James T. Bretzke, *Handbook of Roman Catholic Moral Terms*, 236.

32. John Ford and Gerald Kelly, *Contemporary Moral Theology I: Questions in Fundamental Moral Theology*, and *Contemporary Moral Theology II: Marriage Questions* (Westminster, MD: Newman Press, 1964).

33. "Ultramontanism" is a theological term derived from putting together two Latin words, "ultra" and "mons," so that the resulting phrase literally means "over the mountains." It refers to the occasional practice in Catholic teaching to appeal debated theological questions from local authorities to a centralized source—an appeal, for instance, from the faculty of Oxford to the pope in Rome (and thus the reference to appealing "over the mountains"). That centralizing tendency reached a high point in the nineteenth century after the declaration of papal infallibility at the First Vatican Council. See Roger Aubert, *Le Pontificat de Pie IX*, vol. 21 of *Histoire de l'Eglise*, eds. Augustin Fliche and Victor Martin (Paris: Bloud and Gay, 1963), 262–310; Richard Costigan, "Tradition and the Beginning of the Ultramontane Movement," *Irish Theological Quarterly* 48 (1981): 27–46; James Heft, "From the Pope to the Bishops: Episcopal Authority from Vatican I to Vatican II," in *The Papacy and the Church in the United States*, ed. Bernard Cooke (New York: Paulist Press, 1989), 55–78.

34. This entire paragraph closely follows the argument made by James Keenan in *History of Catholic Moral Theology in the Twentieth Century*, 116–117.

35. Gerald Kelly, "The Morality of Mutilation," *Theological Studies* 17 (1956): 322. In this paragraph, I follow the argument of James Keenan in *The History of Catholic Moral Theology in the Twentieth Century*, 116.

36. Ford and Kelly, *Contemporary Moral Theology*, I, 3. Keenan, *History of Catholic Moral Theology*, 116.

37. Keenan, *History of Catholic Moral Theology*, 117. Italics in block quote are in Keenan's text.

38. Ibid., 116ff. Richard McCormick, *Notes on Moral Theology, 1965–1980* (Lanham, MD: University Press of America, 1981), 774ff. Richard McCormick, *Notes on Moral Theology 1981 through 1984* (Lanham, MD: University Press of America, 1984), 172ff.

39. "Ford labored over the Latin text, *Status Questionis: Doctrina Ecclessiae ejiusque auctoritas*, 'The State of the Question: The Doctrine of the Church and Its Authority' . . . . It set a tone completely opposed to the majority. Most of Ford's document simply reiterated past teachings—Of ancient theologians, to whom contraception was a 'damnable vice, an anticipated homicide, a serious and unnatural sin.' Of modern popes, even Pope John XXIII (though Pope John spoke on birth control only once). Of the Roman Curia which, Ford contended, had answered questions on this matter 19 times between 1916 and 1928, 'and almost as many times since.' " Kaiser, *The Encyclical that Never Was*, 186.

40. Part B ("A Critique of this Position"), paragraphs 1 and 2, in "Minority Report of the Papal Commission for the Study of the Problems of the Family, Population,

and Birth Rate," at www.bostonleadershipbuilders.com/0church/birth-control-minority.htm.

41. Ibid., "Philosophical Foundations and Arguments of Others, A., A Synthetic Presentation," paragraphs 6 and 7.

42. Ibid., E. "Why Cannot the Church Change Her Answer to this Central Question?," paragraph 1.

43. Ibid., B. "The Value and Dignity of the Church's Teaching Authority," paragraph 1. "Ford asked, 'Why did the Church always teach this doctrine?' Not as a simple reaction against various heresies. Not because the fathers and theologians accepted the Stoic philosophy. Not because, abandoning the principles of the Gospels, they followed some philosophy of nature which is now obsolete. Not because they were ignorant that some conjugal acts are sterile while others are fertile. . . . But because, reflecting on the scriptures and what they found there about the nature of human life and the nature of Christian chastity, they saw that contraception was a violation of human life and the nature of Christian chastity. From the very moment that contraception is first mentioned in Christian literature, no father, no theologian can be quoted who did not acknowledge that contraception violated Christian chastity and violated the inception of human life. Many used the analogy with murder." Kaiser, *The Encyclical that Never Was*, 209.

44. Ibid., B. "the Value and Dignity of the Church's Teaching Authority, paragraphs 2 and 3. The next paragraph goes on: "Other claims that the Church would be better off to admit her error, just as recently she has done in other circumstances. But this is no question of peripheral matter (as for example, the case of Galileo). This is a most significant question which profoundly enters into the practical lives of Christians in such a way that innumerable faithful would have been thrown by the magisterium into formal sin without material sin [i.e., would have been declared sinful by the Church when no real sin had occurred]."

CHAPTER 4

1. The title of this chapter is taken from Curran's autobiography: Charles Curran, *Loyal Dissent: Memoirs of a Catholic Theologian* (Washington, DC: Georgetown University Press, 2007).

2. Ibid., 3, 6.

3. Ibid., 7–8. A number of Curran's professors at the Gregorian were influential scholars sought out by the Vatican—and even by the pope himself—for interpreting church teaching. Thus one of his moral theology professors at the Gregorian, the American Jesuit Edwin Healy, once told his class that he held a number of his positions in moral theology, "even though Father Hurth holds the opposite—although he occasionally writes under the name of [Pope] Pius XII." 8. Healy was referring to German Jesuit Franz Hurth, who was reputedly the primary author of

Pius XI's 1930 encyclical condemning contraception, as well as of most of Pius XII's addresses and pronouncements in moral theology.

4. Ibid., 10.
5. Ibid., 11, 13–14. Typical of Haring's approach in *The Law of Christ* was his discussion of sexual sins and their relation to living the Christian life: "Unfortunately, in popular preaching bodily concupiscence is often depicted as the most grievous consequence of original sin and the root of all evil. . . . A greater and more perilous source of evil is pride rooted in our spiritual nature. This may be called spiritual concupiscence." Bernard Haring, *Law of Christ* (Westminster, MD: Newman Press, 1961), volume I, Part 2, 64.
6. Ibid., 13–14.
7. Charles Curran, "Invincible Ignorance of the Natural Law According to St. Alphonsus: An Historical-Analytic Study from 1784 to 1765," STD Dissertation, Accademia Alfonsiana, 1961. The Accademia Alfonsiana (one of the pontifical colleges in Rome training priests and scholars and famous for its faculty studying moral theology) was named after the great eighteenth-century saint Alphonsus Liguori, and was staffed by members of his religious order, the Redemptorists.
8. Curran, *Loyal Dissent*, 18, 20.
9. Ibid., 20–24.
10. Ibid., 24–25. "These developments indicated that tensions were deepening. I had been called on the carpet on a couple of occasions and told to be more careful; I was advised not to present the views of contemporary German theologians about the teaching of the church. In early 1965 I was called in again and warned about my teaching in general and especially about my call for a change in church teaching on artificial contraception. I could publish in scholarly journals; but anything for a popular journal had to be sent beforehand to the chancery office for approval. I was also told that it would be better if I did not give talks in parishes." 24.
11. Ibid., 29.
12. Ibid., 29.
13. Charles Curran, "Masturbation and Objectively Grave Matter: An Exploratory Discussion," *Proceedings of the Twenty-First Annual Convention of the Catholic Theological Society of America* (Yonkers, NY: St. Joseph's Seminary, 1967). See also Charles Curran, *Christian Morality Today: The Renewal of Moral Theology* (Notre Dame, IN: Fides Press, 1966), 13–26, 67–76, 107–119, 121. "It is a perennial mistake to confuse the repetition of old formulas with the living law of the Church." John Noonan, *Contraception: A History of Its Treatment by Catholic Theologians and Canonists* (Cambridge: Belknap Press of Harvard University Press, 1965), 532.
14. Curran, *Loyal Dissent*, 32. The Latin phrase *sensus fidelium*—meaning "the sense of the faithful"—refers to the Catholic belief that the experience of believers can be a reliable source of faith and practice. Thus "The Dogmatic Constitution on the Church," promulgated by the pope in union with bishops gathered at the Second

Vatican Council, said: "The entire body of the faithful, anointed as they are by the Holy One, cannot err in matters of belief. They manifest this special property by means of the whole people's supernatural discernment in matters of faith, when "from the bishops down to the last of the lay faithful," they show universal agreement in matters of faith and morals." Lumen Gentium, "Dogmatic Constitution on the Church", in *Vatican Council II: The Conciliar and Post Conciliar Documents* (Northport, NY: Costello Publishing Company, 1990), paragraph 12, 363.

15. Among Curran's published works that caused "concern" to the officials at CUA were: "Masturbation and Objectively Grave Matter," (1967); *Christian Morality Today* (1966); "Dialogue with Joseph Fletcher," *Homiletic and Pastoral Review* 67 (July 1967): 821–829; and "The Ethical Teaching of Jesus," *Commonweal* 87 (November 24, 1967): 248–250.

16. Curran, *Loyal Dissent*, 34. Peter M. Mitchell, *The Coup at Catholic University: The 1968 Revolution in American Catholicism*, (2015), chapter 1, 25–29, 44–55. https://books.google.com/books?isbn:1586177567. Albert C. Pierce, *Beyond One Man: Catholic University, April 17–24, 1967* (Washington, DC: Anawim Press, 1967). Francis Connell to Archbishop Egidio Vagnozzi, December 1, 1966, Connell Papers, Holy Redeemer College Archives, Washington, DC. Of the 200-odd Catholic colleges and universities in the United States, the Catholic University of America is the only higher educational institution considered "Catholic" in canon (church) law because it alone is sponsored by the bishops of the United States, and not by a religious order or diocese. Thus the formally correct legal title of the institution: *The* Catholic University of America.

17. Jean R. Hailey, "Groups Protest Priest's Ouster: Contract Expires August 31. Liberal vs. Conservative." *Washington Post*, April 19, 1967; William R. MacKaye, "Father Curran's Hazardous Theological Specialty: No Specifics—Three Negatives," *Washington Post*, April 20, 1967; Jean R. Hailey, "Full Boycott Called at CU after Ouster: Boycott to Protest CU Dismissal," *Washington Post*, April 20, 1967; Jean R. Hailey, "Faculty Backs Ouster Protest: Student Protest Closes Catholic U.," *Washington Post*, April 21, 1967; William R. MacKaye, "Impact of Vatican II Seen in Walkout: News Analysis," *Washington Post*, April 22, 1967; John Carmody, "O'Boyle Summons CU Faculty," *Washington Post*, April 24, 1967; Jim Hoagland, "Catholic University Boycott Goes on without Break," *Washington Post*, April 23, 1967.

18. Jean R. Haley, "Catholic U Rebellion Laid to Faculty: They Made Mistake," *Washington Post*, April 22, 1967; Gerald Grant, "Fight for Academic Freedom Still Wide Open at Catholic U: News Analysis," *Washington Post*, April 26, 1967.

19. John Carmody, "O'Boyle Summons CU Faculty," *Washington Post*, April 24, 1967; Jean R. Haley, "Catholic U Reinstates Fr. Curran: Priest Promoted. Classes for 6600 to Resume Today," *Washington Post*, April 25, 1967

20. Charles Curran, "Physicalism and a Classicist Methodology in the Encyclical," in *Dissent in and for the Church: Theologians and Humanae Vitae* (New York: Sheed

and Ward, 1969), 156–172. See www.natural-law-and-conscience.org/readings/
curran.asp.

21. Ibid., 157. Thomist approaches to moral law (and Catholic approaches to morality
generally) have been termed "realist" because they assert that language about God
in general—and language about our moral duties to that God—actually refers
to something independent of human construction. That is, belief statements
and statements in ethical discourse transcend human intentions and desires, and
have something genuinely *real* as their referent. Moral theology, so understood,
is rooted in the very nature of things (i.e., the "real world"), and is not simply dependent on the belief system of an individual or group. "Theological Realism,"
University of Chicago Divinity School Online, at https://divinity.uchicago.edu/
theological-realism-o.

22. Ibid.

23. Ibid., 158. Among the works referenced by Curran in the article were Bernard
Haring, "The Inseparability of the Unitive-Procreative Functions of the
Marital Act," in *Contraception: Authority and Dissent,* ed. Charles Curran
(New York: Herder and Herder, 1969), 176–192; Robert O. Johann, *Building the
Human* (New York: Herder and Herder, 1968), 7–10; William H. van der Marck,
O.P., *Toward a Christian Ethic* (Westminster, MD: Newman Press, 1967), 48–
60; Donald H. Johnson, SJ, "Lonergan and the Redoing of Ethics," *Continuum* 5
(1967): 211–220.

24. *Lumen Gentium* ("The Dogmatic Constitution on the Church"), chapter 1
("The Mystery of the Church"), 350–358; and chapter 2 ("The People of God"),
359–369. *Vatican Council II: The Conciliar and Post-Conciliar Documents,* ed.
Austin Flannery, O. P. (Northport, NY: Costello Publishing Company, 1975).
See also Avery Dulles, *Models of the Church* (Garden City, NY: Doubleday, 1974),
Introduction and Chapter One; Richard Gaillardetz, "Vatican II: The Battles for
Meaning," *Theological Studies* 73 (2012): 944ff.

25. See pages 42 to 47 in chapter 2 for a more detailed description of Kuhn's argument
on these points.

26. Charles Curran, "Absolute Norms and Medical Ethics," in *Absolutes in Moral
Theology?* ed. Charles Curran (Washington, DC: Corpus Books, 1968), 108.
Italics added.

27. Ibid., 115–116. Italics added in the block quote. "Ethical theory constantly
vacillates between two polarities—naturalism and idealism. Naturalism sees man
[*sic*] in perfect continuity with the nature about him. Nature shapes and even
determines man. Idealism views man completely apart from nature and sees man
as completely surpassing nature. Even Thomistic philosophy, the main Catholic
proponent of natural law theory, knows an ambivalence between nature and
reason." 115.

28. Ibid., 117–118. "The classification of sins against chastity furnishes concrete proof
that 'nature' has been used in Catholic theology to refer to animal processes without

any intervention of human reason. Many theologians have rightly criticized the approach to marriage sexuality used by Catholic natural law theoreticians because such an approach concentrated primarily on the biological components of the act of intercourse. The personal aspects of sexual union received comparatively scant attention in many of the manuals of moral theology." 118.

29. Ibid. Curran utilized the example of Ulpian (a third-century Roman lawyer who influenced the thought of both Albertus Magnus, and Albertus' most famous pupil, Thomas Aquinas) as his prime example of this approach to understanding natural law: "Ulpian defined the natural law as that which nature teaches all the animals. Ulpian distinguished the natural law from the *ius gentium* [literally, 'the law of nations' or human law]. The *ius natural* [the natural law] is that which is common to all animals, whereas the *ius gentium* is that which is proper to men. Albert the Great rejected Ulpian's definition of the natural law, but Thomas [Aquinas] accepted it, and even showed a preference for such a definition. In his *Commentary on the Sentences*, for example, Thomas maintains that the most strict definition of natural law is the one proposed by Ulpian: *ius natural est quod natura omnia animalia docuit* (IV sent. D. 33, q.1, a.1, ad 4.)." 116.

30. Ibid., 118.

31. Ibid., 118.

32. Ibid., 119. "I am not asserting that Thomas [Aquinas] always identified human actions with animal processes or the physical structure of the act. In fact, the general outlines of the hylomorphic theory, by speaking of material and formal components of reality, try to avoid any physicalism or biologism. Nevertheless, the adoption of Ulpian's understanding of 'nature' and 'natural' logically leads to the identification of the human act itself with animal processes and with the mere physical structure of the act. . . . Likewise, Ulpian's notion of nature easily leads to a morality based on the finality of a faculty independently of any considerations of the total human person or the total human community. Catholic theology in the area of medical morality has suffered from an oversimple identification of the human action with an animal process or finality." 119.

33. Ibid., 120. Italics in block quote added.

34. Ibid., 121–122. Italics in block quote added.

35. Ibid., 126. "The Platonic world of ideas well illustrates this classical worldview. Everything is essentially spelled out from all eternity. The immutable essences, the universals, exist in the world of ideas. Everything in this world of ours is a participation or an accidental modification of the subsistent ideas. Man [*sic*] comes to know the truth and reality by abstracting from the accidents of time and place, and arriving at immutable and unchangeable essences. Such knowledge based on immutable essences is bound to attain the ultimate in certitude." 126.

36. Ibid., 128.

37. Ibid., 129–130.

38. Ibid., 131.

CHAPTER 5

1. Russell Shaw, "The Making of a Moral Theologian," in *The Catholic World Report* (March 1996): 4–5. At www.ewtn.com/library/HOMELIBR/GRISEZ.TXT. See also "Grisez and Colleagues: The Way of the Lord Jesus," 6, at http://www. twotlj.org/grisez_collaborators.html. My own reading of Grisez's classic work, *The Way of the Lord Jesus* (Chicago: Franciscan Herald Press, 1983), has been influenced by Robert George's smart reading of the new natural law in *Natural Law and Moral Inquiry: Ethics, Metaphysics, and Politics in the Work of Germain Grisez* (Washington, DC: Georgetown University Press, 1998). The "foundational text" for understanding Grisez's model of the new natural law is *Contraception and Natural Law* (Milwaukee: Bruce Publishing Company, 1964), 20–26.

2. Samuel Gregg, "New Natural Law," *First Principles: The Journal* (July 2012): 1. The Intercollegiate Studies Institute, at www.firstprinciplesjournal.com/index.aspx.

3. Russell Shaw, "Grisez and Colleagues," 6–7.

4. While Grisez and Finnis are usually credited as the major voices in elucidating the New Natural Law movement, other scholars have played significant roles in both exploring and fending its insights. Among these are Robert George, Joseph Boyle, and William May. See Samuel Gregg, "New Natural Law."

5. By "physicalism" I mean an approach to morality that attempts to arrive at moral guidelines from studying the physical structure of human acts. In such an understanding of morality, the rules and guidelines for human action are (almost literally) built into the structure of physical acts, and can be successfully fitted into propositions that themselves structure the discipline of ethics and moral theology. Richard McCormick, "Moral Theology from 1940 to 1989: An Overview," in *Corrective Vision: Explorations in Moral Theology* (Milwaukee: Sheed and Ward, 1994), 1–7. See also "Physicalism" in the *Cambridge Dictionary of Philosophy*, 2nd ed., ed. Robert Audi (Cambridge: Cambridge University Press, 1999). Virginia Woolf, *To the Lighthouse* (New York: Harcourt, Brace, Jovanovich, 1989), 277.

6. [Conventional natural law] requires one to pass from theoretical knowledge concerning human nature to moral obligations governing human actions. This passage is supported by the theoretical presupposition that God will us to act in conformity with nature. But notice that in very many cases the determination of what agrees or does not agree with nature seems to be either arbitrary or question-begging." Grisez, *Contraception and Natural Law*, 50.

7. Grisez, *Contraception and Natural Law*, 47. Italics added. For Grisez's list of four criticisms that could be made against "conventional" (i.e., neo-scholastic) natural law discourse, see ibid., 50–52. Grisez here outlines his four objections to basing the foundation of moral action in the speculative reason, a model of moral action he terms "equivocating": the received model of natural law "requires one to pass from theoretical knowledge concerning human nature to moral obligations governing human actions. . . . If human nature is considered only to the extent that it is an

object of theoretical knowledge, the determination that a certain kind of action would not agree with it seems arbitrary, for the reality which man [*sic*] simply *is* does not seem to settle what he can and ought to be. On the other hand, if human nature is considered to the extent that it already is an object of moral knowledge, the determination that a certain kind of action would not agree with it is prejudiced by the moral knowledge that is assumed. 'Nature' has two senses, and conventional natural law theory rests heavily on this equivocation." 50–51. Francisco Suarez was a Spanish Jesuit who was widely considered the most important scholastic theologian after Thomas Aquinas. Teaching on the Jesuit faculty in Salamanca in the late sixteenth and early seventeenth centuries, he was considered the leading figure marking the "Second Phase of Scholasticism," as it moved from its Medieval into its Baroque form. Daniel Novotny, *Ens rationis from Suarez to Caramuel: A Study in Scholasticism of the Baroque Era* (New York: Fordham University Press, 2013), 17, 296.

8. "[Aristotle's] *Rhetoric* contains important references to natural law. . . . It is here that we are told that the law is either particular or general: general law [e.g., natural law] is that law which, being *acknowledged and recognized by everybody, is not confined to a particular state*. It is basically unwritten law." Max Solomon Shellens, "Aristotelean Natural Law," Notre Dame Law School: NDL Scholarship. "Natural Law Forum." http://scholarship.law.nd.edu/nd_naturallaw_forum. Italics added. In his *Grounding for the Metaphysics of Morals* (1785), Immanuel Kant had argued that the basis for moral action was to be found in a "categorical imperative," which he argued constituted an absolute and unconditional requirement for action that had to be obeyed in all circumstances, and—as such—represented an end in itself. It is probably best known in its first formulation in that work: "Act only according to that maxim whereby you can, at the same time, will that it should become a universal law." Thus, for Kant, precisely because the law of nature was universal and immediately understandable by human beings, the categorical imperative itself offered a perspicacious foundation for moral action transcending rational arguments and cultural differences. Immanuel Kant, *Grounding for the Metaphysics of Morals*, trans. James Ellington (Hackett, 1993), 30.

9. This paragraph was shaped by the very fine insights of Philip Johnson in "In Defense of Natural Law," *First Things*, November 1999.

10. Bretzke, *Handbook*, 223–224. John Finnis and Germain Grisez, "The Basic Principles of Natural Law: A Reply to Ralph McInerny," originally in *The American Journal of Jurisprudence* (1981). Found at Notre Dame Law School: NDLS Scholarship: Journal Articles, Paper 848, at http://scholarship.law.nd.edu/law_faculty_scholarship/848.

11. Germain Grisez, *The First Principle of Practical Reason: A Commentary on the Summa Theologia*, 1-2, Question 94, Article 2, *Natural Law Forum* 168 (1965): 10. Robert P. George, "Recent Criticism of Natural Law Theory," *University of Chicago Law Review* 55 (1987): 1380.

12. My reading of Grisez's purchase on Thomas Aquinas in this paragraph closely follows the argument of Robert George in "Recent Criticism," 1382.

13. The quote is from Samuel Gregg, "New Natural Law," 1–2. Italics added.

14. George, "Recent Criticism of Natural Law Theory," 1382ff.

15. Ibid., 1387.

16. The quote is from Germain Grisez and Russel Shaw, *Fulfillment in Christ: A Summary of Christian Moral Principles* (Notre Dame, IN: University of Notre Dame Press, 1991), 56. Bretzke, *Handbook of Roman Catholic Moral Terms*, 18. See also John Finnis, *Natural Law and Natural Rights* (Oxford: Clarendon Press, 1980), 3ff.

17. My understanding of Grisez's list of basic human goods follows the lucid exposition of Philip Johnson in his fine article, "In Defense of Natural Law," published in *First Things* (November 1999): 2, found at http://www.firstthings.com/article/1999/11/in-defense-of-natural-law.

18. Grisez and Shaw, *Fulfillment in Christ: A Summary of Christian Moral Principles*, 78.

19. Ibid. George, *In Defense of Natural Law*, chapter 3.

20. Grisez, 78ff.

21. Russell Hittinger, *A Critique of New Natural Law Theory* (Notre Dame: University of Notre Dame Press, 1989), 2. I follow Robert George's analysis of Hittinger from "Recent Criticism," 1407.

22. Hittinger, *A Critique of New Natural Law Theory*, 5. George, "Recent Criticism," 1408.

23. George, *In Defense of Natural Law*, 83. Italics added. Russell Hittinger, *A Critique of the New Natural Law Theory* (Notre Dame: University of Notre Dame Press, 1987), 74–79; Lloyd Weinreb, *Natural Law and Justice* (Cambridge: Harvard University Press, 1987), 4–12, 205–263.

24. Hittinger, *A Critique of The New Natural Law Theory*, 5, 6, 8. My presentation of Hittinger's critique of Grisez in this paragraph follows the exposition of Robert George in "Recent Criticism of Natural Law Theory," 1407–1408.

25. John Rawls, "Themes in Kant's Moral Philosophy," in *Kant's Transcendental Deductions*, ed. E. Foster (Stanford: Stanford University Press, 1989): 81–113, 85–88; Adam Cureton and Thomas E. Hill, "Kant on Virtue and the Virtues," in *Cultivating Virtue* (Oxford: Oxford University Press, 2014): 87–110, 91–94; Marcia Baron, "'Acting from Duty' in Immanuel Kant," in *Groundwork for the Metaphysics of Morals*, ed. Allen Wood (New Haven: Yale University Press, 2003), 98–99.

26. George, "Recent Criticism," 1409. George is quoting Henry Veatch, *Human Rights: Fact or Fiction?* (Baton Rouge: Louisiana State University Press, 1985), 98. See also Jean Porter, "Basic Goods and the Human Good in Recent Catholic Moral Theology," *The Thomist* 57 (1993): 28–42.

27. Hittinger, *Critique*, 198. The phrase "declaration of methodological independence" is a direct quote from Robert George's article, "Recent Criticism of Natural

Law Theory," 1409. Natural law theory "by way of shortcuts" is in Hittinger, *Critique*, 198.

28. Hittinger, *Critique*, 62. I follow Robert George closely in laying out Hittinger's critique here.

29. Hittinger, *Critique*, 63. George, *Recent Criticism*, 1412–1413.

30. George, *Recent Criticism*, 1413.

31. Samuel Gregg, "New Natural Law," 2 (www.firstprinciplesjournal.com/articles. aspx?article=262). "Proportionalism" is an ethical theory that argues that it is never morally right to go against a principle unless there is a "proportionate reason" to justify it. Thus proportionalism asserts that one can determine the right course of action by weighing the good and the necessary evil caused by an action, and explaining why moral actors should choose the lesser evil. (Charles Curran, *The Catholic Moral Tradition Today* (Washington, DC: Georgetown University Press, 1999), 71. "Consequentialism" is a school of ethics that holds that the consequences of one's actions form the ultimate basis for any judgment regarding the rightness or wrongness of one's action. The most famous extreme position of consequentialism is encapsulated in the phrase, "the end justifies the means," meaning that if a goal is important enough, any method for achieving it is morally justified. (John Mizzoni, *Ethics: The Basics* (New York: John Wiley and Sons), 104. Grisez's form of new natural law argues strongly against both the proportionalist and consequentialist paradigms by asserting that the basic goods defining the moral life are both "irreducible" (i.e., they can never be sacrificed for a supposedly larger or more important good, or that a lesser evil might result) and "incommensurable" (the mistaken belief that one can sacrifice one such good in order to achieve another). Pope John Paul II utilized these arguments in condemning a form of proportionalism and consequentialism in his 1993 encyclical, *Veritatis Splendor* (#75). Bretzke, *Handbook*, 49, 190.

32. Gregg, "New Natural Law," 2. Gregg has pointed out that H. L. A. Hart, Joseph Ratz, and Philippa Foot stand out as scholars who took Grisez and Finnis' ideas and applied them to important issues in the areas of legal and political philosophy. 2.

CHAPTER 6

1. "Jean Porter, Professor of Moral Theology, elected to the Academy of Arts and Sciences," Lauren Fox, April 17, 2012 (www.amacad.org/news/pressReleaseContent. aspx?i=167). For the list of distinguished members of the Class of 2012 of the AAAS, see (www.amacad.org/news/pressReleaseContent.aspx?i=167). Jason A. Fout, "Nature as Reason: A Thomistic Theory of the Natural Law by Jean Porter," *Reviews in Religion and Theology* 13 (2006): 590–593; Derek S. Jeffreys, "Nature as Reason: A Thomistic Theory of the Natural Law," *Journal of Religion* 86 (2006): 487–489; Patrick McCormick, "Review of Nature as Reason: A Thomistic Theory of the Natural Law by Jean Porter," *Journal of the Society of Christian Ethics* 29 (2009): 253.

2. Jean Porter, "The Natural Law and Innovative Forms of Marriage: A Reconsideration," *Journal of the Society of Christian Ethics* (December 2012), 1. Found online at "The Theology Forum," January 16, 2013, at https://thetheologyforum.wordpress.com/2013/01/16/jean-porter-on-natural-law-and-same-sex-marriage/

3. Jean Porter, *Natural and Divine Law: Reclaiming the Tradition for Christian Ethics* (Grand Rapids, MI: William B. Eerdmans Publishing Company, 1999), 17, 19. Porter expands on this position in "Contested Categories: Reason, Nature, and Natural Order in Medieval Accounts of Natural Law," *Journal of Religious Ethics* 24 (1996): 207–232.

4. Ibid., 29. The words in brackets are my own, which have been added to Porter's quote for emphasis. Porter herself uses the word "paradigm" in a manner specific to her own project and *not* in the way Kuhn defines it. For Porter, a paradigm describes morally significant situations in which moral actors live in a way that is virtuous: "A paradigm represents what the happy life will typically or normally look like, and it is through reflection on this paradigm that we grasp some sense of the overall aims and the point of this way of life." Jean Porter, *Nature as Reason: A Thomistic Theory of the Natural Law* (Grand Rapids, MI: William B. Eerdmans Publishing Company, 1999), 226.

5. Porter, *Natural and Divine Law*, 28.

6. Ibid., 85. Aquinas remarks that understood in one sense, nature is contrasted with reason (*In IV Sent.* 33.1.1 *ad* 4). Nonetheless, the understandings of nature that were mediated to them, both through their authoritative sources and the natural philosophy of their own time, generally emphasized the continuities between nature and reason. Indeed, as D. E. Luscombe observes, "theologians in the first half of the twelfth century frequently equated nature and reason, since they saw the orderly processes of nature as the expressions of the reason of God." 85.

7. Ibid., 90–91. Italics added.

8. Ibid., 93.

9. Ibid., 197.

10. Porter, *Nature as Reason*, 58. Alister McGrath, *A Scientific Theology*, volume 1: *Nature* (Edinburgh: T &T Clark, 2001), 113. The italics in the last line of the block quote from McGrath are in the original; all other italics in the quote have been added.

11. Porter, *Nature as Reason*, 64. I am indebted to Dan Fleming ("Intelligibility in the Natural Law") for this insight into Porter's construction of robust realism (4). I found his commentary on this kind of realism in footnote 17 of his article especially helpful: "[Porter] uses Alasdair MacIntyre's writing on tradition to argue against both relativism and [fundamentalism,] suggesting that collective bodies of thought (traditions) constantly develop both within themselves and with other sources of truth. In this way traditions do not represent only their own truth (relativism) or claim completely objective truth in themselves (fundamentalism) but rather act as mediators and frameworks for dialogue between intellect and reality."

12. Porter, *Natural and Divine Law*, 217.
13. Porter, "The Natural Law and Innovative Forms of Marriage," 1.
14. Porter, "The Natural Law and Innovative Forms of Marriage," 1.
15. Porter, *Natural and Divine Law*, 19–20.
16. Porter, "Jean Porter on Natural Law and Same Sex Marriage," *The Theology Forum*, 2–3.
17. Ibid., 1–2.
18. Ibid., 2.
19. "The Consistent Ethic of Life" is a phrase first elucidated by Joseph Cardinal Bernardin on March 11, 1984, when he (then Archbishop of Chicago) delivered the annual William Wade Lecture at St. Louis University. His lecture was entitled, "The Consistent Ethic of Life: Continuing the Dialogue." The lecture can be found at http://www.priestsforlife.org/magisterium/bernardinwade.html
20. Porter, "Jean Porter on Natural Law and Same Sex Marriage," 2–3. Italics in both paragraph and block quote have been added, and are not in the original text.
21. Porter, *Natural and Divine Law*, 196. Italics added.
22. Ibid., 196–197.
23. She quotes from John Noonan's *Contraception* regarding the views of both Albert the Great and Thomas Aquinas regarding contraction: 284–285. Porter observed that "Albert [the Great] goes so far as explicitly to repudiate the equation of contraceptive practice with homicide, observing that there is no guarantee that a given act of sexual intercourse would produce offspring anyway (*In IV Set. 31.1.8*). In his early writings, Aquinas takes the same line (*In Sent. 31.2.3*). More tellingly, a number of scholastic theologians either do not mention the use of contraceptives at all or they discuss them only in their earlier works." 196–197. John Noonan, *Contraception: A History of Its Treatment by the Catholic Theologians and Canonists* (Cambridge: Harvard University Press, 1965).
24. Porter, *Natural and Divine Law*, 226.
25. Porter, *Natural and Divine Law*, 198. Porter quotes John Noonan's famous observation regarding the basis for the scholastics' condemnation of contraception. Noonan had argued that their blanket condemnation of the practice was actually based on a false syllogism: "Because the sexual act might be generative, and because generation was an important function, the [scholastics] intuited that generation was the normal function [of sexual intercourse]." But a conclusion was—Noonan had argued—problematic, at best. John T. Noonan, *Contraception: A History of Its Treatment by the Catholic Theologians and Canonists* (Cambridge: Harvard University Press, 1965), 295.
26. Ibid., 532.
27. Porter, *Natural and Divine Law*, 197.
28. Ibid., 198. Italics added.
29. Ibid., 225. "At the very least, there is something problematic, from the Christian standpoint, in the deliberate choice to remain childless throughout a marriage.

Many of the critics of *Humanae Vitae* would agree with the encyclical up to that point." 225.

30. Ibid., 226.

31. Ibid., 226–227.

32. Ibid., 227. Italics added. "Nevertheless, the Christian understanding of marriage does imply that children are among the greatest blessings of the marriage relationship, and what is more, that they are a gift that should not be refused lightly. At the very least, there is something problematic, from the Christian standpoint, in the deliberate choice to remain childless throughout a marriage. . . . Why should this be so? In part, these questions can be answered by drawing on the theological arguments for the goodness of procreation, as the scholastics developed them. . . . For the scholastics, the defense of procreation and marriage follows from a doctrinal commitment to the goodness of creation. Many Christians of all denominations share the view that the Christian community should be 'pro-family,' and the scholastic defense of procreation helps us to see that this sentiment reflects a deep and sound doctrinal instinct. This need does not imply that other possible values are unimportant, or much less legitimate, but it does reflect a sense that a commitment to procreation should have a central place in the public witness of the church." Ibid., 225–226.

33. Lisa Sowle Cahill, "Toward Global Ethics," *Theological Studies* 63 (2002): 324–344, 325. "In any event, international relations seem more determined by economic than by moral forces. The global dominance of transnational economic institutions and corporations, evading governance by national states or international bodies, has almost demolished the idea that relations among peoples can be promoted cooperatively under an effective world authority." 325.

34. To make her point, Cahill quotes from the famous encyclical, *Pacem in Terris* of Pope John XXIII: "The common good touches the whole man, the needs both of his body and of his soul. Hence it follows that the civil authorities must undertake to effect the common good by ways and means that are proper to them; that is, while respecting the hierarchy of values, they should promote simultaneously both the material and social welfare of citizens." John XXIII, *Pacem in Terris*, paragraph 57. In David O'Brien and Thomas Shannon, eds. *Catholic Thought: The Documentary Heritage* (Maryknoll, NY: Orbis, 1998), 140.

35. Cahill, "Toward Global Ethics," 326.

36. Ibid., 331. "What ideas or definitions of moral rationality and universality are rejected by skeptics if global ethics or a 'common rationality' who do address this problem out of Western academia's civil war among liberalism, foundationalism, and postmodernism? Most are motivated precisely against the imperialist tendencies and pasts of their own cultural traditions. Jean Porter, for instance, is wary of a 'global ethic' that claims that 'all moral traditions share a fundamental core, which amounts to a universal valid morality,' since statements of very general principles are uselessly 'platitudinous,' and specific derivations will be controversial

and incompatible. It would be better simply to seek practical consensus ad hoc."
331. Quoting Porter from her article "Search for a Global Etic," *Theological Studies*
62 (2001): 119–121.

37. Ibid., 326.

38. Porter, *Natural and Divine Law*, 108, 141–144.

39. Porter, "Search for a Global Ethic," 110, 111.

CHAPTER 7

1. William Bole, "No Labels Please: Lisa Sowle Cahill's Middle Way," *Commonweal*
(January 2011): 3. Of Cahill's many articles, the following are especially
helpful: "The Natural Law, Global Justice, and Equality," in *Searching for a
Universal Ethic: Multidisciplinary, Ecumenical, and Interfaith Responses to the
Catholic Natural Law Tradition*, eds. John Berkman and William Mattison (Grand
Rapids: Eerdmans, 2015); and "Natural Law: A Feminist Reassessment," in *Is There
a Human Nature?* ed. Leroy Rouner (Notre Dame: University of Notre Dame
Press, 1997).

2. Ibid., 4.

3. Lisa Sowle Cahill, "Catholic Feminists and Tradition: Renewal, Reinvention,
Replacement," *Journal of the Society of Christian Ethics* 34 (Winter, 2014), 28, 38.

4. See Lisa Sowle Cahill, "Toward Global Ethics," *Theological Studies* 63 (2002): 324.

5. Lisa Cahill, "Natural Law: A Feminist Reassessment," in *Is There a Human Nature?*
ed. Leroy Rouner (Notre Dame: University of Notre Dame Press, 1997), 78–678.
See also Lisa Cahill, "Nature, Change, and Justice," in *Without Nature? A New
Condition for Theology*, ed. David Albertson and Cabell King (New York: Fordham
University Press, 2010), 282–283.

6. Cahill, "Natural Law: A Feminist Reassessment," 78.

7. Cahill, "Toward Global Ethics," 325, 326.

8. Mike Collins, "The Pros and Cons of Globalization," *Forbes Online*, May 6, 2015.
Nikki Lisa Cole, "What Is Globalization? A Sociological Definition," *Globalization
101*, The Levin Institute, The State University of New York, at www.globaliza-
tion101.org/what-is-globalization/. "Policy and technological developments of the
past few decades have spurred increases in cross-border trade, investment, and migration so large that many observers believe the world has entered a qualitatively
new phase in its economic development. Since 1950, for example, the volume of
world trade has increased by 20 times, and from just 1997 to 1999 flows of foreign
investment nearly doubled." Cole, 1.

9. Cahill, "Toward Global Ethics," 324.

10. Ibid., 328. Cahill was quite critical of the actions of the United States on the issue of
the Kyoto Protocol: "The fact that in 2001 the United States reneged on a previous
commitment and became the lone dissenter to the Kyoto Protocol . . . was met by

disapprobation both internationally and domestically. The Protocol's supporters, including the European Union and Japan, proceeded with implementation."

11. Ibid., 329. Cahill was thus proposing a rejection of both poles of a false dilemma— on the one hand "objectivist foundationalism" (the belief that there really *was* an objectively true natural law ahistorically applicable to everyone all the time, regardless of historical or cultural location), and on the other hand, "relativism nonfoundationalism (the belief that it was impossible to ever achieve anything like a universal, common set of moral principles or guidelines, morality being thus simply "relative" to one's specific cultural location). From Cahill's point of view, this was to pose a false dilemma, both poles of which were problematic and simplistic.

12. Cahill, "Natural Law: A Feminist Reassessment," 85.

13. Cahill, "Toward Global Ethics," 338. Cahill references Daniel Westberg, *Right Practical Reason: Aristotle, Action, and Prudence in Aquinas* (Oxford: Clarendon Press, 1994), 82, 84, 246–247.

14. Ibid.

15. Cahill, "Catholic Feminists and Tradition," 39.

16. Cahill, "Toward Global Ethics," 86.

17. Cahill, "Catholic Feminists and Tradition," 41, 43. Italics added.

18. Lisa Cahill, "The Natural Law: Global Justice and Equality," in *Searching for a Universal Ethics,* ed. John Berkman and William Mattison (Grand Rapids: William B. Eerdmans Publishing Company, 2014), 239, 242.

19. Cahill, "Toward Global Ethics," 329. Italics added.

20. Ibid., 326. "Jean Porter takes the position that a global ethic is impossible, and that it is moreover unnecessary because cultures can overcome moral disagreements by proceeding on an ad hoc and pragmatic basis. William O'Neill, SJ, writing about African thought, avoids any antithesis between universal and particular moralities by recasting the debate as a discussion of how narrative traditions critically reinterpret themselves using rhetoric and symbols such as 'human rights.' Neither Porter nor O'Neill is prepared to endorse an objective, universal, or common ethic in fact or in principle, though both allude to the fact that people from very different cultures do come together to debate and even agree on paths toward resolution of difficult social problems." 326.

21. Ibid., 331. "Others similarly reject the 'misleading and impossible quest for a moral Reason which stands outside the flow of time and contingency.' While such characterizations find their target in some form of Kantianism and liberalism, and rightly battle dogmatism and imperialism, there may be other, less pernicious forms of moral realism available to serve as part of a liberative strategy. Not surprisingly, Roman Catholic authors often see promise in an Aristotelian-Thomistic understanding of moral rationality, linked to 'narrative' or traditions and practices as historically reappropriated."

22. Ibid., 333.

23. Ibid., 333. See also Michael B. Crowe, "The Pursuit of the Natural Law," in *Readings in Moral Theology, No. 7: Natural Law and Theology* (New York: Paulist, 1991), 296–332.

24. "A point to be stressed perhaps more strongly is that human nature, its ends, its flourishing, and its moral standards are not 'discovered' as already existent and unchanging entities. They too are 'contingent' and perhaps in some degree mutable; the extent to which this is the case is a matter of debate." Ibid., 334. Pamela Hall, *Narrative and the Natural Law: An Interpretation of Thomistic Ethics* (Notre Dame: University of Notre Dame Press, 1994), 94.

25. Cahill, "Toward Global Ethics," 334.

26. Cahill, "Catholic Feminists and Tradition," 34.

27. *Praxis*—itself a postclassical Latin word that transliterated the Greek original ("praeksas") from which the English words "practical" and "pragmatic" derive— means "action or practice; the practice or exercise of a technical subject or art, as distinct from the theory of it." *Oxford English Dictionary Online.* http://www.oed.com/view/Entry/praxis.

28. Cahill, "Toward Global Ethics," 334. "The intellectual virtues, including prudence, are 'directed to the apprehension of truth.' But truth and reason in moral contexts have to be understood as integrally bound to action, indeed as emerging within action, not only as 'leading to it' as their effect. Since prudence is 'right reason about things to be done' (*ST* 1–2, q. 57, a.4), practical truth, the truth of practical reason, 'arises only within contingent states of affairs,' and by means of an 'inevitable choice between competing options.' Moral truth as practical truth is a truth of action." 334.

29. Ibid., 335. Italics in the quote have been added.

30. Ibid., 335. Italics added.

31. Ibid., 335. Italics added.

32. Ibid., 335. Cahill is quoting from Peter Phan, "Method in Liberation Theologies," *Theological Studies* 61 (2000), 59, 60, 61, 63.

33. Jean Porter, *Natural and Divine Law*, 108, 141–144.

34. Cahill, "Toward Global Ethics," 335.

35. Ibid., 337. Italics added. Among the international resolutions Cahill offers as evidence for her argument are the "General Assembly Declaration of Commitment on HIV/AIDS," June 28, 2001 (excerpted from the article, "From the U.N.'s Statement on AIDS: 'Prevention Must Be the Mainstay,'" *New York Times*, June 9, 2001, A8; and the "Resolution Adopted by the General Assembly 55/2," *United Nations Millennium Declaration*, September 8, 2000 (http://www.un.org/millennium/declaration/ares552e.htm). Cahill draws on the arguments of Robert Drinan, SJ, in *The Mobilization of Shame: A Worldview of Human Rights* (New Haven: Yale University Press, 2001).

CHAPTER 8

1. "In the years immediately after the Second Vatican Council, reception referred to the process by which some teaching, ritual, discipline, or law was assimilated into the life of the local church. . . . Within [that] legal framework reception, strictly speaking, must be 'exogenous'—that is, it is a reception of something within a community which comes from the outside. [But Yves Congar] had a much broader conception of reception. For him, reception denoted a constitutive process in the Church's self-realization in history." Richard Gaillardetz, "The Reception of Doctrine: New Perspectives," chapter 7 in *Authority in the Roman Catholic Church: Theory and Practice* (New York: Routledge, 2002).

2. Among the works I've found most insightful are Gould's *Time's Arrow, Time's Cycle: Myth and Metaphor in the Discovery of Geological Time* (Cambridge: Harvard University Press, 1987) and *Bully for Brontosaurs: Reflections in Natural History* (New York: Norton, 1991). I've found David Prindle's study of Gould—*Stephen Jay Gould and the Politics of Evolution* (Amherst, NY: Prometheus, 2009)—especially helpful in understanding Gould's place in the history of science.

3. John P. Meier, *A Marginal Jew: Rethinking the Historical Jesus*, volume 2: *Mentor, Message, and Miracles* (New York: Doubleday, 1994), chapter 23: "The So-Called Nature Miracles," 919.

Index